AMAZIGH ARTS IN MOROCCO

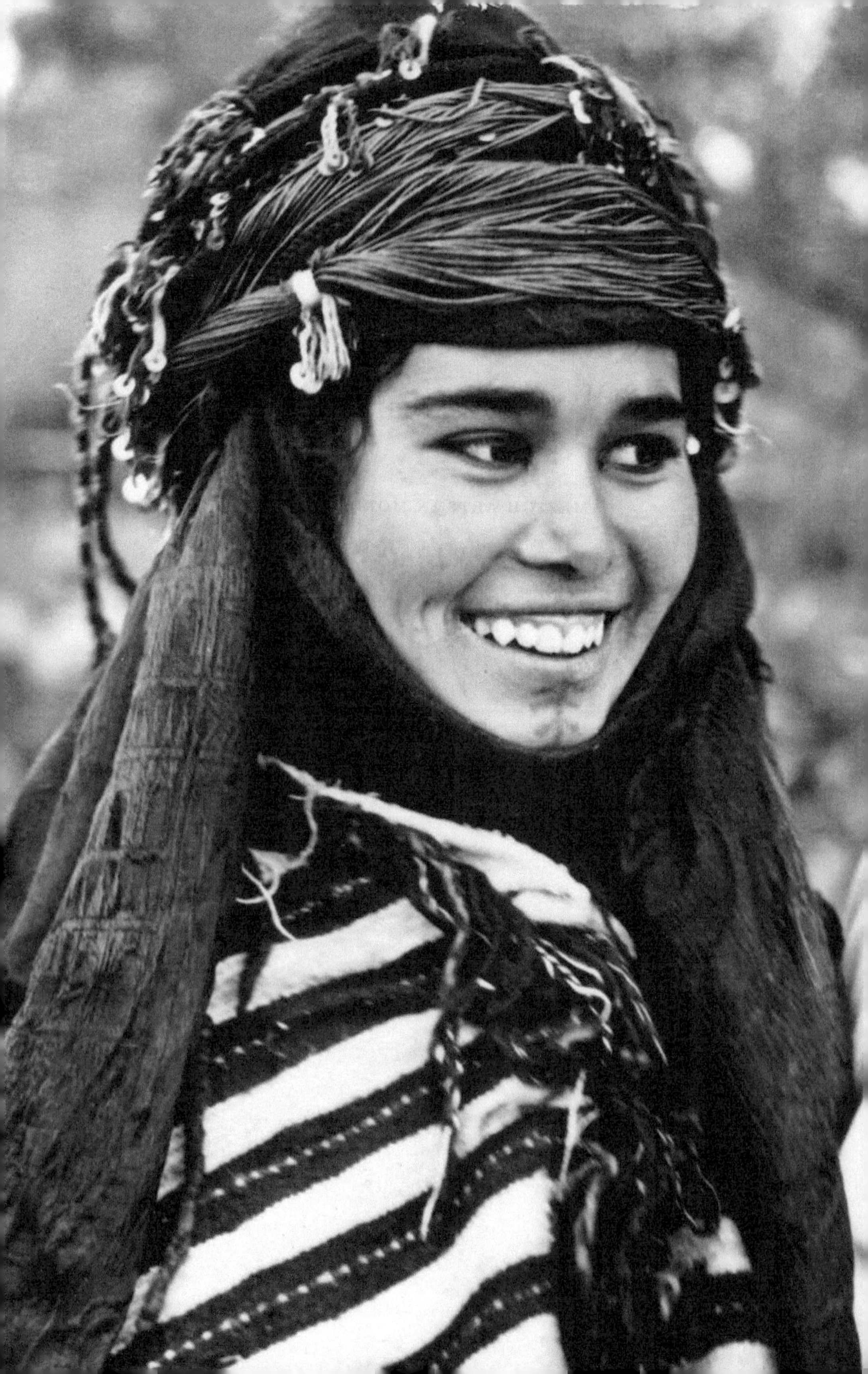

Amazigh Arts in Morocco

Women Shaping Berber Identity

Cynthia J. Becker

University of Texas Press, Austin

Library of Congress Cataloging-in-Publication Data
Becker, Cynthia.
Amazigh arts in Morocco : women shaping
Berber identity / Cynthia Becker. — 1st ed.
        p.   cm.
Includes bibliographical references and index.
ISBN-13: 978-0-292-71295-9 (cloth : alk. paper)
ISBN-10: 0-292-71295-2
1. Arts, Berber — Morocco.   2. Women artists —
Morocco.   3. Ethnicity in art.   4. Identity
(Psychology) in art.   5. Berbers — Morocco —
Social life and customs.   I. Title.
NX587.75.A1B43 2006
704'.0420964 — dc22
                                        2006002245

To my parents, Kathleen and George Becker
And to Addi and the entire Ouadderrou family

Contents

A Note on Transcription and Transliteration

The Ait Atta, the focus of this book, speak an Amazigh language called Tamazight, found in the Middle Atlas Mountains and the southeastern region of Morocco. The term "Tamazight" is also used more generally by scholars to refer to a group of closely related Afro-Asiatic languages spoken throughout northwestern Africa. In this book the term "Tamazight" refers both to the specific Amazigh language spoken by the Ait Atta and to Amazigh languages as a whole.

The Amazigh songs and phrases in this book are from the Tamazight language specifically spoken by the Ait Atta. Addi Ouadderrou did the transcriptions, basing his work on the system created by Salem Chaker (1984). Addi Ouadderrou and I did the translations from Tamazight to English. The following is a guide to the system used by Addi Ouadderrou.

Letter	Tamazight Example	English Translation
a	*aẓul*	hello
e	*amellal*	white
i	*iẓli*	song
o	*oreɣ*	gold
u	*afus*	hand
w	*aẓwu*	wind
y	*kuyan*	everyone
b	*aberkan*	black
c	*icwa*	sharp
d	*tudert*	life
f	*tiflut*	door
g	*agadir*	wall

h	*uhu*	no
j	*iledjigen*	flowers
k	*akal*	earth
l	*tamlalt*	antelope
m	*asmun*	companion
n	*alni*	brain
q	*aqrab*	bag used by men
r	*irifi*	thirst
s	*tislit*	bride
t	*itran*	stars
x	*axdil*	stomach
â	*aâerrim*	teenager
γ	*aɣbalu*	water source
ḍ	*aḍar*	foot
ḥ	*tiḥli*	beauty
ṣ	*ṣber*	patience
ṭ	*imeṭṭawen*	tears
ẓ	*Iẓẓay*	heavy

Doubled letters indicate stress during pronunciation.

Acknowledgments

This book was a communal endeavor that involved numerous people, including my family in Morocco: Mama Lhacen and her children Zohra, Brahim, Fatima, Erqia, Ali, and Khira Ouadderrou. Brahim's wife, Khadija, and their children Najat, Nora, Seham, Muhammad, and Hamza further enriched my life in Morocco. Ali's wife, Fatima, and their children Hamid and Hassan as well as Fatima Ouadderrou's daughter Erqia and her granddaughter Khadija welcomed me every time I visited Morocco, ensuring that I will feel at home for years to come. In addition, Youssef Kherbouch always offered a helping hand. Their acceptance and unconditional love provided me with entrance into Mezguida, a place I consider to be my second home. I especially wish to acknowledge the young women of Mezguida, many of whom have married and left the village, for their companionship and for dancing with me at weddings as well as the female elders who shared their intimate knowledge of wedding songs and life in the past. I am also thankful to the many people in Mezguida, Rissani, Erfoud, Merzouga, Haselbait, Khamlia, Tabat el Khir, and Hafira for inviting me to join in their wedding celebrations and tolerating the presence of my camera, allowing me to participate in and record their lives. The Bouganig and Taghlaoui families opened their homes to me. The Ismkhan of Khamlia patiently shared with me the details of their annual festival and healing ceremonies.

Many others have assisted me in Morocco since my first visit in 1993. Thanks to all of those involved in the Sijilmasa project, especially Jim Miller, and the Centre d'Études et de Recherches Alaouites in Rissani, in particular Zohra Meddiki and Fatima Boualwan. The artists Farid Belkahia, Mohamed Mallal, Fatima Mellal, Mohamed Ziyani, Muhand Saidi, and Hamid Kachmar and the poet Omar Taws shared their ideas and artistic inspiration with me. Abdeltif

Kich from the Musée de Marrakech provided me with insight into contemporary art in Morocco. Salem Chaker from the Institut National des Langues et Civilisations Orientales (INALCO) in Paris, Rachid Ouzennou from the Abrid Association in Erfoud, and Mustapha Berhouchi shared their knowledge about contemporary Amazigh issues.

The support of my former colleagues at the University of St. Thomas was invaluable to me. Joanne Eicher and an anonymous reviewer read the entire manuscript, providing me with useful commentary. I especially wish to thank Lotus Stack, the textile curator at the Minneapolis Institute of Arts, who generously shared her knowledge of Moroccan textiles and always encouraged my scholarship. Evelyne Disdier at the Maison Méditerranéenne des Sciences de l'Homme, Cécile Blouin Boquien from the Institut du Monde Arabe, and the National Anthropological Archives at the Smithsonian Institution assisted me with images. David Kelley made the book's map.

Special thanks to my colleagues from the Department of Art History and the African Studies Center at Boston University. I would also like to thank the faculty at my alma mater, the University of Wisconsin–Madison, and the friends I made while I was a graduate student, especially Andrea Frohne and Professor Lois Anderson, the ethnomusicologist who encouraged me to analyze Ait Khabbash performances. My former graduate advisor Henry Drewal provided the intellectual support that made this book possible. He continues to mentor my academic endeavors and inspires me with his great energy and passion for African arts. Most of all he is a well-respected and cherished friend.

Financial support for this study was provided by a long-term and short-term grant from the American Institute of Maghreb Studies, a Fulbright Grant, a Title VI Foreign Language Fellowship for Arabic, and a University Fellowship from the University of Wisconsin–Madison. Research assistance grants from the University of St. Thomas provided me with release time for further research and writing. I also thank Wendy Moore from the University of Texas Press for assisting me with the publication process.

Finally, I thank my entire family in New Orleans and especially my parents, George and Kathleen Becker, and my brother Scott, who supported my interest in African arts and my travels around the world without question. In particular I am grateful to my mother, whose initiation to international travel was her trip across the Atlantic to Morocco to check on her daughter. Andrée Bouterie and Victoria Giambrone provided friendship and emotional support. And I profoundly pay tribute to Addi Ouadderrou for all his patient help in Morocco and in the United States. He nurtured my understanding of life in Morocco and spent numerous hours transcribing and translating cassette recordings and videotapes of Ait Khabbash songs from Tamazight to English. He happily accompanied me on my numerous jaunts to remote desert villages and to nomadic weddings, expertly navigating our Renault IV on desert roads, always ready for the next adventure.

Introduction

When I first arrived in Morocco in 1993 with the intention of learning about Berber art, I soon discovered that women rather than men were the artists in Berber societies. Berber women wove brightly colored carpets. They decorated their faces with tattoos, dyed their hands and feet with henna, and painted their faces with saffron. They also embroidered brightly colored motifs on their indigo head coverings and wore elaborate silver and amber jewelry. Women both created the artistic symbols of Berber identity and wore them on their bodies, making the decorated female body a public symbol of Berber identity.

These connections and intersections of art, gender, and identity are the subject of this book. This study considers women and their participation in the process of identity construction by examining the centrality of the textiles, jewelry, and other art forms created by women to the social relations and ethnic identity of the Berbers of Morocco, the indigenous peoples of North Africa. Unlike Arab groups in North Africa, in Berber societies women rather than men are the primary producers of art, and women's arts identify the group as Berber. This examination, in addition to revealing a rich body of art, is meant to illuminate the complexity of women's roles in the Islamic societies of Africa and to demonstrate the role of women's agency in negotiating complex social and religious issues. Its central argument is that women's control over the visual symbols of Berber ethnic identity grants them power and prestige yet also restricts them to specific roles in that society.

I use the term "ethnic identity" in this book to refer to Berber attitudes regarding group membership. Ethnic categories, according to Nira Yuval-Davis (1998: 169), are based on constructs of collectivity, centering on the notion of a "common origin and/or destiny and engaging in constant processes of struggle and negotiation." As I demonstrate here, Berber groups, who typically trace their heritage to a common male ancestor, attempt to guard female sexuality and fertility to maintain the purity of their group's bloodline and by extension its ethnic purity. Therefore, the forms, colors, and designs of Berber women's arts are public identity symbols that are clearly linked to concepts of contained and controlled female fertility. Since ethnic identity is a process that is subject to historical, political, and social dynamics, this book illustrates that, as concepts of Berber ethnicity change, women's arts have been transformed from localized ethnic symbols to symbols that represent a transnational Berber identity.

To examine the complexity of identity construction and its relationship to gender and artistic production, this study introduces the reader to the art of the Ait Khabbash, who are part of the largest Berber group in southern Morocco— the Ait Atta. The Ait Khabbash are one of the many groups (but one of the only Berber groups) living in and around the Tafilalet oasis of southern Morocco. Various Arab groups, both sedentary and nomadic, have lived here with the Ait Khabbash Berbers since the beginning of the nineteenth century. This diversity has kept the Ait Khabbash Berbers conscious of their difference from others in the area.[1]

Issues of ethnic identity are of crucial importance to Berbers, who consider themselves the indigenous inhabitants of northern Africa, a land they call Tamazgha. Berbers believe themselves to be ethnically, culturally, and linguistically distinct from Arabs, who arrived in North Africa in the seventh century CE after various groups such as the Phoenicians and the Romans had previously conquered portions of Tamazgha over the centuries. In contemporary North Africa, pockets of Berber settlements can be found from Egypt to Morocco, with approximately a million in Mali, Niger, Burkina Faso, and Libya and 140,000 in Tunisia, Egypt, and Mauritania. The largest Berber populations can be found in the westernmost regions of North Africa. It is estimated that 25–30 percent of Algeria's 30 million people are Berber; and Morocco has the largest Berber population, which accounts for 40–60 percent of the country's 31 million people (Chaker 1998: 14). It is this large Berber population that differentiates Morocco from other African countries.

The arrival of Arabs in Morocco in the seventh century resulted in the gradual conversion of some Berbers to Islam. It was not until the thirteenth century, however, with the arrival of large numbers of Arabs from the Middle East, that the majority of Berbers accepted Islam, learned the Arabic language, and were assimilated into the Arab culture. Yet many Berber groups living in inaccessible remote areas, such as the mountainous regions of Morocco or its desert fringes, continued to speak their own languages and retained their political autonomy from the urban-based Arab dynasties that ruled Morocco over the centuries.

Berbers in contemporary Morocco can be found in three major geographical regions, each with its own Berber language: Tarifit in the Rif Mountains of northern Morocco, Tamazight in the Middle Atlas Mountains and southeastern desert oasis, and Tashelhit in the Sus Valley, High Atlas Mountains, and Anti-Atlas Mountains.[2] Although speakers of Tamazight and Tashelhit can communicate with each other, communication with speakers of Tarifit is difficult.[3]

Rather than calling themselves "Berbers," a pejorative term derived from the Latin word *barbarus* or "barbarian," they refer to themselves by the name of their particular group. Berbers also use the overarching term "Imazighen." "Amazigh" is the adjectival form of the word. While the word "Imazighen" has become more common in the last fifty years, particularly among Amazigh political activists, who define it as "the free people," several scholars have argued that the term is indeed an ancient one.[4]

When referring to their particular group, Imazighen commonly use a two-word name: "Ait," meaning "people of," and the name of their male ancestor. For example, the Ait Atta, who are the largest Amazigh group in southern Morocco, trace their ancestry to a man named Atta.[5] According to the origin story of the Ait Atta collected by the anthropologist David Hart, Atta (who lived in the Jebel Saghro region of southern Morocco in the sixteenth century) had forty sons, who were all married in one communal marriage ceremony. During the wedding a man from a rival Amazigh group filled the barrels of the sons' flintlock guns with water. The rival group, knowing that the marriage festivities would leave Atta's sons distracted and vulnerable, attacked later that night. The sons left their new wives, rushed to their guns, and, finding them unusable, were all killed. But Atta and his daughters-in-law survived the attack. All of his sons had impregnated their new wives before they were killed, and nine months later thirty-nine sons and one daughter were born. Atta went to live on his own, leaving the women to take care of the children. The thirty-nine sons grew up and joined their grandfather, henceforth known as Dadda Atta (meaning "Grandfather Atta"), declaring unrestricted warfare on their fathers' attackers and driving them out of the region (Hart 1981: 11). The forty sons founded all of the subgroups of the Ait Atta, who currently live in southern Morocco between the Valley of Dades in the west to the Tafilalet oasis and Boudnib in the east.

Whether this Ait Atta origin story is historically accurate is unknown. The story's historical correctness is less important than what it reveals about Ait Atta identity construction. As Benedict Anderson (1991) has suggested, the way in which a community subjectively imagines itself should be the basis for our understanding of that community. This origin story not only demonstrates that the Ait Atta consider themselves a distinct ethnic group that shares a common bloodline but also reveals Amazigh attitudes concerning female fertility. It was women who survived the attack, giving birth to the next generation and teaching them what it means to be Ait Atta.[6] Due to their ability to give birth, Ait Atta women ensured the group's continuation into the future.[7]

Blood is only one substance that unites people. Among Amazigh groups, women's breast milk also has the ability to forge kinship relations. When unrelated children are nourished by one woman's breast milk, the children become *awlad laban* or "milk children." This is a common occurrence among women, who typically breast-feed until a child is two to three, providing many opportunities to offer their breasts to other small children. Women may desire to create kinship bonds between themselves and others or simply to quiet a crying child, but milk bonds are taken as seriously as blood ties. Children sharing the breast milk of one woman are transformed into siblings, establishing a pact based on milk kinship known in Tamazight as *tafargant* or "prohibition" that prohibits marriage between the two children.[8] The fact that breast milk, a woman's bodily substance, can create kinship bonds illustrates that women unite and bind the society together through their reproductive abilities.[9]

This book demonstrates that the generative power of women is metaphorically extended to the creation of the artistic symbols of ethnic identity. Amazigh women recognize that their individual status is reliant on their ability to give birth and incorporate symbols and colors referring to female fertility in their art. Women's arts not only laud female fertility but also serve as public symbols of ethnic identity.[10] Identity depends on difference; and symbolic systems, such as arts, express difference and create a sense of belonging. Unlike Arab groups in Morocco, where men generally dominate artistic production, women are the artists in Amazigh societies: they create and wear the public visual symbols of Amazigh ethnic identity, such as woven textiles, tattoos, and particular styles of jewelry and dress. Women weave the wool cloaks and gowns once commonly worn by Amazigh men. Women tattoo their faces, hands, and ankles with symbols marking their ethnic identity; and women weave those same symbols into textiles and paint them on ceramics. Except for woven garments made by women, men do not wear clothing that distinguishes them as Imazighen. Amazigh men do not practice tattooing or wear silver jewelry.

This complex relationship of art, gender, and ethnic identity in Amazigh culture defies many stereotypes and generalizations about women's lives in the Muslim world that are commonly found in the literature. The most common interpretation is the notion that in Muslim societies women are associated with the inner, domestic world and men with the outer, public world; this has been used as a model for most of the Mediterranean and Islamic world, thus dividing Muslim cultures into binary categories (Antoun 1968; Bourdieu 1977; Dwyer 1978; Joseph 1980). This binary model is often used to suggest a hierarchical relationship in which women are subordinated to men. According to Lila Abu-Lughod (1986) and Guity Nashat and Judith Tucker (1999: 102–103), binary categories such as public and private do not acknowledge the complex and sometimes ambiguous gender overlapping and mixing that occur in North African societies. As Bernhard Venema and Jogien Bakker (2004: 52) state in their study of Amazigh women in the Middle Atlas of Morocco, "There is in fact no separate world between men and women and no strict hierarchical model of sex roles." In fact, women in North Africa and more specifically Amazigh women have always been active agents who influence both the domestic and the public sphere. They play an important role in their communities by providing commodities such as tents, clothing, rugs, sacks, and ceramic pots, in addition to acting as healers, marriage brokers, midwives, cooks, agriculturalists, and pastoralists (Clancy-Smith 1999: 27).

While women's artistic production is indeed crucial to the economic survival of their communities, this study shows that women's arts also serve as public symbols of Amazigh ethnic identity, although the relationship between gender and ethnicity can be a burden for women. Nickie Charles and Helen Hintjens (1998: 2), for example, have argued that, when identity is based on ethnic ties determined by blood relationships, tight control over a woman's sexuality is necessary in order to define and maintain the boundaries of the group. This study reinforces their statement. Ultimately, it is through the control of female sexuality and fertility that ethnic purity can be maintained. The result is that women serve as potent symbols of ethnic identity with considerable power and prestige, but they are also restricted by specific societal constraints.

This book fills a void in the current literature concerning African and Islamic art and history. Previous books in English tend to provide descriptive and often superficial information about Amazigh art without a thorough cultural analysis, typically discussing Amazigh art in the ethnographic present as if it has remained untouched from ancient times (Courtney-Clarke and Brooks 1996; Fisher 1984; Jereb 1995; Reinisch and Stanzer 1991). This book moves the discussion of Amazigh art from the ethnographic past into the present, avoiding terms such as "traditional" and "authentic." This study also places art forms such as textiles and jewelry within a dynamic cultural context, considering how they interact with verbal and performing arts. Rather than presenting Amazigh art as a timeless, exotic remnant of a folkloric past, this book places it within its cultural and historical context, examining women's arts in Morocco from the early twentieth century to the present. Unlike previous studies, this one looks at Amazigh art in Morocco within a larger framework that takes into consideration the impact of French protectorate policies, Moroccan nationalism, changing gender roles, state education, and the transnational Berber movement on artistic production.

Most studies of Amazigh arts do not consider how the lives of Imazighen in Morocco have drastically changed in the last century due to colonialism and nationalistic agendas. Morocco was made a French protectorate in 1912, and the French implemented a policy of divide and rule. For example, in 1930 the French created the Dahir Berbère, where Imazighen were allowed to follow their customary laws, while Arabs abided by the Islamic *shariâa* law. During this time, many French anthropologists were sent to the country to learn about the people living in North Africa in order to facilitate colonial rule of the region. Many of these studies argued that Amazigh beliefs and artistic forms were the result of ancient Roman and Christian values, making Imazighen appear more European in order to reinforce the French justification of colonialism as their duty to reunite Imazighen with their European heritage and Christian roots (Cola Alberich 1949; Doutté 1909; d'Ucel 1932; Laoust 1920; Marcy 1931).[11]

These policies contributed to the rise of an Arab-Islamic nationalist sentiment in Morocco after independence in 1956. The public recognition of Arab-Amazigh differences was viewed by the Moroccan monarchy and Morocco's urban Arab bourgeoisie, who controlled much of the government after independence, as a colonial vestige and an attempt to divide the country. The Moroccan postcolonial government emphasized the nation's common Islamic faith and the Arabic language (which has considerable status as the written language of the Qur'an), attempting to subsume the Imazighen and the Amazigh languages and to unify the country. An Arab-Islamic identity also served to legitimize and strengthen the rule of the Moroccan monarch, a descendant of the Prophet Muhammad. For the first decade after independence, the government failed to recognize Morocco's Amazigh heritage (Denoeux and Maghraoui 1998: 122).[12]

This changed in 1967, with the creation of the first Amazigh association in Morocco, called Association Marocaine de Recherche d'Échange Culturel (AMREC), which led to the founding of approximately forty Amazigh associations throughout the country (Kratochwil 1999: 154). These groups dedicated themselves to the preservation and promotion of the Amazigh heritage, and the government tolerated them as long as they did not engage in political activity. Even as the Moroccan government attempted to suppress the political mobilization of the Imazighen, Amazigh artistic and cultural activity remained publicly visible. Photographs of Imazighen were featured on travel brochures, and Amazigh musicians commonly performed at government-organized tourist festivals. In addition, Morocco's many markets were filled with Amazigh ceramics, carpets, and silver jewelry for sale. Amazigh activists angrily complained that the government was reducing Amazigh culture to a folkloric commodity for tourists while marginalizing the Imazighen and preventing them from accessing the country's economic and political resources to the same degree as Arabs (Almasude 1999: 119).

In the 1990s Amazigh political activists became involved in more aggressive actions and public protests, insisting on Amazigh language instruction in schools and the incorporation of Amazigh languages in the media.[13] They argued that since the Tamazight language and the Amazigh culture are the basis of Moroccan society, they must be preserved in order to safeguard Morocco's distinct cultural heritage.[14] They demanded that Tamazight not be referred to as a dialect of Arabic, the official policy of the Moroccan government at the time, but be recognized as a national language.[15]

Imazighen in Morocco drew strength from Imazighen in France and Algeria, looking across national borders to become part of a transnational Amazigh group called the World Amazigh Congress. In 1994 seven members of an Amazigh cultural association (located in Goulmima) called Tilelli, meaning "Freedom" in Tamazight, were arrested after publicly protesting in Errachidia and carrying banners with political slogans that promoted the recognition of Morocco's Imazighen.[16] Three of the seven men (all teachers) were sentenced to prison for terms of one to two years. Widespread publicity and public outrage led to a reduction of their sentences by the Moroccan king, and the three were released two months after their arrest. Protests like this and the public and international support for these protesters increasingly pressured the Moroccan monarchy to recognize the political necessity of heeding Amazigh demands (Maddy-Weitzman 2002: 161).

Four months after the protest, King Hassan II publicly announced that it was time to consider teaching Amazigh "dialects" in primary schools but that Arabic would remain the mother language of the country.[17] Amazigh activists continued to make demands on the government. After the death of Hassan II in 1999, his son King Muhammad VI continued his father's concessions to the Moroccan Amazigh population. In 2001 he ordered that a Royal Institute of Amazigh Culture (IRCAM) be established to study the Amazigh language and culture in an academic fashion.[18] The government introduced Amazigh languages into a limited number of Moroccan primary schools in 2004.

While Amazigh activists tirelessly work to preserve and promote their Amazigh identity, there is a strict gap between their political agenda and the daily life of the majority of Imazighen in Morocco. As noted by David Crawford (2002), Amazigh activists are a largely male-dominated group run by college-educated intellectuals, living far different lives than the rural Imazighen who have greatly contributed to the survival of Amazigh heritage. Ironically, the factors that create the differences between rural Amazigh and political activists are also those that have contributed to the survival of Amazigh cultural and linguistic heritage in Morocco: illiteracy and the association of the Amazigh language and culture with women. Amazigh men, even those in rural areas, are more likely than women to work outside the home and to receive formal education in Arabic, French, English, or Spanish, while rural Amazigh women are more likely to be monolingual and illiterate (Sadiqi 2003: 225). By speaking Tamazight on a daily basis in their homes and teaching it to their children, women thereby preserve the language and the culture.[19]

Southeastern Morocco, the focus of this book, is an ideal region for the consideration of issues of Amazigh art, gender, and ethnic identity. Southeastern Morocco was one of the last areas of the country to be colonized and was not controlled by the French until the 1930s. Therefore, artistic production in the area was not heavily influenced by the French colonial government's policy to control artistic production by creating artificial stylistic divisions among the different geographic regions of Morocco.[20] The Tafilalet, Morocco's largest oasis, is located in southeastern Morocco, fifty kilometers west of the border with Algeria (Fig. I.1). The oasis has hundreds of thousands of palm trees covering an area thirteen miles long and nine miles wide and is home to the ancient trading city of Sijilmasa. Caravans from Sijilmasa traversed the Sahara to western Africa and returned with gold, slaves, and other commodities destined for northern Africa and Europe. Southeastern Morocco has historically been a crossroads where people of diverse origins and backgrounds have long interacted, and the area continues to contain much ethnic diversity.

The Tafilalet is somewhat isolated from the rest of the country. To get there, it is necessary to take a rigorous ten-hour bus ride from Casablanca on thin, winding roads that eventually lead to the provincial capital of Errachidia, and from there another bus or taxi for the hour-long ride to the Tafilalet oasis. In addition to its early historical importance and ethnic diversity, the Tafilalet also holds the distinction of being the home of the Alaouite dynasty that ruled Morocco in the seventeenth century and continues to rule today. The Alaouite dynasty, founded by Mulay Ali Sherif in 1666, claims descent from the Prophet Muhammad, giving the region considerable religious significance. Mulay Ali Sherif's tomb is located just outside of Rissani, the largest town in the oasis, with 40,000 people. The town is small and sleepy except on market days, when it becomes vibrant and full of activity.

The Ait Khabbash, who are part of the largest Amazigh group in southern Morocco, the Ait Atta, reside in and around the oasis. Prior to colonization, the Tafilalet oasis could be described as an Arab oasis surrounded by an Amazigh sea. Until recently, sedentary Arab farmers (who called themselves Filala after the name "Tafilalet") inhabited the oasis, while Ait Khabbash populated the surrounding desert landscape. The Ait Khabbash controlled approximately 25,000 square kilometers of land that extended from Boudnib in the northeast to Tabalbala in the south. Ait Khabbash also traveled north into the Atlas Mountains and west to the area near Zagora (Joly 1951) (Fig. I.2).

Even though the Ait Khabbash did not live in the numerous walled mudbrick villages (called *qsour*) that dot the oasis, the Tafilalet oasis was still considered Ait Khabbash territory, because the Ait Khabbash would threaten to invade Arab villages to collect financial tribute from the sedentary Arab farmers. Arab farmers paid the Ait Khabbash one-third to one-fourth of their total harvest as tribute; in exchange, the Ait Khabbash were obliged to dispatch a number of men whenever necessary (Dunn 1977; Spillman 1936).

In the late nineteenth century three Arab villages on the fringe of the oasis, under threat of invasion from another Amazigh group, invited the Ait Khabbash to live with them. Ait Khabbash still occupy these villages today. For more than two years I lived in one of these villages, Mezguida (five kilometers outside of Rissani), in a large, two-story mud-brick house with my husband's Ait Khabbash family, where I learned about Amazigh arts and culture by par-

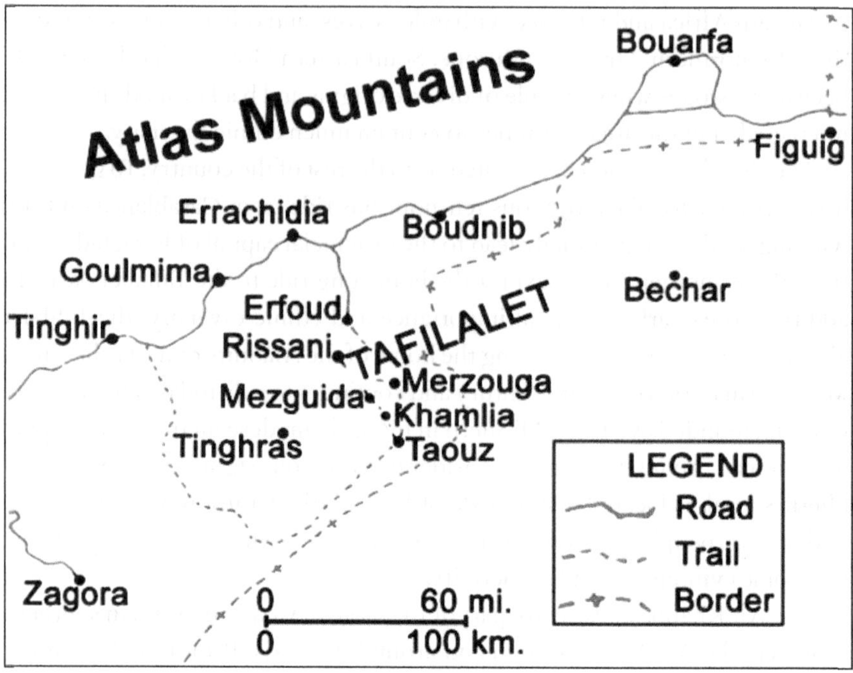

Figure I.1. Detail of the Tafilalet oasis. Map by David Kelley.

ticipating in everyday life, attending scores of Ait Khabbash weddings, collecting wedding songs, photographing and filming wedding ceremonies, and discussing my interpretations with numerous Ait Khabbash women and men.

My fluency in Moroccan Arabic and basic knowledge of Tamazight, the language of the Ait Khabbash, made possible one of the central and original insights of this book: the interrelationship of the visual and the verbal arts in Amazigh society. Addi Ouadderrou transcribed the oral text from tape recordings and videocassettes, using the system of transcription developed by Chaker (1984), and together we translated the text into English. I had the opportunity to spend considerable time speaking with women and photographing their arts, which would not have been possible for a male scholar. A man would not have been allowed to sit with women while the bride was dressed. Male scholars would not have been privy to women's conversations about marriage, sexual relations, and other private matters. Women freely shared this information with another woman, however; hence my gender contributed to my understanding of women's arts in the region. My experience living and studying in Morocco and my familial connections have given me an intimate view of Moroccan culture and an appreciation for the nuances and complexity of Amazigh art and culture.

The majority of images in this book are my own, allowing me to place textiles, jewelry, and other forms of artistic expression in their original cultural contexts. In certain instances, women asked that their individual identities not be revealed in publication. Hence, I covered their faces using a photo-editing program and refrained from using their names in the photos' captions. The generic captions used in this book are not intended to objectify people but simply to protect their requested anonymity.

Although the Tafilalet oasis is somewhat marginalized from the rest of Morocco, lifestyles of people in southeastern Morocco have changed drastically over the last century. This has led to similar changes in the arts, which I discovered in conversations with friends and participation in their lives. I also learned about Ait Khabbash life in the past from older women, who sometimes

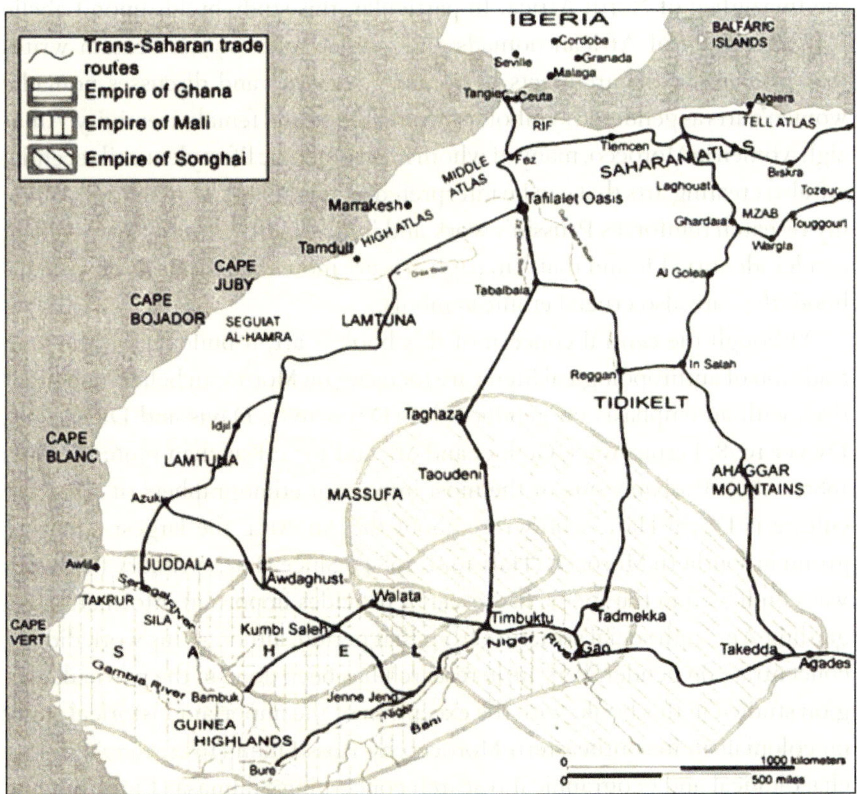

Figure I.2. Map of the trans-Saharan trade routes. Map by David Kelley.

continued to make and wear older art forms. Visits to Ait Khabbash families still living nomadic lifestyles outside the oasis and colonial photographs dating from the 1930s to 1950s provided additional information on nomadic lifestyles.

As this study demonstrates, French colonization and its aftermath caused Imazighen to abandon or modify many of their art forms, which in turn profoundly influenced gender roles. After independence, increased contact with Arabs living in the Tafilalet oasis also influenced Ait Khabbash art and culture. Therefore, this study presents Amazigh women's arts as living, dynamic cultural forms that have changed and continue to change in response to external and internal pressures. This allows women to negotiate their social position, which is dependent on their connection to Amazigh identity.

In the field of African art there is increased interest in incorporating North Africa into the art history canon, and this book fills a significant gap in the understanding of textile production, dress, and performance modes among the Imazighen of North Africa. In particular, this study builds upon Labelle Prussin's study of African nomads and gender roles (1995). Prussin writes that women are the architects in nomadic societies and discusses nomadic women's arts as gendered symbols of womanhood and female creativity. Amazigh women in Morocco, many of whom lived nomadic lifestyles until recently, are also creating arts that can be interpreted as symbols of womanhood. While my research reinforces Prussin's work and indicates that Amazigh arts reflect gender identity, I found that Amazigh arts are more than symbols of womanhood: they are also crucial ethnic symbols.

Although the central concern of this book is art, it builds upon the long tradition of anthropological literature focusing on Moroccan beliefs and practices with an emphasis on gender roles (Davis 1983; Davis and Davis 1985; Dwyer 1978; Fernea 1998; Gellner and Micaud 1972; Kapchan 1996; Mernissi 1987, 1989). Probably one of the most important ethnographers of Amazigh culture is David Hart, who wrote about the Ait Atta, the largest Amazigh group in southern Morocco (Hart 1981, 1984). Since Hart's primary fieldwork was conducted in the 1960s, his research provides important information regarding Amazigh social structure from that period, although his work did not concentrate on gender. Very little research has been done in the particular region studied in this book, with the exception of the important historical study on colonialism in southeastern Morocco by Ross Dunn (1972, 1977), the archaeological and geographical research concerning Sijilmasa (Lightfoot and

Miller 1996; Miller 2001), and a recent anthropological study on Ait Khabbash concepts of honor by the French scholar Marie-Luce Gélard (2003).

Chapter One focuses on the performative practice of weaving textiles, which for Ait Khabbash women has included nomadic tents, clothing, blankets, and grain sacks. This discussion of the process of textile manufacture itself as well as the finished product demonstrates that Ait Khabbash women are cultural carriers who give life to the society both literally and metaphorically.

In Chapter Two, the description of Ait Khabbash women's art forms is extended to dress, including hairstyles, tattooing, and embroidered headscarves. This chapter considers how gender identity is learned as a person passes through the life cycle and analyzes the gender identity inscribed through dress at birth, childhood, and puberty. In particular, it discusses women's tattooing and the implications of permanently carrying symbols of the group's identity on the body.

In Chapter Three, the focus is on *ahidous,* a collective dance commonly performed at weddings by Amazigh groups throughout Morocco. The dance incorporates many forms of expressive culture, such as movement, singing, musical instruments, and specific forms of dress. This examination of the aesthetics of *ahidous* performances considers women's agency and use of dress to negotiate the tension between contemporary modesty requirements and the source of their power in Amazigh society — their connection to female fertility.

Chapters Four and Five analyze Amazigh weddings and their associated art forms. Through their central role in Amazigh weddings, women express and preserve the cultural distinctiveness of their group despite other societal influences that have changed the nature of their daily life. Although the styles of everyday clothing and jewelry have continued to change for Amazigh women and men, the adornment of the bride and groom, the focus of Chapter Four, has remained the same. Chapter Five concentrates on the dances, songs, and ceremonies that make up the three-day wedding ceremony itself. Together, these two chapters demonstrate that control over symbolic systems such as the arts earns women considerable respect in Amazigh society, as weddings and their associated art forms are among the few concrete symbols that continue to unify the Amazigh community.

Chapter Six considers how Ait Khabbash art forms have been shaped by their participation in the trans-Saharan slave trade. The Ait Khabbash enslaved peoples from Sudanic Africa (the area of Africa south of the Sahara between the Nile and the Atlantic). The descendants of those enslaved have been assimilated into the Ait Khabbash; but, at the same time, the groups do not intermarry. Despite the fact that slavery was outlawed in the 1930s, the descendants of the enslaved continue to refer to themselves as Ismkhan, the plural form of the word *ismkh* or "slave" in Tamazight. This chapter discusses the visual and performing arts found at Ismkhan ceremonies, which unite them with the Ait Khabbash but also express their difference.

As the concluding chapter demonstrates, far from being fixed in an essentialized, stagnant past, Amazigh artistic production and its relation to gender roles continue to be subject to the changing discourses of history, culture, and power. Morocco's Amazigh heritage makes it distinct from the rest of Africa and the Middle East; thus the artistic heritage of Amazigh women is crucial to the creation of a new "Moroccan" identity that embraces the cultural diversity that is part of the country's history and visually expresses the concerns of the emerging Amazigh cultural and political movement.

In sum, these chapters consider various artistic forms, examining both the process of artistic creation and finished products to provide an original view of women's lives in southeastern Morocco. Artistic production not only reveals the complexity of women's roles but also demonstrates women's agency. These chapters argue that the control over artistic production is a mechanism through which women can negotiate complex religious and social issues while restricting them to limited roles in their society, thereby demonstrating the complexity of women's lives in Islamic Africa.

ONE

Ait Khabbash Textiles

WEAVING METAPHORS OF IDENTITY

A woman who weaves forty carpets is guaranteed a place in heaven.

—MOROCCAN PROVERB

A commonality among Amazigh art across Morocco is the predominant place of textiles. Amazigh women are renowned for the brightly colored carpets, blankets, and clothing that they weave from goat, sheep, and camel wool, and Ait Khabbash women are no exception. In addition to the functionality of these art forms, the colors and motifs that adorn Ait Khabbash textiles refer to female fertility and also serve as symbols of Ait Khabbash ethnic identity. Thus an examination of these textiles illuminates both the aesthetic system that informs Ait Khabbash art and the central role of women in artistic production.

As this chapter illustrates, the formal qualities of this art have been primarily shaped by two factors: the nomadic history of the Ait Khabbash and beliefs concerning female fertility. The process of weaving itself is central to the discussion because of its reliance on collaboration and mutual assistance, reflecting a nomadic lifestyle that is based on cooperation. Women dominate the weaving process, metaphorically giving life to textiles that serve as public symbols of Ait Khabbash Amazigh identity. With this cultural background, we shall see that women have a crucial role in the maintenance and public expression of Ait Khabbash identity.

Ait Khabbash Art and Their Nomadic Past

"Why do they have a tent set up next to their house?" I asked my sister-in-law Khera after visiting an Ait Khabbash family living on the outskirts of Mezguida. She explained that the family, who were among the last remaining Ait Khabbash to abandon their nomadic way of life, had illegally settled on the village's communal land. Aware that the village's governmental council did not want nomads to settle on land that could be used for agriculture and might forcefully remove them at any time, they hastily built a one-room mud-brick house so that they could claim permanent residence. They used the familiar tent as an extra sleeping area for their children and a place to pass the cool desert evenings.

Mezguida is one of four villages in the Tafilalet oasis occupied by Imazighen (Fig. 1.1). The majority of the Ait Khabbash, who arrived in the area from the Ait Atta–controlled territory of south-central Morocco in the early nineteenth century, advanced into the Tafilalet oasis and forced Arabs living in the oasis into submission (Hart 1981: 15). Although the Ait Khabbash survived on grains and dates given to them in the form of tribute by Arabs in the oasis, the majority lived a nomadic lifestyle even after French occupation of this region in 1934 (Spillman 1936). The Ait Khabbash raised goats, sheep, and camels in this Saharan region of southeastern Morocco, which receives less than four inches of rainfall per year. These tents — woven, constructed, and taken down by women — protected families from the scorching desert sun, the frequent sandstorms, and the cold desert nights. Nighttime temperatures can be as cold as 30 degrees Fahrenheit during the winter and daytime temperatures in the summer months can be as hot as 120 degrees.

The wide-open landscape of the region, called the *hamada* in Arabic, is covered with black stones and divided by dry riverbeds that seasonally fill with water. The flat *hamada* is disrupted by massive dunes of gold-colored sand that house enormous reserves of fresh water. Nomads built wells on the fringe of the dunes, and the seasonal flooding of dried riverbeds supplied them with much-needed water. Ait Khabbash subsistence was different from that of other Ait Atta in Morocco, who were transhumant, herding sheep and living in mud and stone houses in the fall and winter and in tents in the spring and summer (Hart 1981: 5). Unlike other Ait Atta, the Ait Khabbash were nomadic year round and herded camels (Joly 1951). The herding of camels (which required large amounts of fodder), coupled with the harsh desert environment of southeastern Morocco, meant that the Ait Khabbash traversed larger expanses of land than most Amazigh nomads or transhumants, searching for food sufficient for their livestock. Ait Khabbash crossed the Sahara, participating in the trans-Saharan caravan trade into western Africa via Tabalbala in Algeria.

As with most nomads, a family measured its material wealth by the amount

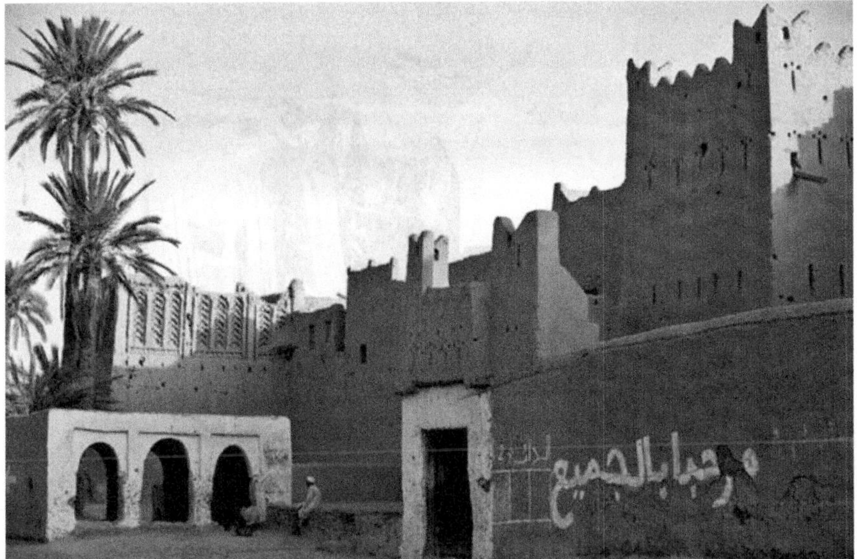

Figure 1.1. Qsar Mezguida in the Tafilalet oasis.

of livestock it owned. Livestock provided meat, milk, and wool. Wool was used to make items necessary for daily life. Unlike more sedentary peoples, the Ait Khabbash did not purchase their blankets, carpets, and bags in the local market; instead the women used the wool from their animals to weave them. The soft hair from sheep and camels was used to make the floor coverings on vertical looms set up inside a nomadic tent between two upright poles that supported its frame. The strong, coarse goat hair was reserved for creating the long, narrow brown tent panels called *aflidj* (plural *iflidjen*). Women wove these tent panels on horizontal ground looms, called *azetta n iflidjen,* that ran parallel to the ground (Fig. 1.2). They created the horizontal ground loom by pounding four pegs into the ground and tying two cross-poles to them. Since the warp threads were long, a weaver worked sitting in the open air. The loom had a fixed heddle rod and shed stick that held the warp threads apart so that a weaver could pass the weft through the warp with her hand. Weavers pounded the weft threads in place with an iron comb called a *taska.*[1]

Each *aflidj* was at least two feet wide and thirty-two feet long, and they were sewn together to create a tent. A medium-sized tent consisted of approximately seven *iflidjen,* each of which took about three weeks to weave; and a woman typically wove one new *aflidj* every year. Many other utilitarian textiles were also woven on the horizontal loom. A sack for transporting grain

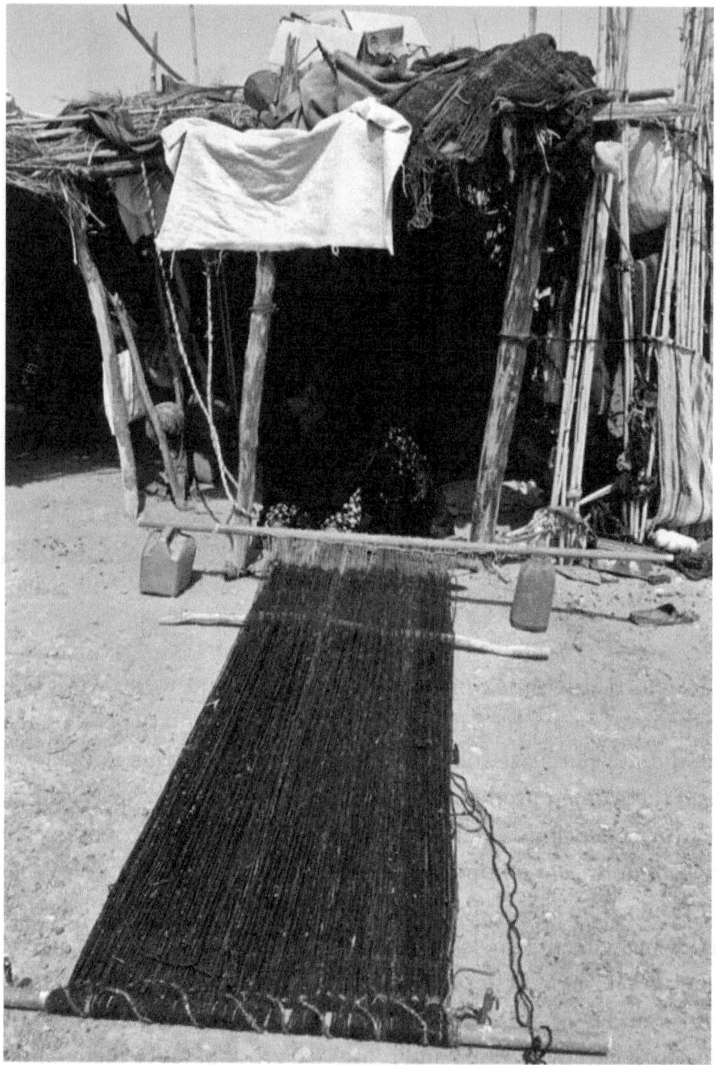

*Figure 1.2. An Ait Khabbash woman living outside the Tafilalet oasis weaves
a panel for her nomadic tent, 2002.*

and other goods on a camel or donkey's back could be made from a single *aflidj*
folded over, with its bottom and sides sewn together. Women also wove wool
bags that were hung inside the tent to store valuable items such as jewelry,
tobacco, henna, and various herbs.

The textiles woven by the women, while crucial to daily survival, also
served as symbols of Ait Khabbash group identity. Sedentary Arab women,

such as those living in the Tafilalet oasis of southeastern Morocco, typically did not weave textiles, because they did not have access to wool from large herds of livestock; while Arab nomads living in the desert also wove tents similar to those of the Ait Khabbash, they did not fill their tents with woven wool bags and blankets. Arab nomads instead made nonwool blankets, called *bu sharwiṭ* in Moroccan Arabic, which were woven from old clothing torn into strips.[2] Until quite recently, the Ait Khabbash had taboos that prevented women from making similar nonwool textiles. Fatima, a friend living in Haselbait, explained:

> The *bu sharwiṭ* was made from old clothes, and in the past clothing was not as bright and colorful as it is today. A *bu sharwiṭ* was very dull looking and only poor people used them. We don't make these because we believe they bring bad luck to the family. My sister sent me one a couple of years ago, and I asked my mother-in-law if I could keep it. She said it was okay if I did not start making them myself.

The reliance of the Ait Khabbash on animal wool to weave bedding and shelter and on animal meat and milk for subsistence meant that during times of drought they necessarily developed a symbiotic relationship with the Arab farmers living in the nearby Tafilalet oasis. Although the oasis is surrounded by the vast, open desert, its water supply supports more than a hundred villages or *qsour* (singular *qsar*), historically occupied by Arab farmers. A *qsar* consists of adjoining two-story square mud-brick houses set along narrow alleyways and surrounded by a massive wall and can house 200 to 2,000 people (Fig. 1.1). The oasis of the Tafilalet provided the Ait Khabbash relief from the harsh desert landscape and a source for the foods upon which they became dependent. Barley and wheat cultivated on small plots of land provided grains for bread and couscous, and palm trees were a rich supply of the highly desired dates. Although the Ait Khabbash relied on these crops for their survival as nomads, they did not respect anyone who worked the land, preferring to sell their livestock to buy dates and grain from the Arabs living in the oasis. Ait Khabbash often collected these products in the form of tribute, first raiding a village and then demanding *râaya* or "protection money": Arab farmers typically paid a quarter or third of their harvest to the Ait Khabbash. The fear of being pillaged or having their date palms cut down forced most of the cultivators into paying regular tribute to the Ait Khabbash (Dunn 1972, 1977).

After the French occupation of the Tafilalet oasis in 1934, life changed drastically for everyone living there and in the surrounding desert, but especially for the Ait Khabbash. The French occupation stopped the free movement of Ait Khabbash with their herds; although they still raided *qsour* for wheat and dates, they were no longer able to collect tribute from their previous clients. The French presence also restricted the extent of their grazing land and ended their trade across the Sahara. Together these factors forced many families to abandon their nomadic lifestyle and sell their livestock, especially in light of a policy that the French enacted to encourage the settlement of nomads in the region. By 1959, according to Frank Trout's *Morocco's Saharan Frontiers* (1969: 151), only 10 percent of the Ait Khabbash in southeastern Morocco continued to be nomadic. By this time, most nomadic Ait Khabbash had folded up their tents and built mud-brick villages on what had been their traditional grazing territory, creating desert towns such as Hafira, Tabat el Khir, Merzouga, Khamlia, Taouz, and Haselbait (Fig. I.1). These towns were built near the water supplies found under the desert's sand dunes, providing water to drink and to irrigate newly planted crops of wheat and vegetables. Despite making the transition to a sedentary lifestyle, Ait Khabbash women still kept small herds of sheep and goats, traversing the landscape looking for fodder rather than letting them graze.

In the 1970s further changes occurred in the lifestyle of the Ait Khabbash when the Moroccan government built a dam at the River Ziz in Errachidia that prevented seasonal flooding, which, together with drought, caused the landscape to dry up. Lack of grazing land meant that most of the remaining nomads sold their sheep and goats, left their tents, and built houses in the previously established oasis towns of Rissani and nearby Erfoud.

As a result of all these changes, textile production by Ait Khabbash women has also changed in many ways. For example, because the weaving of tents was no longer necessary, by the 1960s the horizontal ground loom had virtually disappeared from use. Instead the vertical loom became more common, and it is currently the most widely used loom in Morocco.

Since wool working, which includes washing and combing the wool and then spinning it into thread, is labor intensive, women do not work alone but rely on the aid of their daughters, daughters-in-law, friends, and neighbors. Among the Ait Khabbash every aspect of weaving, from start to finish, is a communal endeavor, demonstrating the Amazigh concept of *adwal* or "cooperation," a type of mutual aid involving shared labor in which members of the group assist each other with a particular task until everyone has been

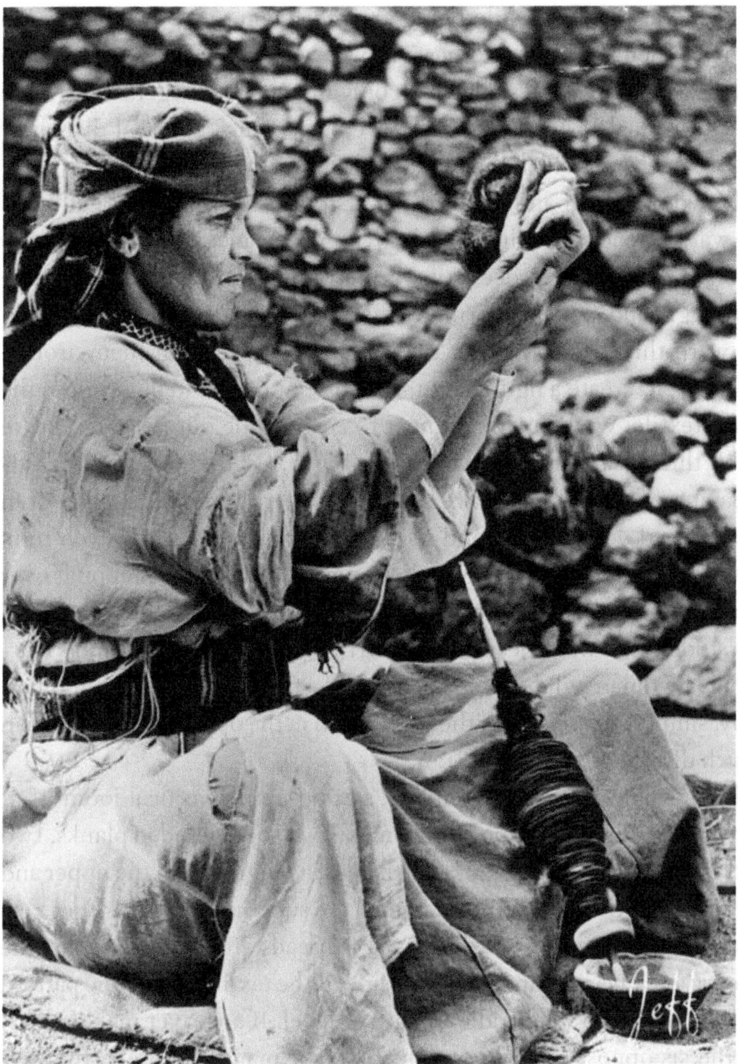

Figure 1.3. A woman spinning wool. Photo courtesy of the National Anthropological Archives, 1930–1959. Smithsonian Institution/04072800.

helped with it.[3] Even with such help, the preparation of wool for the loom is a time-consuming process. First the women must card the warp threads using long-toothed combs, and a small drop spindle called a *tizdit* creates fine, strongly twisted threads that are wound into a ball for later use (Fig. 1.3). To create the more loosely twisted weft threads, they use short-toothed brushes and large leg-twirled spindles called *izdi*. They may or may not dye the weft threads, depending on the textile being created. Dying wool also often involves many women working together. The weavers I spoke with did not have any knowledge of natural dyes, although only mineral and vegetal dyes were once used. Instead, they told me, they have been using chemical dyes ever since they became available in the nineteenth century.

After the wool is spun and dyed, three or four women work together to mount the warp threads onto the loom, providing a chance to gather together and socialize. To begin the process of warping, they hammer a row of three stakes into the ground, which determines the length of the textile. One woman wraps the warp threads around the two outer stakes, turning them around the central stake to create a figure eight; the amount of thread determines the width of the textile. Women who sit next to each of the outer stakes ensure that the weft threads are adequately spaced (Fig. 1.4).[4] In the beliefs regarding the weaving of textiles that have developed over the centuries, the loom itself is considered very potent, and its power begins before it is even fully constructed. According to Amazigh beliefs, people must avoid stepping over the warp threads before they are attached to the loom or risk a life filled with bad luck: a student will never learn, an unmarried person will never find a marriage partner, a woman will become barren, and a man will become impotent. Fortunately, simply stepping over the warp again in the opposite direction can forestall such disaster (Reswick 1981: 60).

After the warping process is complete, setting up the vertical loom itself requires the cooperation of numerous women. Two solid wooden planks, two inches thick by six inches wide and over six feet in length, form the upper and lower horizontal portions of the loom, which are supported by two other vertical planks. Women carefully leash the warp threads around a single heddle rod. Weavers typically sit facing the underside of the textile so that the pattern does not face them with the heddle rod at eye level. If a weaver makes a flat-woven textile, as opposed to a knotted carpet, she manually inserts the weft threads horizontally through the warp threads held apart by the heddle rod and shed stick (Fig. 1.5). A small iron comb with a wooden handle called a *taska* is then used to pound the weft threads into place. As the women work, they unwind the warp from the top beam and roll the completed portion around the lower beam, limiting the height of the loom so it can be used indoors rather than outdoors. As I observed in Mezguida, two or more women often worked together on the same loom; or, on days when there was a great deal of other work to be done around the house, the women would take turns weaving. Sometimes my mother-in-law would weave in the morning, for instance,

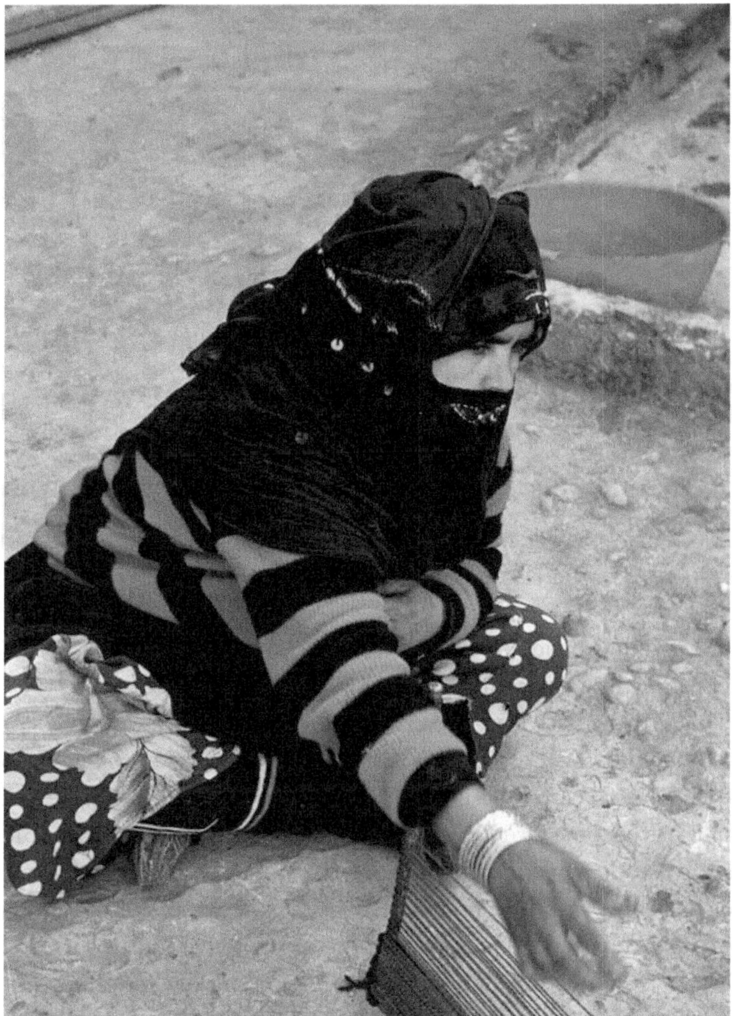

Figure 1.4. An Ait Khabbash woman prepares the warp threads of her loom, 1996. (The woman in this photograph requested anonymity, so her image was altered using photo retouching software, extending her head covering to conceal her lower face.)

and her daughter would take over in the afternoon. The weaving process suggests that weaving is a communal endeavor intended to benefit the entire household.

Ait Khabbash textiles are unusual: unlike Amazigh textiles found in other areas of North Africa, they do not have geometric motifs. Ait Khabbash women weave flat-woven blankets, floor coverings, bags, and pillows that con-

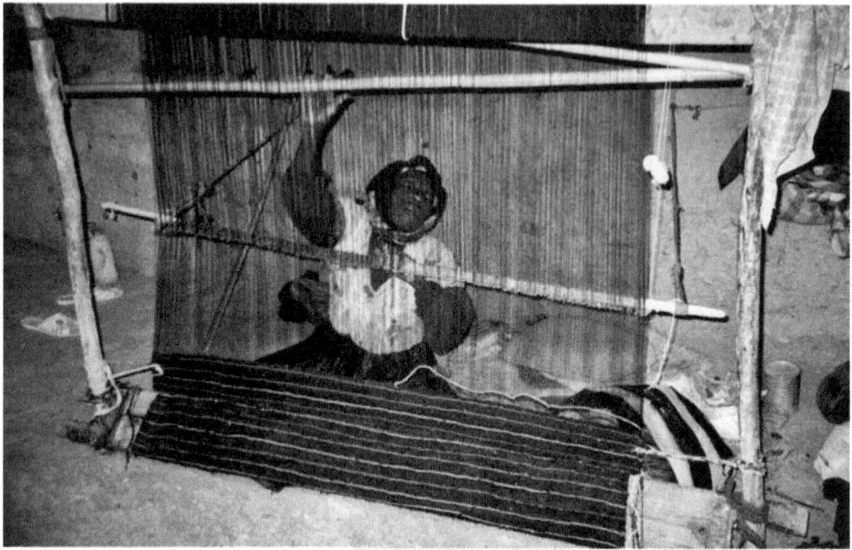

Figure 1.5. An Ait Khabbash woman in Khamlia weaves on her vertical loom, 1999.

sist of solid horizontal bands of undyed wool or of alternating red, green, yellow, black, and white horizontal bands (Fig. 1.6).

Until the mid-1980s these were the primary types of textiles woven by Ait Khabbash women; however, in the last twenty years weavers have begun to make long-pile knotted carpets (Fig. 1.7). Wool continues to be the preferred material, but it has become rarer in recent years. Although Ait Khabbash sold most of their livestock when they settled, many families continued to keep a dozen or so sheep and/or goats, requiring women to spend numerous hours walking the desert landscape to find food for them. Women proudly continued to weave carpets from this wool until recently. As a result of drought conditions and increased desertification in the last twenty years, the Ait Khabbash started to keep fewer livestock. By the 1980s most women purchased some or all of their wool in the market. Because wool is expensive, women started to economize by unwinding sweaters and leggings made from synthetic fibers and used that thread to create knotted carpets. These new materials also mean that the number and variety of colors used in textile production have greatly increased (Fig. 1.8). Women still prefer to use wool; but since the Ait Khabbash rarely own large herds of sheep, they use synthetic fibers out of necessity. Some women told me that they prefer synthetic fibers, because their colors do not fade over time, while wool dyed with chemical dyes is rarely color-fast.

The style of textiles has also changed. Unlike the horizontal lines typical of

Ait Khabbash flat-woven carpets, knotted carpets often adopt repetitive triangle motifs that are sometimes combined to create a diamond motif (Fig. 1.7).
The use of the triangle is common to Amazigh art forms. For example, the
silver bracelets once commonly worn by Ait Atta women consist of a series of
triangular projections, and silver triangular pendants once commonly adorned
a woman's headdress (Fig. 1.9). Women also wore brightly colored beaded
chokers with repeating triangular motifs (Fig. 1.9) and painted triangular red
and green motifs on dyed yellow skin bags, which they used to carry henna
and perfumed herbs (Fig. 1.10). Triangular tassels dangle from the ends of an
Ait Khabbash bride's large amber necklace and her wool belt, mimicking the

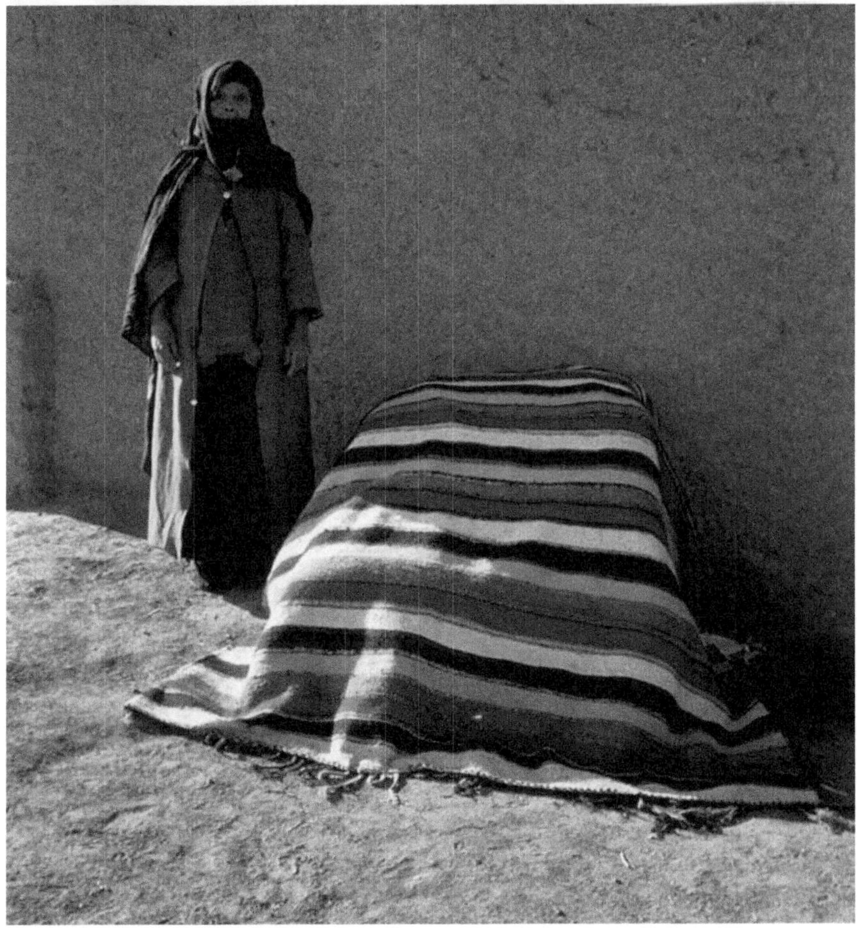

Figure 1.6. An Ait Khabbash woman stands near the textile she wove, 1995.

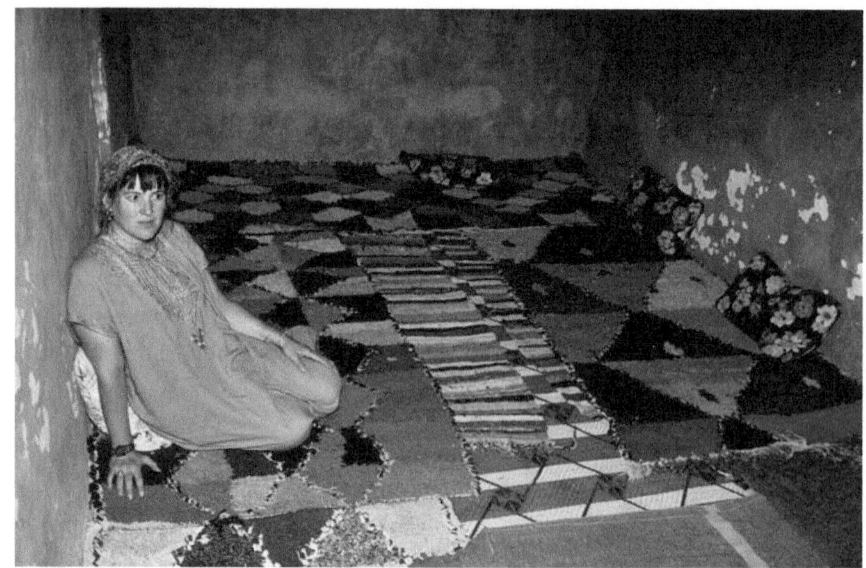

Figure 1.7. Interior of an Ait Khabbash home at Khamlia, 2002. Photo by Addi Ouadderrou.

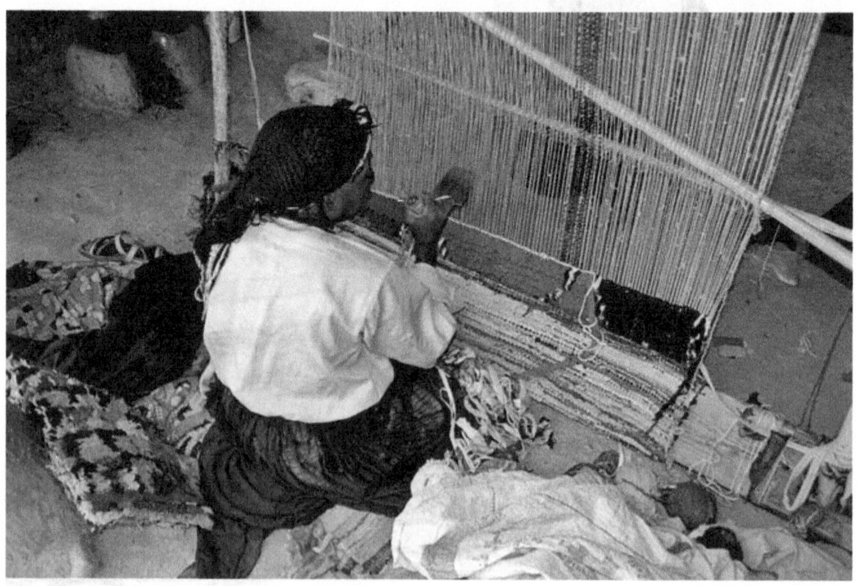

Figure 1.8. An Ait Khabbash woman weaves a knotted carpet from synthetic fibers, 2000.

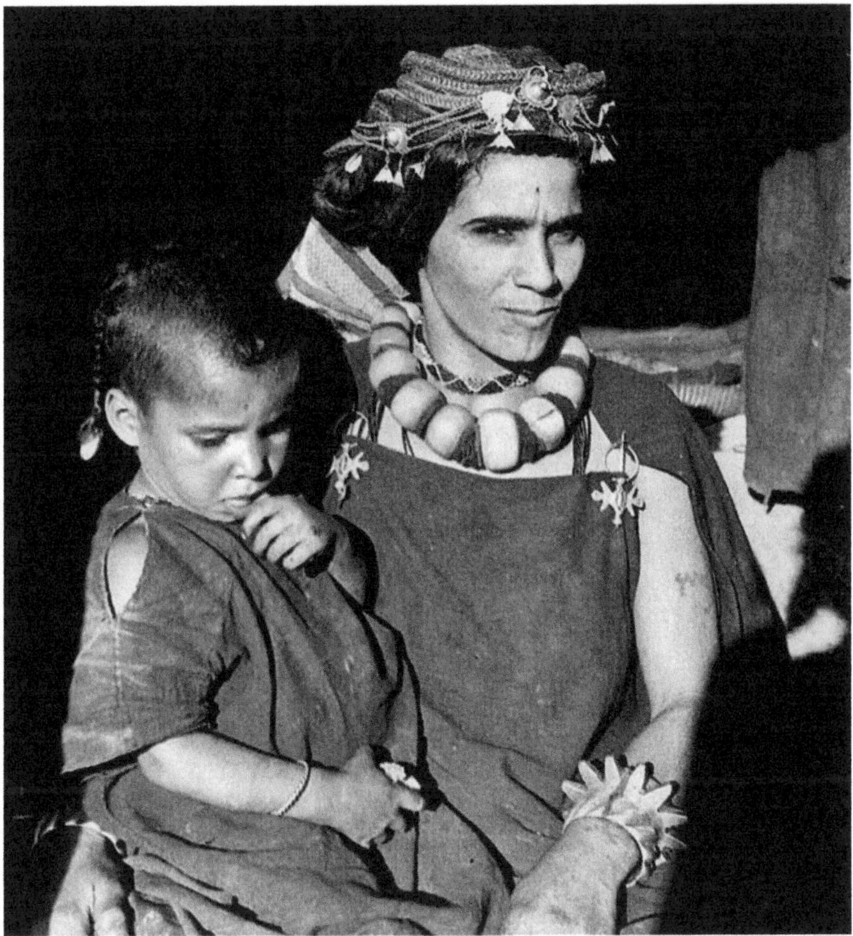

Figure 1.9. This photo from the 1950s shows an Ait Atta woman wearing the headdress and large silver bracelets once commonly worn by Ait Khabbash women on a daily basis. Photo by Mireille Morin-Barde, 1950–1952 © Édisud.

triangle motif also embroidered on Ait Khabbash women's head coverings (Fig. 1.11).

Amazigh women throughout Morocco commonly weave motifs derived from the triangle (such as the zigzag and diamond) into their carpets, as seen in the contemporary Zemmour carpet in Figures 1.12 and 1.13. These various geometric motifs are given different names in the literature on Amazigh art. Authors refer to the zigzag pattern as the sickle, scissors, or saw—pointed objects that can pop and burst the evil eye. They commonly interpret the diamond and triangle as representing a mirror or an eye. Overlapping triangles

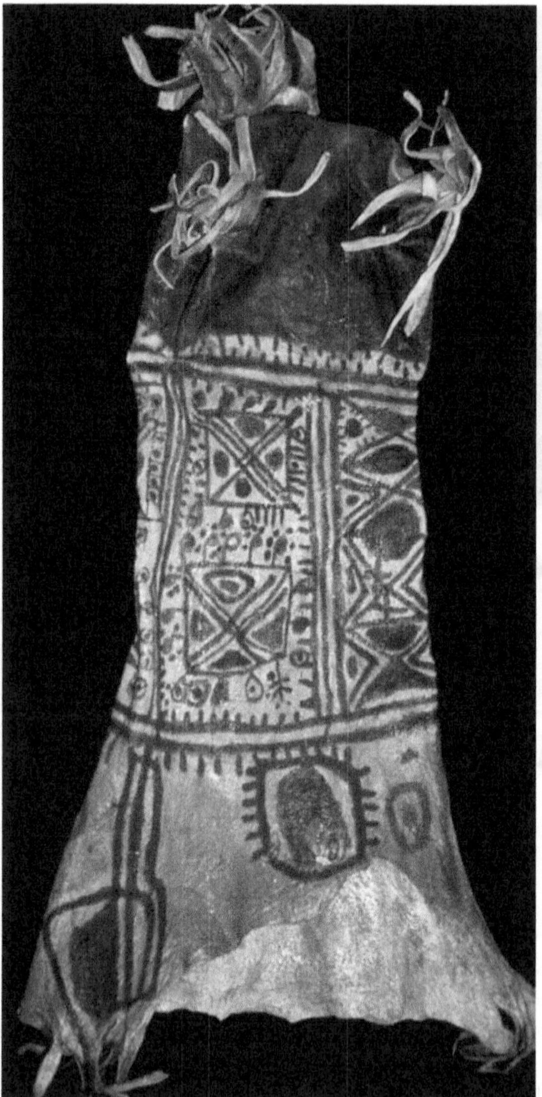

Figure 1.10. An Ait Khabbash woman's painted leather bag.

are often called spiders or chameleons. Scholars also interpret the triangle as a stylized hand motif that is protective (Bynon 1984; Reinisch and Stanzer 1991: 60–63; Westermarck 1926 [1968], 1: 465–466).

My own interpretation, based on both the literature and discussions with Amazigh weavers themselves, is that, while motifs used in Amazigh art remain the same from generation to generation and are transferred to various

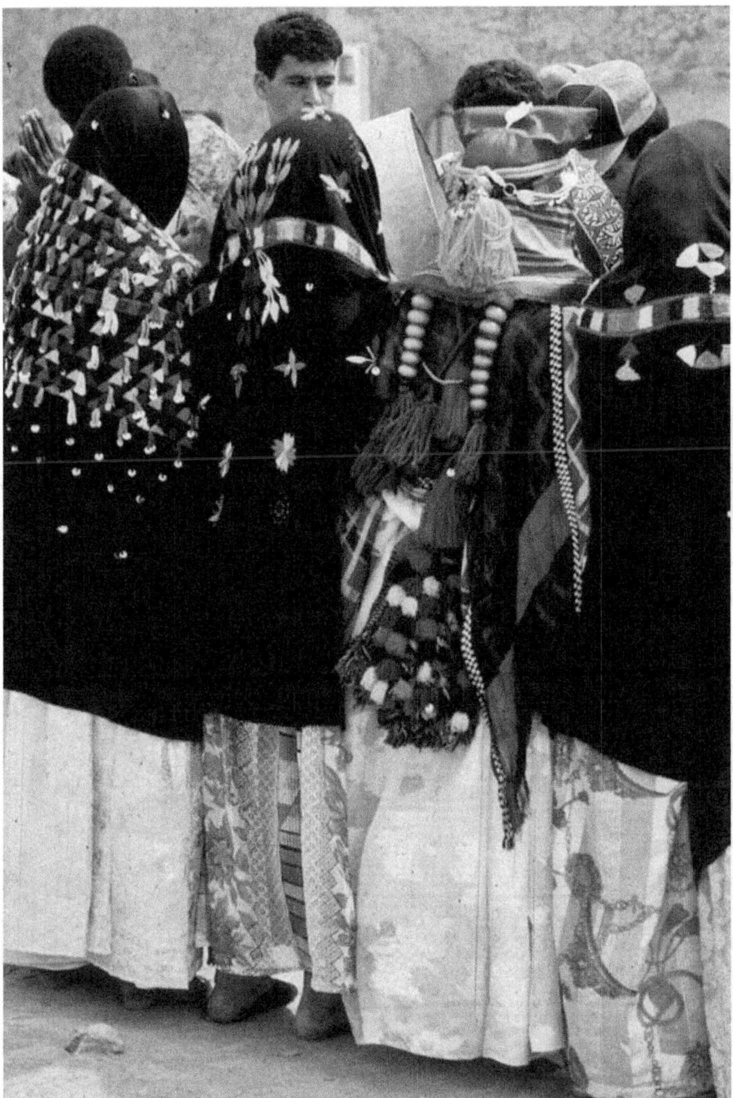

Figure 1.11. The bride participates in aḥidous *performance in Ḥafira, 1999.*

artistic media (such as textiles, tattoos, jewelry, and ceramics), most are based on the basic form of the triangle. The names given to the motifs change from generation to generation, however, depending on the historical and political circumstances of the time. For example, until the 1970s Ait Khabbash women commonly wore necklaces made of triangular silver pendants interspersed with colored plastic and glass beads (Fig. 1.14). The pendants themselves were

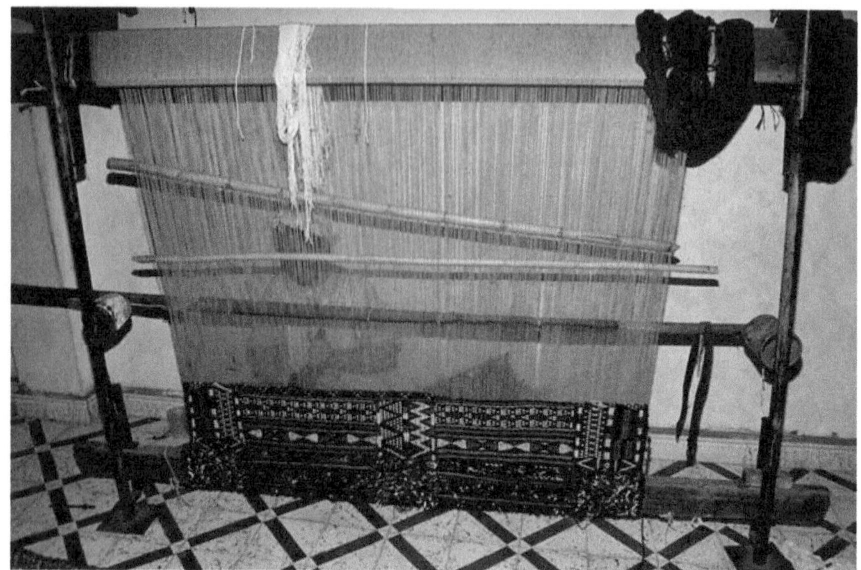

Figure 1.12. A Zemmour woman in Khemisset weaves at her loom, 2002.

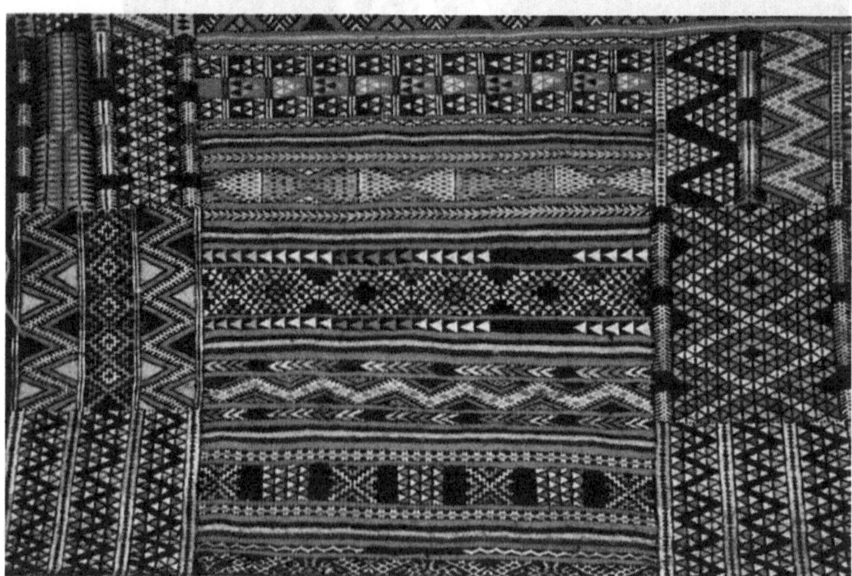

Figure 1.13. Close-up of a Zemmour woven carpet.

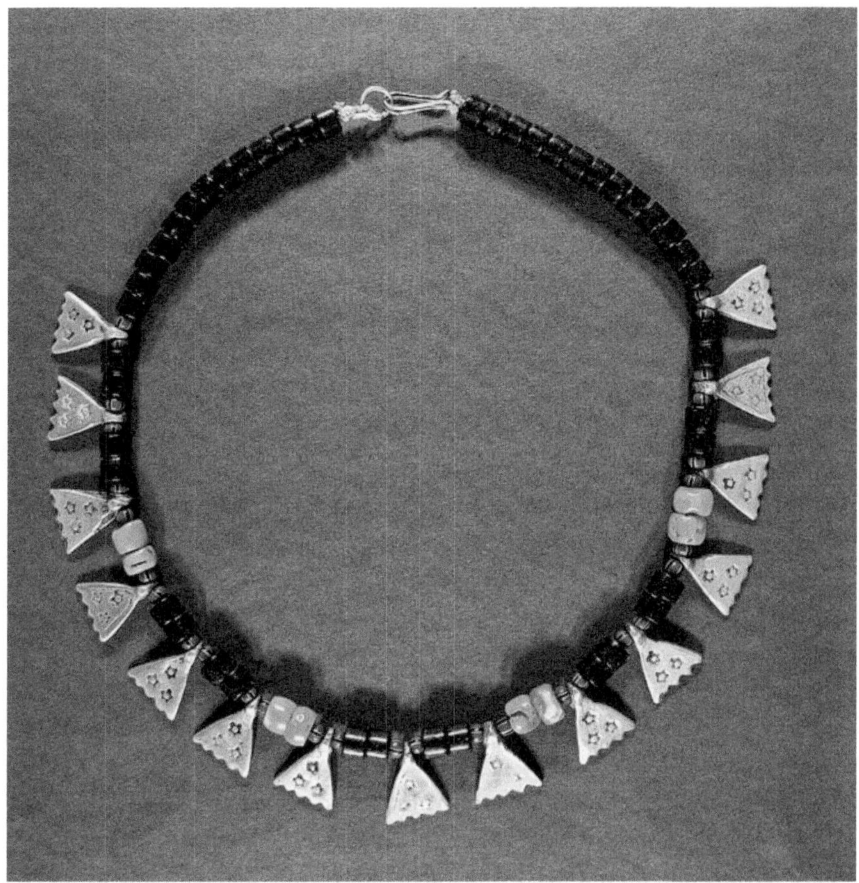

Figure 1.14. An Ait Khabbash necklace made from tiferfrin *pendants, said to resemble a pigeon's tail feathers.*

called *tiferfrin,* a term that comes from the Moroccan Arabic word *ferfer,* meaning "to fly." Women explained to me that beautiful women are often referred to as pigeons; hence the name was given to these pendants because their triangular shape reminded them of the tail feathers of this bird. Ait Khabbash refer to the triangle or diamond motif found on woven textiles as *taḥanut* ("room"). The nomadic tent-dwelling Ait Khabbash historically did not live in rooms or weave motifs based on triangular forms into their textiles until recently, so I interpret this as a reference to the relatively recent settlement of Ait Khabbash in houses. Women who were once responsible for creating their homes out of wool in the form of a tent are now transferring symbols of their new homes to textiles.

As Bert Flint (1980: 62) has noted, the triangle or diamond motif in textiles represents a settled existence, where life is contained within a physical boundary. I argue that its use in Ait Khabbash textiles reflects both the setting of boundaries for Ait Khabbash nomads who freely wandered the landscape prior to French colonialism and increasing restrictions placed on the physical movements of women. The recent settlement of the Imazighen in ethnically diverse urban areas in which houses have running water and cooking is done with gas means that women do not have the freedom of mobility they once had. Women often stay within their homes to avoid the Arab male strangers who are now their neighbors. Thus the triangle, a familiar visual symbol in Amazigh art, has been reused and redefined by the Ait Khabbash, taking on new meanings in the context of their changes in lifestyle and reflecting the process of adaptation and creativity.

Although Ait Khabbash women no longer weave clothing for their families and weaving is no longer crucial to daily survival, both men and women continue to praise women who excel at weaving blankets, pillows, and carpets. The Ait Khabbash women I encountered were proud that their weaving abilities significantly contributed to the economic well-being of their families. For instance, my friend Touda, a married woman in her late forties, told me that she gained satisfaction from helping her family materially and economically:

> Good women help their husbands by making carpets and blankets. My husband does not need to buy them at the market. The blankets at the market are terrible and do not keep you warm like a wool blanket made by an Ait Khabbash woman does.

Although the act of weaving still brings Ait Khabbash women status, fewer and fewer young women are learning how to weave blankets and carpets; it is rapidly becoming an art that is restricted to the older generation.

Textiles as Metaphors of Female Fertility

In order to understand Ait Khabbash textiles beyond their formal and functional characteristics, one must consider the metaphorical meanings they carry. Imazighen throughout Morocco commonly create metaphors based on things that share similar visual qualities. For example, I often heard the Ait Khabbash families tell riddles at night to pass the time.[5] These riddles, called *timeẓẓra,* use visual metaphors to compare *lemsayel-dey aksulent* or "things that are similar."

The word *tikselt* in Tamazight, translated as "a similarity," is derived from the verb *siksel,* which means "to be the same" or "to look alike" and is related to the concept of a metaphor. Most metaphoric associations emphasize objects found in the natural environment, such as these two metaphors that I heard while living in Morocco:

Question: *Zrey-awent-nit. Ticict n walluzen mi ylla wadduj ammas.*
[A plate of almonds with a walnut in the middle.]
Answer: *Igenna d yitran d wayur.*
[The sky, the stars, and the moon.]

Question: *Zrey-awent-nit. Tetey d-twrirt tgen.*
[It circled the mountain and slept.]
Answer: *Tawenza.*
[Bangs: the mountain represents the head, and "it" represents bangs.]

Metaphors are not only used in riddles: metaphors relating to fertility are attached to the actions and products of weaving. For example, the wool used in weaving itself is so important to the Ait Khabbash that it has taken on a metaphorical dimension and spiritual importance. Along with other natural substances (such as henna and wheat) that represent the fertility of the earth, wool is associated with fertility and believed to have *baraka,* "divine blessing." Wool in particular is attributed to God's generous nature, as God causes the rain that makes the grass grow that supplies animal herds with food. According to my mother-in-law:

Wool and bread are the same. If you see a piece of bread or a small piece of wool on the ground, you must pick them up. These things come from Allah and must be respected.

Thus Ait Khabbash women who work wool are highly respected, and it is even said that a woman who makes forty carpets during her lifetime receives the ultimate *baraka* or blessing: her passage to heaven is guaranteed after she dies. The Ait Khabbash also believe that some of the *baraka* of the wool is transferred to its user when wool blankets are used and wool clothing is worn. For that reason, clothing made from wool is highly valued, and an old wool garment is never discarded. Rather, the wool threads are unraveled and reused to create a new carpet or piece of clothing. Just as wool garments protect the wearer against the elements, they can metaphorically insulate and safeguard the larger community. My mother-in-law recounted that wool garments were believed to be so sacred that a white wool garment could be used to resolve disputes between two people. If two men angrily quarrel in public, for instance, a bystander may remove his white wool cape (called *asilham* in Tamazight and in this particular situation referred to as *aâban n Rebbi,* which means "clothing of God") and place it in front of them, signaling them to resolve their differences. Not obeying the command of *aâban n Rebbi* and refusing reconciliation is considered by the Ait Khabbash a shameful desecration of one of God's most important gifts.

The loom and the act of weaving are also believed to have *baraka* and, like the wool itself, are metaphors relating to fertility. When the warp threads are attached to the vertical loom, the textile is said to be metaphorically born and have a "soul" (*ruh*), echoing women's role in human reproduction and the propagation of the Ait Khabbash as a people. In some areas of Morocco, weavers physically straddle the warp threads and beams of the loom before they are raised, symbolizing the metaphoric birth of the textile;[6] according to the weaving lore of the Ait Khabbash, it then moves through youth, maturity, and old age as it is woven.[7] And when a textile is finished and its warp threads are cut, it is believed to die. The textile is splashed with water, just as Muslims wash a dead person before he or she is buried, and the following expression is recited: "Drink, loom. You will drink tomorrow in heaven." Not only do women have the power of life over the textile, but the personification of the textile underlines women's reproductive and creative powers and reinforces their role in the propagation of Ait Khabbash identity and the preservation of the Ait Khabbash as a people.

The Ait Khabbash also believe that the symbolic connection between textiles and the human life cycle leaves women weaving textiles especially vulnerable to attacks by the *jnoun* (singular *jinn*), spirits that prey on people passing through the major transitions of life. These supernatural beings are mentioned in the Qur'an:

> And surely We created man of sounding clay, of black mud fashioned into shape. And the jinn, We created before of intensely hot fire. (15: 26–27)[8]

This Qur'anic verse refers to the *jnoun* as beings made from fire, suggesting that they are hotheaded and uncontrollable, with a rebellious nature. They are contrasted with humans, who, made from an unpretentious lowly substance like clay, have a self-controlled and calmer nature.

Throughout Morocco, people believe the *jnoun* are temperamental beings who can be helpful one minute and angry and harmful the next. They are said by the Ait Khabbash to live in entrances to villages, doorways, drains, and wells. Pouring hot water down a drain is dangerous, because the *jnoun* may be burnt and take revenge against the person. *Jnoun* are also drawn to metaphorical passages, such as circumcision, marriage, and childbirth.[9] If the *jnoun* are provoked into action, it is said that they can cause serious illness or death. Possession by the *jnoun,* people believe, is the cause of epilepsy, strokes, convulsions, and mental illness, and a person whose body is possessed by the *jnoun* is said to be *mejnoun.* Just as people passing through life's transitions must protect themselves from the wrath of the *jnoun,* so must weavers. Thus, prior to mounting the warp threads, a weaver sprinkles the area surrounding a loom with salt, guarding her from the *jnoun,* who are referred to in Tamazight as *wida tsentel tisent,* "those who are hidden by salt."

The prevalence of fertility symbolism in Ait Khabbash aesthetics is also revealed by the colors and patterns used to weave textiles. As previously mentioned, the most common type of textile once woven by Ait Khabbash women on a vertical loom is the *taberraknut* or "flat-woven textile," which can be used as a blanket or a floor covering; a typical example of *taberraknut* can be seen in Figure 1.6. Its overall composition consists of repeating horizontal bands of solid color that proceed across its surface in a steady, rhythmic progression. Except for the absence of geometric patterning, it is similar in composition and color to Middle Atlas textiles made by the Zemmour, such as the carpet in Figures 1.12 and 1.13.[10] The colors red, green, yellow, purple (used in the place of black), and white dominate the Zemmour textile and are especially evident in the thin bands of solid color that divide the bands filled with geometric motifs. While this carpet is contemporary, most early twentieth century Amazigh textiles from Morocco have similar compositions and color schemes.

At first glance Ait Khabbash textiles appear to have no overall pattern that unites the composition; however, weavers organize the horizontal bands according to a very definite color scheme, in which a red band is followed first by a green one, then by a yellow band, and then by a black one. These same four colors are also used in the Ait Khabbash necklaces made from silver money and glass beads shown in Figure 1.15; and red, green, and yellow are used to adorn their leather bags (Fig. 1.10).

The Ait Khabbash divide the colors red, green, yellow, and black into a light/dark dichotomy; a dark color is always placed near a light color, giving a feeling of order and balance to the composition. Light colors, which include

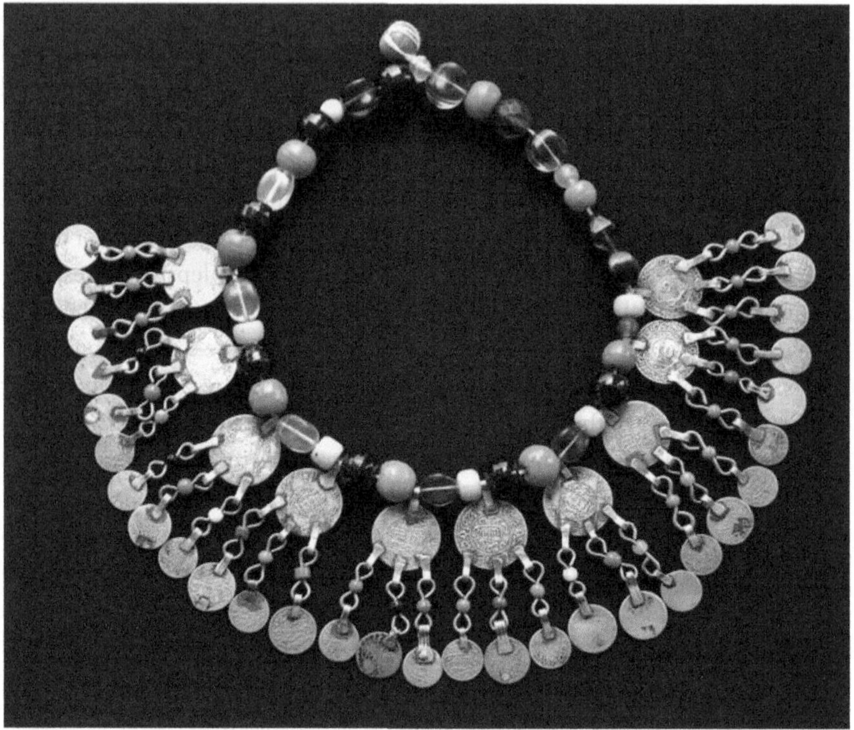

Figure 1.15. An Ait Khabbash necklace made from early-twentieth-century silver money and strung with red, green, yellow, and black beads. Photo by Addi Ouadderrou.

red and yellow, are called *llun issuddan*, which derives from the noun *asidd*, "light," because of their similarity to sunlight. Dark colors, such as black and green, are called *llun illasn*, from the noun *tillas*, "darkness." The four bands of alternating colors are sometimes separated by intervening bands of white repeated at the same regular intervals, establishing the orderly, steady rhythm of the woven textile.

I found that these five colors (red, green, yellow, black, and white) are the basic colors common to Amazigh textiles throughout Morocco.[11] In my conversations with them, Ait Khabbash women associated the colors red, green, yellow, and black with the life cycle of familiar things in their natural environment. Several women likened them to ripening dates, which turn from green to yellow and then red and an almost black dark brown, and an analogy can be made between ripening dates and the blossoming of a girl's body into that of a woman. Women also referred to these four colors as the hues of henna. Green is the color of henna leaves and of henna paste when it is first applied to the skin, and good henna will stain the skin black and then fade to red and to an almost yellow-orange color. The association of these colors with the natural life cycle also extends to the fertility of women and their ability to give life: they are worn by brides during the Ait Khabbash wedding ceremony.

Women also told me that the rainbow inspired their use of the colors red, green, yellow, and black (purple is often substituted for black). While these are only a sample of the actual colors in the rainbow, the rainbow is an important metaphor of female fertility. The name of a rainbow in Tamazight is *tislit n unẓar,* meaning "bride of the rain." Ait Khabbash highly value rainbows due to their rarity. Southeastern Morocco receives less than four inches of rainfall annually, making the sighting of a rainbow a rare treat. Ait Khabbash women may spontaneously hold "bride of the rain" ceremonies called *telyunja* once or twice a year, asking God to send rain and connecting women even more to the fertility of the land. The word *telyunja* derives from the word *ayunja,* referring to a large wooden ladle used by women to mix soup. During "bride of the rain" ceremonies, women outfit a ladle to look like an Ait Khabbash bride, who wears red, green, yellow, black, and white clothing (Fig. 1.16). Women, accompanied by their children, go from house to house (or tent to tent in the past) collecting wheat, tea, and sugar and singing:

Telyunja asey urawn s-igenna; yer i Rebbi ad-dik anẓar s-kigan.
Diy ar agmadin xes anẓar ayd-id iruran.
Tislit a Rebbi d-am wayur awa tiwey aman s-widda stedda awa.
Iqqur wattub a mulana, yit-tid a Rebbi.

[*Telyunja,* raise your hands to the sky; ask God to give a lot of rain.
I went until the other side of the river, and the rain made me
    come back.
Oh God, the bride looks like the moon taking water to the community
    where she is going.
Oh God, the soil is dry; bring rain.]

After collecting offerings, women march with their "bride" to a dried-up riverbed, turning her upside down and putting her head-first into the riverbed. The *telyunja* ceremony clearly connects women, especially newly married women, to fertility. The colors used in women's textiles, those worn by the bride during the actual wedding, and those worn by "the bride of the rain" suggest a connection between the fertility of the land and the fertility of women, celebrating a woman's reproductive power. Thus not only the textiles them-

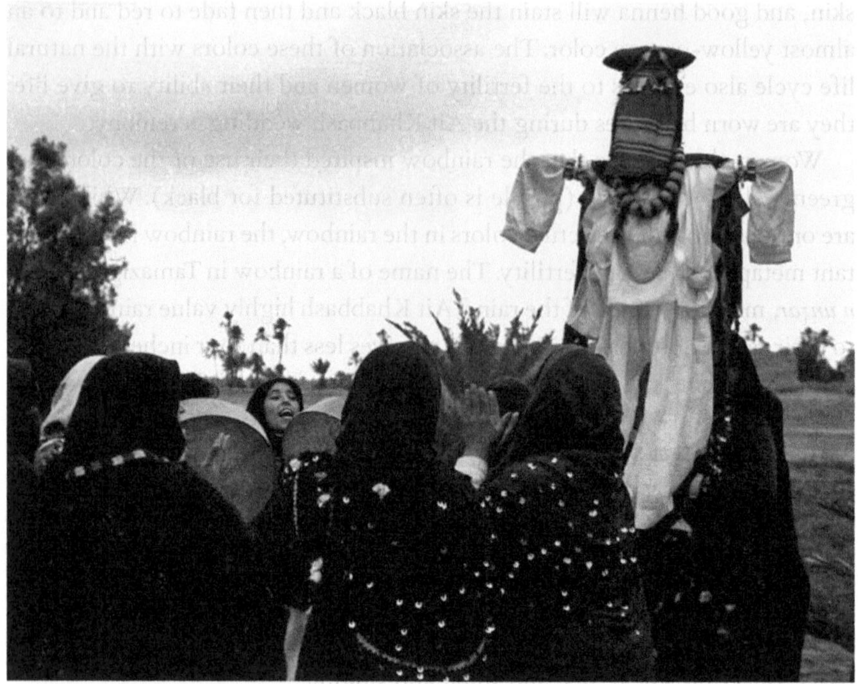

Figure 1.16. Ait Khabbash women in Mezguida carrying telγunja *"bride of the rain" to a dry riverbed, 1997.*

selves but the design elements and colors within them express female fertility and creative powers.

A woman also carries the symbols of her fertility on her body in the form of a woven shawl, called *taynast*. A *taynast* was woven by mothers for their daughters and given to them at marriage and until the 1970s was worn by Ait Khabbash women to protect against the cold desert nights typical of southeastern Morocco. The *taynast* typically measures forty-seven inches by thirty-five inches and is worn draped over the shoulders and tied in front by means of braided red, green, yellow, and black ties. The overall pattern consists of alternating stripes of black and red wool separated by thin solid white bands. Thin checked bands of red, green, yellow, black, and white squares divide the black and red bands in half (Fig. 1.17). Another version of the *taynast* (commonly worn by Ait Khabbash women living near Errachidia, where the winter temperature is colder than in the area of Mezguida and Merzouga) follows the same basic format. It is slightly heavier, with wide, rather than thin, bands of white wool and long warp threads left at one end to protect the neck from cold, such as the *taynast* shown in the colonial-era photograph in Figure 1.18.

After the *taynast* was woven, women sometimes embroidered specific motifs symbolizing fertility onto its surface. One such motif consists of a series of chevrons joined by a straight line to create a *tasṭ,* which means "the branch of a palm tree." Southeastern Morocco is famous for its dates (as noted above), and my interpretation is that the palm tree was adopted as a reference to the fertility of the land and, by extension, to women's fertility. Another motif em-

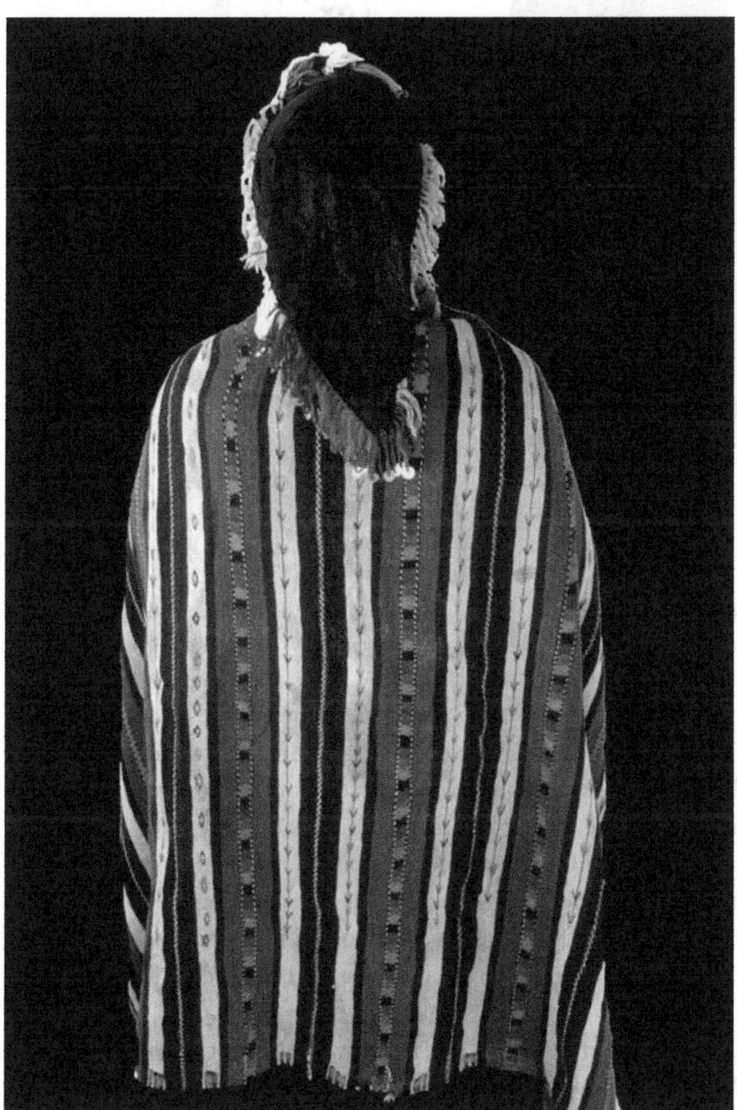

Figure 1.17. An Ait Khabbash woman's shawl. Photo by Addi Ouadderrou.

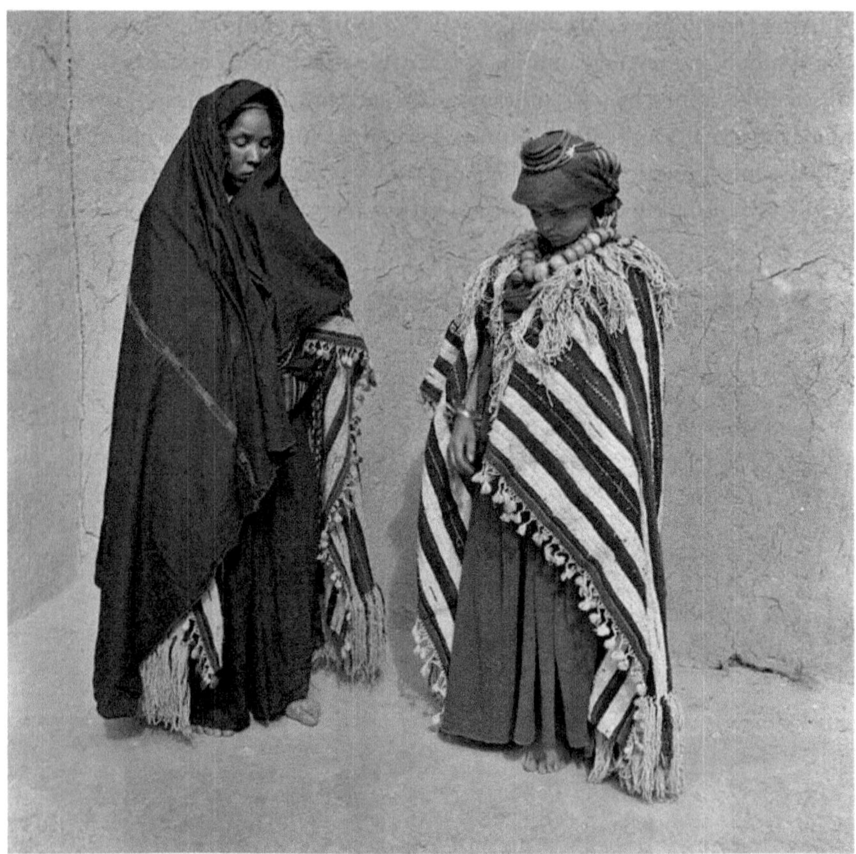

Figure 1.18. Ait Khabbash women from the 1930s from the Ziz Valley near Errachidia. Photo by Jean Besancenot, 1934–1939. Image courtesy of the Institut du Monde Arabe, Paris.

broidered on the *taynast,* the *tazra n Ismkhan,* meaning "slave's necklace," consists of a series of four or five diamond patterns of different colors, with red, green, yellow, and black predominating. Ait Khabbash women told me that the motif resembled the large glass and plastic beaded necklaces once worn by enslaved women, reinforcing my earlier statement that the names given to particular motifs vary from generation to generation, depending on historical circumstances. Many Ait Khabbash were involved in the trans-Saharan slave trade until its prohibition in the 1930s and some had enslaved women working for them.

Another motif called *tigdaḍ* or "little birds" was incorporated into the actual weaving. Woven out of black and red wool on the edges of a woman's *taynast,* the *tigdaḍ* motif was said to resemble pigeon's claws. The Ait Khabbash often associate pigeons with the fertility of the land, because a dry, barren landscape does not attract birds; and, as previously mentioned, there is a metaphoric association in Ait Khabbash culture between women and pigeons.

Color symbolism is gender specific. This becomes especially evident when the women's *taynast* is compared to the equivalent outer garment woven for men, a hooded wool gown called a *tajellabiyt*. The word *tajellabiyt* comes from the Arabic word for the same type of garment, *jellaba*, which the Imazighen "Berberized" by adding a *t* as a prefix and a suffix. The *tajellabiyt*, common across Morocco, is a tailored tunic fitted with sleeves and a hood. Women presented their sons with their first hand-woven *tajellabiyt* when they were around thirteen or fourteen years old, publicly marking their transition in status from boyhood to manhood and the taking on of male responsibilities. As my mother-in-law explained, "You had to wait until the boy was strong enough to wear it," which was meant both literally and metaphorically. Boys of this age began accompanying their fathers to the market and spending nights in the open desert with the herds, where the *tajellabiyt* protected them from the harsh desert environment.

Unlike the *taynast*, the Ait Khabbash *tajellabiyt* was woven from undyed sheep's wool. The patterns woven into the *tajellabiyt* consisted of a series of vertical brown stripes that alternated with brown and white checked stripes (Fig. 1.19). Although the *tajellabiyt* lacked any obvious motifs, Ait Khabbash women explained to me that the colors used and some of the patterns created during the weaving process also represented living things found in the natural environment. For example, the area in the checked band where the threads of adjoining colors slightly overlap is called *ticcaf*, which means "spikes at the ends of wheat or barley." Similarly, the thin black and white band embroidered around the neck is referred to as *iyjden*, which means "little goats," because it resembles the black and white markings on the bodies of goats.

In addition to the striped *tajellabiyt*, Ait Khabbash men, like Ait Atta men throughout southern Morocco, commonly wore white wool cloaks called *asil-ham* (as shown in the market scene from the Ait Atta–dominated town of Tinghir in Fig. 1.20). For Moroccans, white is not merely a color but represents moral qualities and good fortune. Moroccans believe a good-natured agreeable person has a "white heart." White foods such as milk and eggs are prestigious; and during a wedding an Ait Khabbash bride sprinkles her wedding guests with milk for good luck, called *fal amellal* in Tamazight, literally meaning "white luck." Across North Africa, men commonly wear white or light-colored clothing, such as the *tajellabiyt*, white cotton robes and under-

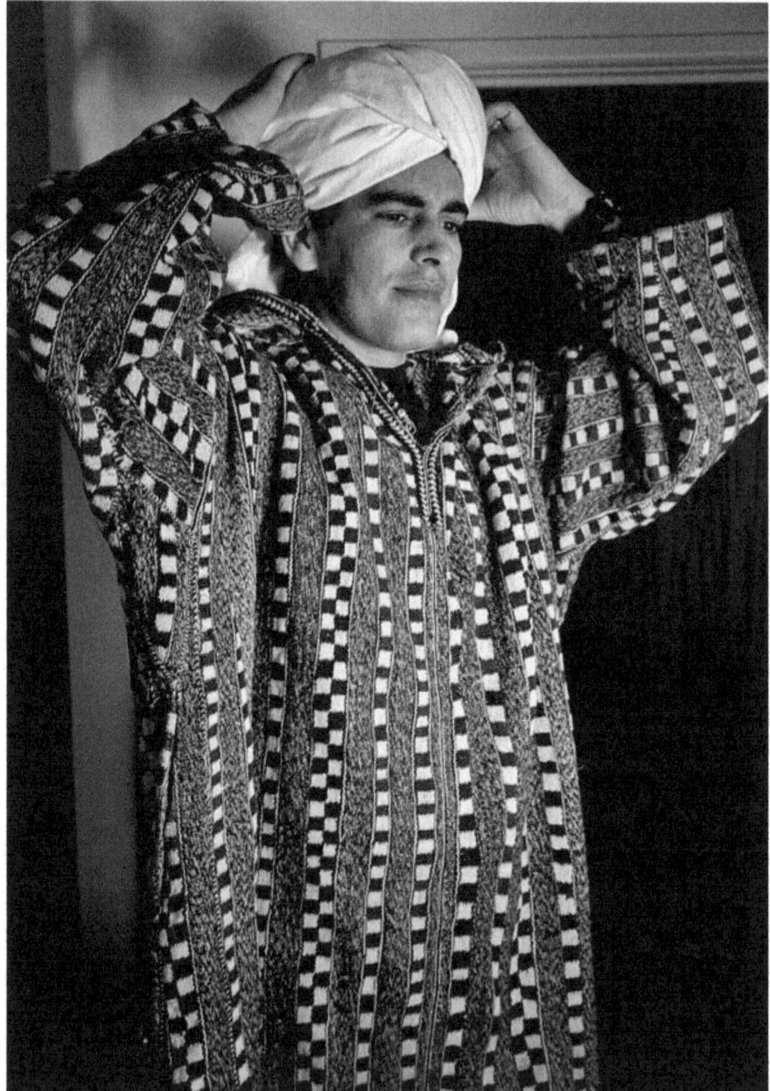

Figure 1.19. An Ait Khabbash man wearing a tajellabiyt, *1998.*

garments, and white wool capes, which (as other scholars have shown) is associated with purity, piety, and Islam (Fig. 1.21).[12] Men throughout the Muslim world typically wear white clothing while performing their Friday prayers in the mosque; hence white connects them with pious behavior and prayer.

The light-colored wool used to create the *tajellabiyt* thus symbolically imbues Ait Khabbash men with virtue, piousness, and honesty, reinforced by the hooded gown serving as a modesty garment. An elderly friend of mine, for instance, became upset when her twenty-year-old son wore a T-shirt and long pants in front of her. Although she did not reveal her feelings directly to her son, when he left the room she told me that she found his clothing distasteful:

When I was young, men did not wear pants in front of women. Today they wear pants and jeans and you can see their "things." Men should be modest in front of a woman and wear something long.

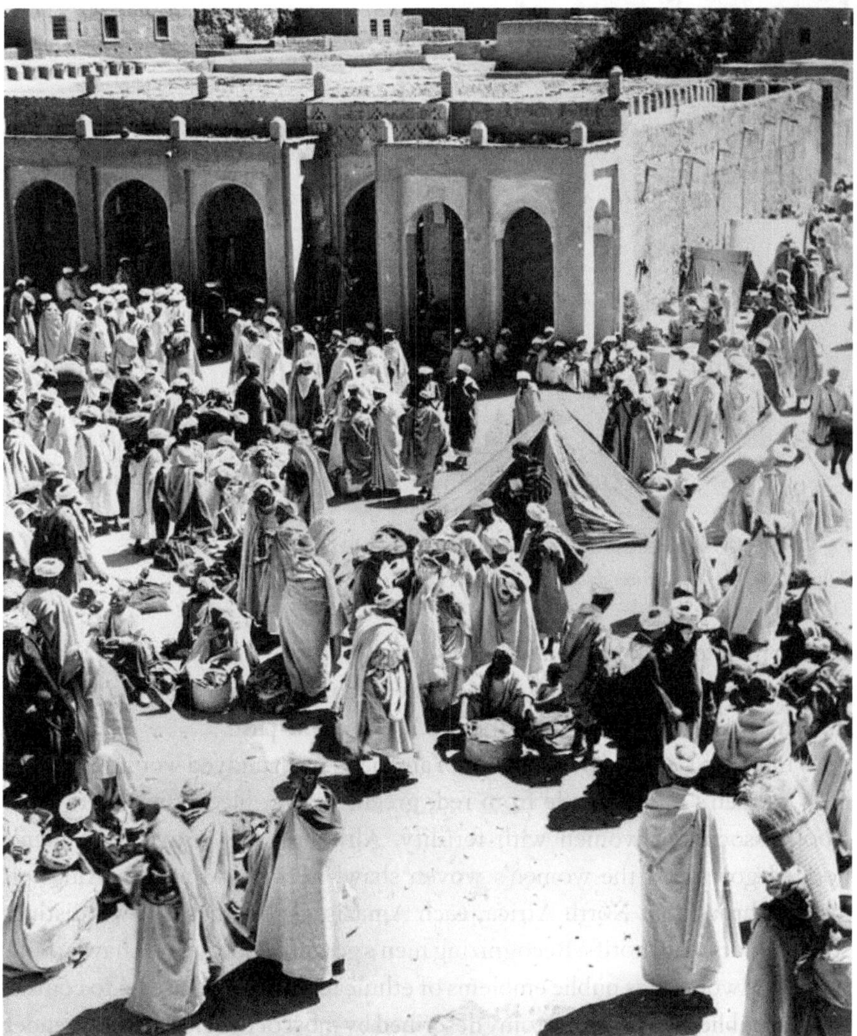

Figure 1.20. Men typically wear white clothing in the Ait Atta–dominated town of Tinghir. Photo courtesy of the National Anthropological Archives, 1930–1959. Smithsonian Institution/04068800.

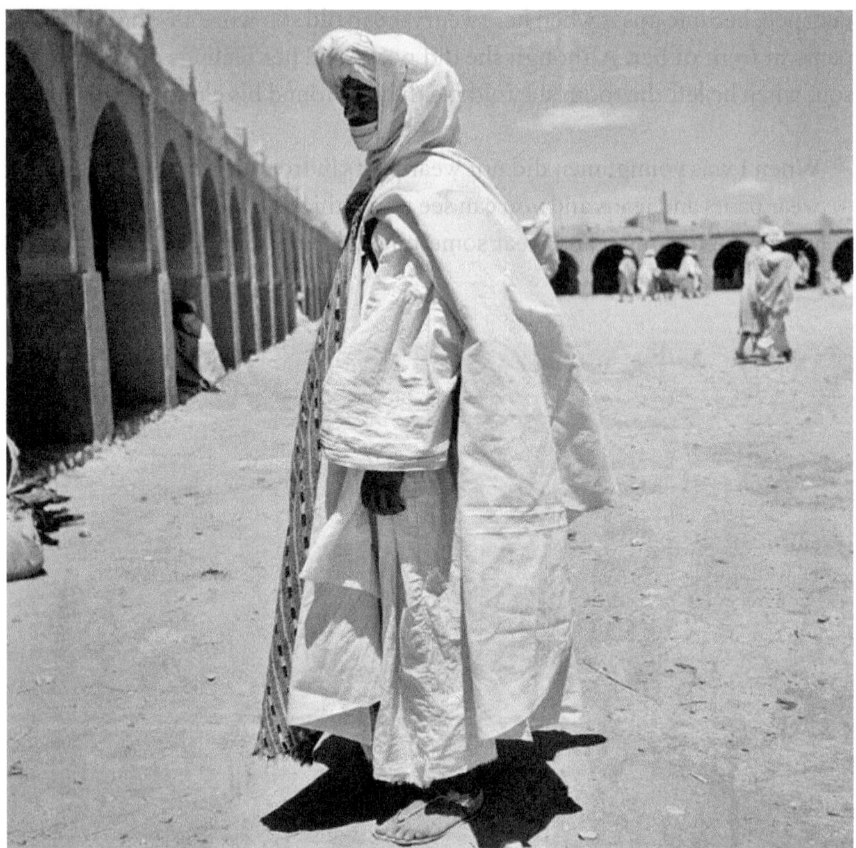

Figure 1.21. An Ait Khabbash man. Photo by Jean Besancenot, 1934–1939. Image courtesy of the Institut du Monde Arabe, Paris.

The woman felt that her son was not showing her the level of respect that she deserved by wearing clothing she considered inappropriate, and she admitted that she preferred men to wear the *tajellabiyt* of the past.

While men's *tajellabiyt* and *asilham* are made from undyed wool, Ait Khabbash women's shawls made from red, green, yellow, black, and white dyed wool, associating women with fertility. Although the form of the men's hooded gown and the women's woven shawl is common among Amazigh groups throughout North Africa, each Amazigh group has its own distinct styles, colors, and motifs. Recognizing men's gowns and women's shawls, both woven by women, as public emblems of ethnic identity would seem to contradict the public-private dichotomy described by most of the literature on gender relations in North Africa. In that view women are associated with the inner, domestic world and men with the outer, public world, leading to men being more socially valued and powerful than women.[13] I found that women create the public symbols of ethnic identity and wear them on their bodies, revealing the important role that women play in the maintenance and public expression of Ait Khabbash identity.

The central paradox of this study is that the very association of women, art, and ethnic identity that gives women their social power also limits their life choices and exerts control over female sexuality. For example, many Ait Khabbash women laughingly explained to me how the loom is used to ensure the virginity of young girls. Before a completed carpet is cut off the upper warp beam, a woman with an unmarried daughter will make a small opening for her to squeeze through.[14]

A young girl's passage through the loom is a form of *thiqaf* (which comes from the Arabic word for "stop" and means use of a particular action to prevent someone from doing something), because it is intended to guard her virginity until her marriage. When the time comes for her to be married, she must once again squeeze through the loom before her marriage is consummated so that she will be "opened up" and can pass through another one of life's phases to become a wife and a mother.

In Ait Khabbash culture, female virginity is connected to family honor, and a girl who is not a virgin at marriage is typically divorced by her husband and brings shame to her family. As noted in Marie-Luce Gélard's study of honor among the Ait Khabbash (2003: 52), women play an important role in controlling the behavior of their daughters, while men rarely intervene. Ait Khabbash women's metaphoric control of their daughters' fertility through their looms thereby protects their daughters, themselves, and their family from social disgrace and ensures the future of their families and their people. The use of the loom to guard their daughters' virginity is one form of women's agency that works within the social system to protect women from social dishonor. The role of women in the creation of the artistic symbols of ethnic identity and the gender-specific color symbolism that associates women with fertility suggest that, although women are empowered by the association of female fertility, art, and ethnic identity, it also limits their life options and results in the control of their sexuality.

This discussion of textiles, the manufacturing process, and weavers illustrates that women play a central role in artistic production. Women weave textiles that are believed to come alive, demonstrating that the propagation of Ait Khabbash identity depends on the creative and reproductive powers attributed to women. In addition, the color symbolism associated with women's wool shawls emphasizes female fertility and publicly expresses ethnic identity. Women, rather than men, create the artistic symbols of Ait Khabbash identity. However, the artistic process is dynamic. Textiles patterns, forms, and colors change in response to social and economic factors. Even though the Ait Khabbash have abandoned their nomadic lifestyle, my analysis of textiles indicates that women embody identity through art, giving them an agent to hold onto their power and status through socially acceptable means. While art provides women with a means by which they can publicly enhance their social position, it also results in the control of their sexuality. Ait Khabbash women typically marry Ait Khabbash men and are expected to be virgins until their marriage. Women who give birth to many children, especially sons, are rewarded with considerable status in their households. Elderly and married Ait Khabbash women with children benefit from the social system that rewards mothers as propagators of the group's ethnic identity. These women continue to make and wear art that stresses the association of women, fertility, and ethnic identity. In the next chapter, we will see that these women still largely control artistic production, although younger women are beginning to feel that the connection between women and identity is a burden that limits their life choices.

TWO

The Art of Dressing the Body

Eat according to your own taste but dress with the taste of others.

—MOROCCAN PROVERB

Ait Khabbash gender roles are conveyed by more than just the color and design of their woven textiles. Women also use dress, which includes body painting, tattooing, jewelry, hairdos, and headgear (both in the way it is worn and in its design), to convey their gender identity.[1] It is through the objects and materials that adorn the body that gender is first inscribed; thus the process of dressing the body further illustrates the gendered discourse on Ait Khabbash identity introduced in the previous chapter.

Beyond their artistic qualities, dress and adornment begin early among the Ait Khabbash, as in other cultures. Each stage of a person's life is marked through a particular style of dress, inscribing social meanings, constructing values, and teaching identity constructions that are internalized as second nature, exerting a powerful influence on the socialization of individuals.

Although the art of dressing the body begins at birth, its earliest function in Ait Khabbash culture is not to mark gender distinctions but to protect the very young from the *jnoun* and from the evil eye. The first seven days of a child's life are believed to be the most dangerous. My mother-in-law, for instance, shared with me a story about the birth of her eldest son:

When Brahim was born, I was home alone with the new baby and my two small daughters, who were sleeping. I heard something like people talking. I woke up and saw two women looking at Brahim. They did not see me, but

I heard one woman ask the other if they should steal my baby. The other woman said, "No, leave the woman her baby."

When I asked her who these women were, she replied:

They were *jnoun*. This is why a woman who gives birth should not be left alone as my husband left me. Sometimes they [*jnoun*] bring their children and when they find a good [human] baby they change them with their babies. Children of the *jnoun* do not live and they become skinnier and skinnier until they die.

If a child dies within seven days of its birth, local beliefs explain the death by saying that the *jnoun* successfully exchanged their child for the human child. In addition to such practices as leaving a candle constantly burning next to the newborn child to discourage the *jnoun,* who thrive in darkness and dislike bright spaces and shiny things, Ait Khabbash women adorn their children with objects and materials containing *baraka* or "divine blessing" to protect them during this crucial period. The child's body is rubbed with dry henna, which is believed to protect and strengthen the skin; in southeastern Morocco, the child is dressed in a white seamless cloth, called *tamneqebẓrout,* connected to ideas of purity and goodness. Women make this garment by folding a cloth in half and pounding one corner with a rock, creating a hole through which the child's head is placed. The women with whom I spoke associated the *tamneqebẓrout* with the *iḥram,* a white seamless garment worn by men making the pilgrimage to Mecca that symbolizes their separation from the profane world.[2] The white *tamneqebẓrout* is a visual symbol of the moral purity and goodness of children. Throughout Morocco, women also typically swaddle their children by wrapping them in a thin strip of fabric to which glass beads, a silver coin, and a bag containing ground harmel (a local plant) may be tied to safeguard against the *jnoun* as well as the evil eye.[3]

The evil eye, referred to as *tiṭ* in Tamazight or *el âin* in Arabic, can be described as a glance or look accompanied by a compliment, which is considered dangerous because compliments are believed to be connected with envy and covetousness.[4] Hence it is commonly thought that one's good fortune, health, or looks may cause jealous people *wten-ten s-tiṭ,* "to hit them with the evil eye." The evil eye is greatly feared by people living throughout the Muslim world,[5] who believe it can cause bad luck, illness, and even death. When I asked people to explain the powers of the evil eye to me, they typically responded with the

Moroccan commonplace that one-third of people die by the sword, one-third from illness, and the other third from the evil eye. Because the first glance of a person is considered the most dangerous, many people in Morocco and elsewhere wear beads and other pendants to attract a negative first glance and prevent the person from being harmed. Similarly people sometimes respond to a compliment by saying *Falek fal ẓarri, mayhart maydarri* ("May your wish be the dung beetle's wish, can't cultivate, can't harvest").[6] Because the dung beetle is considered hideous, the recitation of this phrase is believed to stop harmful sentiments embedded in a compliment. The evil eye not only afflicts people but can destroy fruit trees and crops, kill animals, and cause houses to collapse or objects to break.

I witnessed how intensely people believe in the evil eye when our family's cow fell and broke its leg while grazing outside the house, leaving everyone shocked and heartbroken when the animal had to be killed. Since this was the first time the cow had been grazed near the main thoroughfare that led to their village, they did not hesitate to blame their misfortune and the cow's death on the evil eye of a jealous passerby. In the next few days, more than fifty women visited the house, offering condolences on the cow's untimely death, blaming *el âin* or "the eye." Our family's cows were never allowed to graze near the road again, and the family attached pendants with cowrie shells to the remaining cows for protection.

On the seventh day after a child's birth, parents hold a naming ceremony called *sbuâ* in Arabic or *sibâ* in Tamazight. An animal is sacrificed, and friends and relatives are invited to celebrate their child's passage through this initial critical period.[7] On the day of the naming ceremony, a child's mother or another woman paints the eyebrows and outlines the eyes of the newborn with kohl, a silvery gray powder made from antimony sulfide, expressing standards of beauty held throughout Morocco: dark eyes, eyelashes, and eyebrows. This adornment with kohl not only enhances a child's appearance but also marks the beginning of a child's life as a social being.

Even after this initial period, a Moroccan mother and child live a somewhat secluded lifestyle for the first forty days after childbirth. A generation ago children throughout Morocco would have their heads shaved after forty days, signaling the end of the child's precarious, dangerous state.[8] Among the Ait Khabbash, a single cowrie shell was attached to a circular patch of hair on the crown of the child's head. Although this hairstyle can still be found on children in rural areas of southeastern Morocco, it is becoming increasingly rare.

At the end of these forty days gender differences also begin to be expressed through dress. The children start to wear beaded necklaces made by their mothers that incorporate substances venerated for their protective powers. These materials, which may include multicolored beads, amber, cowrie shells, silver coins, Qur'anic amulets, and other protective substances such as gazelle's horn, depend largely on the gender of the child. The birth of a boy is highly desirable and gives women a certain level of prestige. Women adorn their newborn sons with elaborately beaded necklaces to distinguish them from girls, who wear a single beaded strand. This is not to say that female children are not appreciated. Girls spend large amounts of time with their mothers on a daily basis, forming strong emotional bonds between them. Ait Khabbash women frequently remark that sons marry and forget their mothers, but girls always remember them. However, both parents recognize that financial security in their old age depends on their male children, who are expected to provide for their parents later in life. A son brings his wife into his parent's household, giving a mother-in-law a position of power and authority and allowing her to live out her old age in security and prestige, with her daughter-in-law and her grandchildren taking care of her. A daughter, in contrast, is expected to marry and leave the household.

The beaded necklaces that mothers construct for their sons include shells, beads, and other pendants strung on a heavy cord and hung over the child's shoulder so that it drapes across his chest (Fig. 2.1).[9] At the end of the necklace is placed a small knife pendant made of silver or copper, mimicking the *koummiya*, a dagger with a curved blade and an engraved silver or brass sheath commonly worn by Ait Khabbash men until the 1960s.[10] A man's knife was attached to a silk cord, hung on the left side so that it could easily be grabbed by the right hand. Thus the knife pendant links boys to the history of Ait Khabbash men, who were involved in raids, the caravan trade, and the military defense of the group. Although such knives are no longer used, the pendant worn by Ait Khabbash boys continues to refer to the warrior-like quality once associated with the identity of Ait Khabbash men. The knife pendant is also believed to protect against the *jnoun*, who dislike white, shiny objects and are repelled by the knife's steel blade, and to guard against the evil eye, which it can symbolically pop or burst. (Women often place knives under their children's beds to protect them from both the evil eye and the *jnoun*.)[11]

Other protective items commonly used by women to construct a boy's necklace include a white goat's tail (preferably from the animal sacrificed after the seventh day of the child's birth), cowrie shells, and silver coins (their white color again symbolizing purity and goodness), and a black bead (believed to be

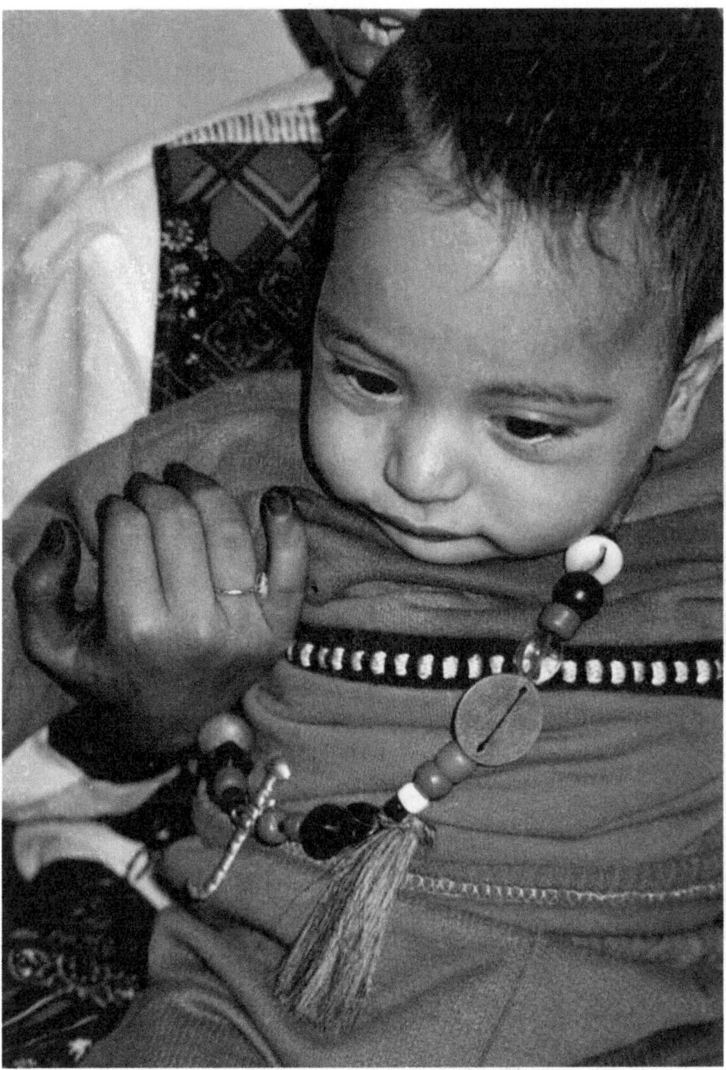

Figure 2.1. A boy in Mezguida wears protective beads and a silver knife pendant to protect him from the evil eye, 1997.

hideous) or a pendant embedded with a mirror to attract and deflect the negative gaze of the evil eye. Women may also use amber beads or pieces of gazelle's horn because of their association with wealth and prestige. Other common protective items are leather pendants decorated with five cowrie shells in a formation often referred to as a *khamsa*, meaning "five" in Arabic, or *afous*, "hand" in Tamazight, symbolizing the human hand (Fig. 2.2).[12] Five is also

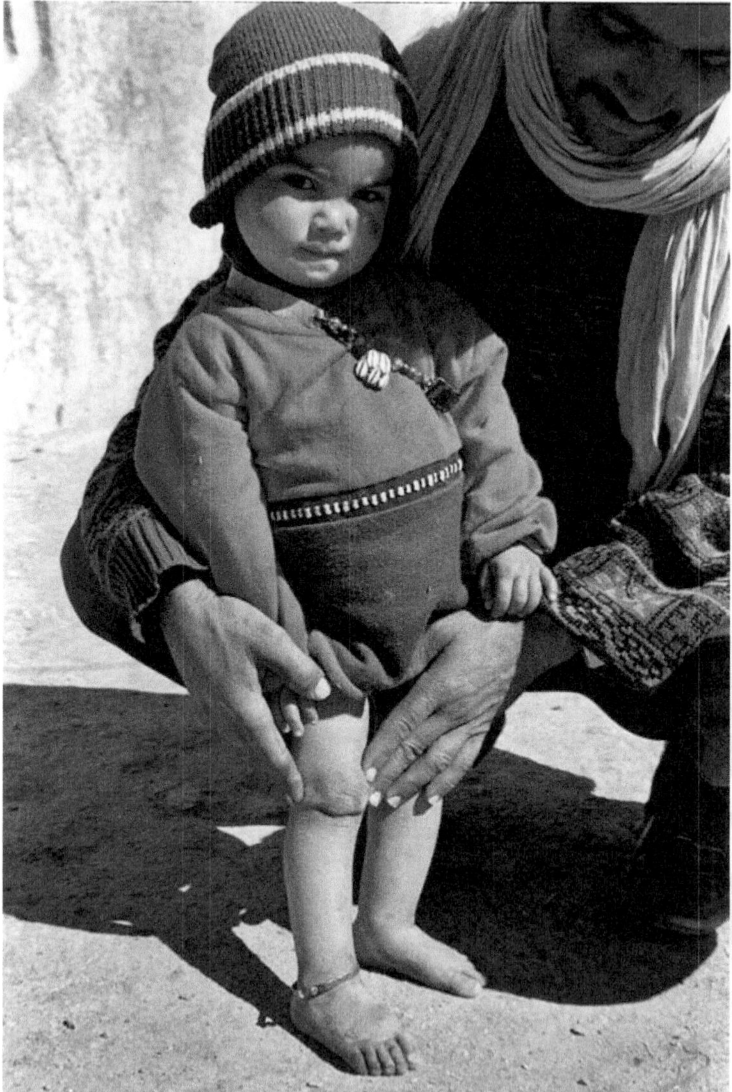

Figure 2.2. A child wears a cowrie shell pendant, 1996.

considered an auspicious number: there are five pillars or obligations of Islam, and Muslims pray five times a day. The expression *khamsa fi âin-ek* or "Five in your eye" is another response to compliments used throughout Morocco, figuratively poking the eye as protection; and people may also respond by holding up their hands to block the negative gaze of the evil eye.

Sometime between the age of one and two years, Amazigh and Arab chil-

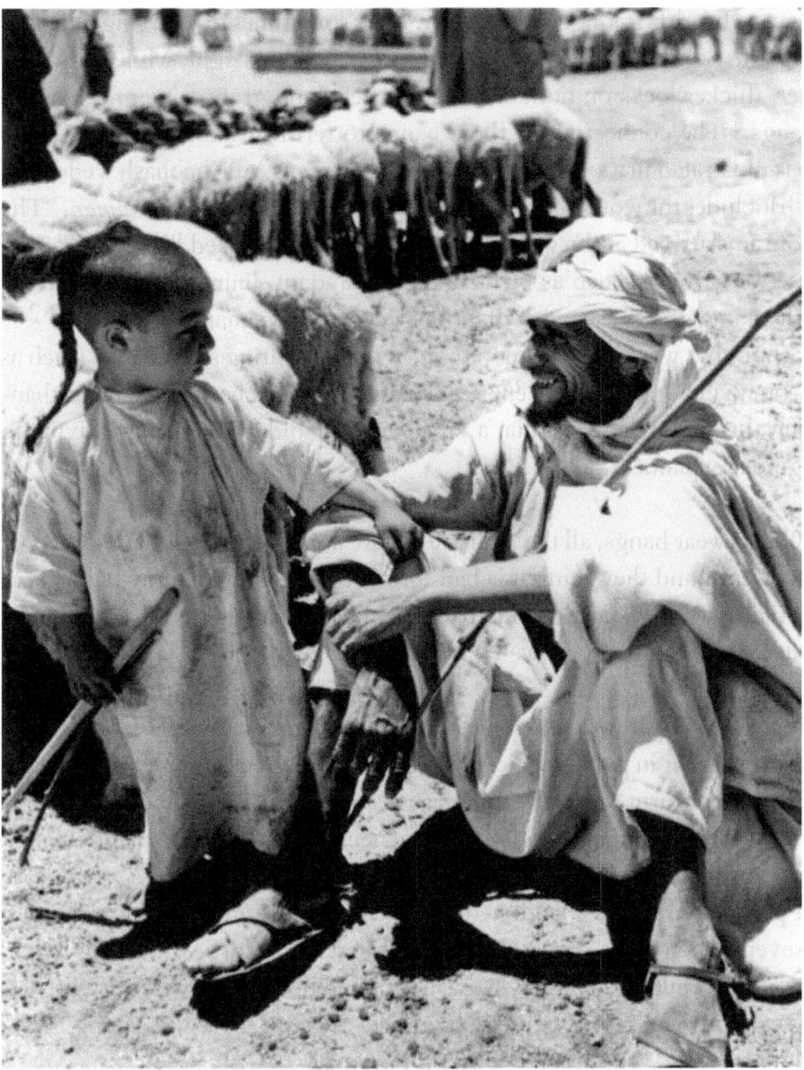

Figure 2.3. An Amazigh boy with the azag *hairstyle. Photo courtesy of the National Anthropological Archives, 1930–1959. Smithsonian Institution/04072400.*

dren alike are given gender-specific hairstyles, which vary slightly in each region of Morocco.[13] Although these particular hairstyles are rarely seen in urban
areas today, people living in rural regions continue to style their children's
hair in the older gender-specific styles. The hairstyles of both Ait Khabbash
boys and girls include an *azag,* a thin, vertical band of hair that runs from the
front or middle of the head to the nape of the neck (Fig. 2.3), although the

a˞ag worn by girls is longer and thicker. Boys sometimes grow a single lock of hair on the right side of the head called a *takiot* in Tamazight, while girls wear longer, thicker locks on both sides of the head and grow *tawen˞a*, "a fringe of bangs." The connection of these bangs to fertility among the Ait Khabbash is illustrated in a song praising the bride during Ait Khabbash weddings, which includes the words *Zwarn-id i˞amarn ulli gan tawen˞a ddan s-aman*, "The line of rams arrived at the water before the ewes and looked like bangs." This phrase, describing sheep as plentiful and abundant, lining up near a stream and drinking, serves as a wish that the bride will have many children.

Although it was once common to see women wearing short bangs (such as the woman in Fig. 1.9), in recent years young Ait Khabbash women are abandoning this hairstyle. As Erqia, a nineteen-year-old friend of mine living in Mezguida, explained:

When I wear bangs, all the Arab girls stare at my hair. Their hair is covered by a scarf, and they think it is bad for me to show some of my hair. I kept noticing women staring at my bangs while they talked to me. That's when I decided to let them grow.

Erqia felt that Arab women's stares signaled their disapproval that she was showing her hair in public, which is considered religiously inappropriate, and decided to conform to a more conservative style of dress. In addition, some Moroccans feel that the bangs and beaded necklaces worn by Imazighen mark them as provincial; perhaps for that reason, these forms of dress, once worn until puberty, are now abandoned when children begin attending school at age seven. When Yadir, an Ait Khabbash friend in his thirties, laughingly told me about his childhood hairstyle, he mentioned that a child who currently attends school wearing one of these hairstyles is called *âroubi*, meaning "from the countryside," "rural," and "unsophisticated."

Circumcision is typically performed when a boy is anywhere from seven days to ten years old.[14] Male circumcision in Morocco is called *tahara*, meaning "purification," and is viewed by Muslims around the world as a necessary step to prepare boys for their entrance into the *umma*, "Islamic community."[15] As Edward Westermarck ([1926] 1968, 2: 418) notes, boys are circumcised in a local sanctuary in some areas of Morocco, making the connection between circumcision and the Islamic community even more explicit. Furthermore, only men are allowed to participate and witness the actual procedure, indicating that the practice of circumcision is intended to initiate boys into the male

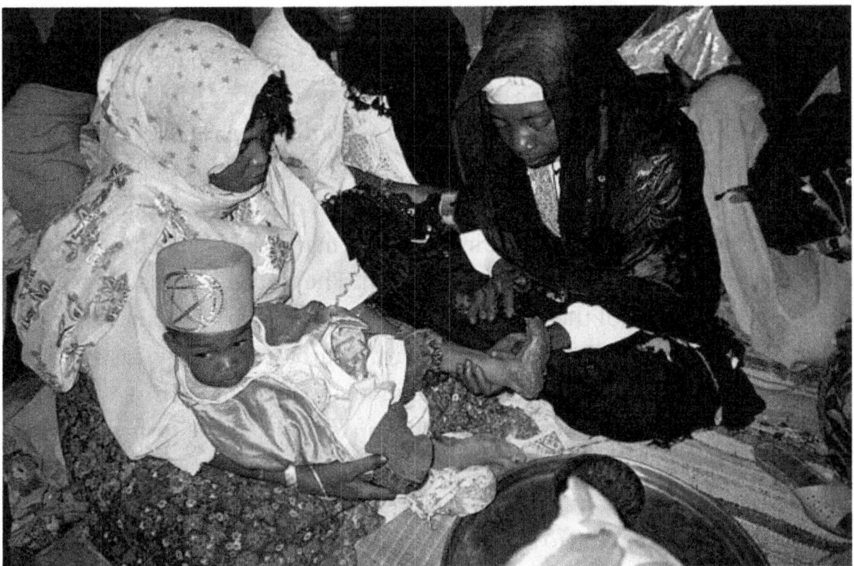

Figure 2.4. *A young boy in Khamlia has his feet covered with henna in preparation for his circumcision, 1997.*

community. Yet because boys are considered especially vulnerable to attacks from the evil eye and *jnoun* during circumcision, women dress them in such a way as to protect them. The clothing worn by boys for this ceremony is intended to protect them as they symbolically cross the boundary from boyhood to manhood, wearing substances and colors associated with *baraka*. A boy is typically dressed in a white gown and sometimes a green cape and green flat-topped hat called a fez (Fig. 2.4). A string with coins, beads, and a small bag with salt and harmel is tied around his right ankle for protection. Salt protects the boy from the *jnoun,* who are often referred to in Tamazight as *widda tsentel tisent,* meaning "those who are hidden by salt." Women apply henna to the boy's hands and feet the night before the ceremony and rub saffron on the top of his head, and his family members typically wear white bands decorated with vertical stripes of saffron (Fig. 2.4).

At puberty, the dress of both males and females drastically changes. As part of this transition, boys wear a *tajellabiyt* (the hooded gown discussed earlier), shave their distinctive hairstyles, and wrap an *arezziy,* "turban," around their heads. The Ait Khabbash *arezziy* is made from a long, thin piece of white cotton fabric approximately four feet long that is typically purchased in the market. Women told me that they once wove the turban out of wool; but when imported fabric was introduced into the area in the 1930s, men began to use white cotton fabric bought in the market. Men would wind the turban around the crown of the head several times (Fig. 2.3). Sometimes they wrap one fold across the entire face, leaving a narrow slit for the eyes. According to the men I spoke with, turbans carry important social meanings, symbolizing honor and respect. The Tamazight phrase *tbedda tarezziyt-nnek,* used to describe an honorable person, means "your turban is standing up." If a man has been dishonored, Ait Khabbash men say that his turban has fallen. The turban is therefore a metaphor for the fragility of the honor that men must work to maintain. Although fewer and fewer Ait Khabbash men wear the turban on a daily basis, it continues to be worn during important ceremonial occasions such as weddings. Thus elements of male dress such as the *tajellabiyt* and the turban embrace imagery that associates men with Islam and the qualities of modesty, honor, and dignity.

Although it is common to see men in their fifties and sixties proudly wearing hooded gowns and turbans, in recent years young men have been abandoning this style of dress for European-inspired pants and shirts. The dress and body art of Ait Khabbash women have also changed in recent years, and nowhere is this seen more dramatically than in the case of tattooing. Although tattooing is no longer practiced by the Ait Khabbash, in the recent past an Ait Khabbash girl's mother, aunts, or family friends would tattoo her face and wrists when she reached puberty. The Ait Khabbash women I talked with recounted that their faces and wrists had been tattooed sometime between the ages of eleven and fourteen, a time that generally coincided with their first menstrual cycles. Unlike the ceremonial nature of male circumcision, an attitude of casualness surrounded tattooing. The responsibility for tattooing was not inherited or religiously consecrated; nor were there tattoo specialists. Rather, female friends and family members tattooed girls, and groups of girls were most often tattooed at the same time, making it a very social activity shared and passed on among Ait Khabbash women.[16]

When I asked middle-aged or elderly Ait Khabbash women about their bluish-green tattoos, many told me stories similar to that of Fattou, an elderly Ait Khabbash woman living in Mezguida who had been tattooed when she was twelve or thirteen. "I did not want these tattoos," she insisted, stroking the long tattooed line running down the center of her chin. "I was held down by some girls in my village. You see, I did not have tattoos, and the other girls said I had to have them like everyone else, because without them I looked like a man." I was unable to tell whether these women actually had been tattooed against their will or whether the current stigma attached to tattoos caused them to use this story to avoid embarrassment. Although previous generations of both Arab and Amazigh women commonly tattooed their faces, wrists, hands, and ankles, more recently understandings of Islam have led to few women younger than thirty years old having tattoos. Today tattooing is believed to be in violation of Islamic beliefs: they permanently alter the body, and Islamic tradition holds that anything that permanently changes God's perfect creation is prohibited. According to the Hadith, the Prophet prohibited tattooing, cursing women who tattoo and those who get themselves tattooed.[17] Furthermore, people told me that tattoos render ineffective the ritual ablutions proscribed before daily prayers because they stop water from penetrating into the skin.[18]

In past generations, Arabs and Imazighen living in rural areas were tattooed more frequently than urban women, since the rural women (not living near centers of religious education) were often unaware of Hadith that rejected tattooing. In general, nomadic groups like the Ait Khabbash rarely had access to formal religious training. An Ait Khabbash man in his eighties explained to me how nomads learned about Islam:

> People did not send their children to school in the past, because during the time they would be sitting in schools, they could be searching for food. In the past there was not much food available as there is now. Also people did not study in school when the French were here, because the people here were afraid they would become Christians and be like the French and forget their religion. Also the Qur'anic schools were in the villages. In the Qur'anic schools people learned about Islam. But those nomads in the desert, they did not study in the schools. The nomads learned from people in the *qsour* [mud-brick villages in the Tafilalet oasis] who traveled to the Sahara and passed time in the desert. Nomads learned about Islam from them.

When nomadic populations began to settle in towns, such as Erfoud and Rissani, however, they began sending both male and female children to Qur'anic schools. As a result of increased exposure to Islamic teachings and social pressure from Arabs, by the 1970s the Ait Khabbash had abandoned their practice of tattooing the faces and wrists of adolescent girls. Fatima, an Ait Khabbash woman in her fifties with facial tattoos, recited an Arabic song condemning tattooed women that she recounted being sung in Mezguida ten years earlier:

> God insults the women who do tattoos, the women with tattoos,
>   and the women who rest near them.
> He also insults the wall near them.
> Why doesn't it fall on these tattooed women?

Today it is very rare for a young Ait Khabbash girl to be tattooed, and many older women try to use natural herbs and chemicals to remove their tattoos, without success. Tattooed Ait Khabbash women believe that after death their marks will be burned off their bodies in the afterlife, rendering them perfect once again.

Nonetheless, tattooing was an important art form practiced by Ait Khabbash and other Moroccan women for centuries. As described by various writers, the techniques used appear to have been basically the same all over Morocco. Women would draw the tattoo design on the skin with charcoal or pot-black (the soot that is deposited on the bottom of a cooking pot) then prick the design onto the skin with a pointed object such as a prickly pear spike, knife, or needle and apply alfalfa to the wound to give the design a green color.[19] My fifty-year-old sister-in-law Erqia described how this was done when she received a facial tattoo:

> I was around twelve years old. A neighbor did the tattoo for me. I asked her to do it for me. She painted the design on my chin and forehead with charcoal and then pricked my chin with a needle. It really hurt. When she pricked my lip, it was like someone was poking the whites of my eyes with a needle. She went over it three times and put alfalfa on the marks. I wrapped up my chin and left the alfalfa on it for three days to make sure it became green. I wouldn't let her tattoo my forehead then, because the first one hurt too much.

Although scholars typically describe Moroccan tattoos as blue-black, Ait Khabbash women told me that the best tattoos were a deep green color. One scholar has gone so far as to suggest that Moroccans erroneously refer to their tattoos as green because they are unable to distinguish between green and blue;[20] but those I met were clearly aware of the difference between the two colors and had different words for them. Further, Ait Khabbash women consciously chose green vegetation to achieve the color because of its association with *baraka*.

Throughout Morocco substances containing *baraka*, such as saffron or henna, are believed to infuse the body with positive healing energy and are applied during rites of passage that typically coincide with the flow of blood.[21] I believe it is not coincidental that Moroccan women tattooed their bodies with substances containing *baraka* for symbolic purification of their bodies during female menstruation, providing women with an agent to enhance their bodies during a crucial moment in the life cycle. In her discussion of pollution categories in Turkey, Julie Marcus (1992: 74) writes that the basis of Islamic pollution categories is that the human body has an inner and outer body, which are separated into discrete, mutually exclusive realms that must be kept apart in order for the body to be pure. When bodily fluids like blood and semen flow from the inner to the outer body, the body is made unclean; then participation in religious practices is forbidden. In other words, the human body and its orifices should be closed and contained in order for a body to be pure and prevent bodily fluids from crossing from the inner to the outer body, a quality that many groups in northern Africa strive to maintain.[22] Thus, menstruating women are instructed not to pray, enter a mosque, perform the pilgrimage to Mecca, or have sexual relations until blood flow stops and they have been purified through ritual washing.[23]

Just as ritual washing removes physical dirt from the outer body, it symbolically cleanses impurities from the inner, spiritual body. Likewise, substances containing *baraka* are believed to have the ability to cross the outer physical body and purify its inner spiritual essence. Hence henna is used during male circumcision ceremonies to purify the body.[24] Because of this connection between tattoos and menstruation, tattoos can be seen as a means of both purifying women's bodies at the onset of first menstruation and publicly marking their transition from childhood to womanhood; they are a physical and ever-present symbol of women's prestige as useful members of the society who ensure the survival of the group through their ability to give birth.

Particular tattoo motifs, composed of a variety of geometric designs, varied from group to group in Morocco, thereby allowing a woman to express ethnic identity publicly and permanently through her tattoos. The Ait Khabbash women I encountered during my fieldwork felt that their tattoos continued an ancient artistic tradition into the present and frequently evoked the proverb *Sker mayd skern imeʒwura,* "Do what the first ones did." While most scholars would agree that tattoos have been a means of expressing ethnic identity, there is very little agreement concerning the names and significance of individual tattoo designs.[25] Although they did not have a specific name for the patterns they used, on their foreheads Ait Khabbash women typically tattooed

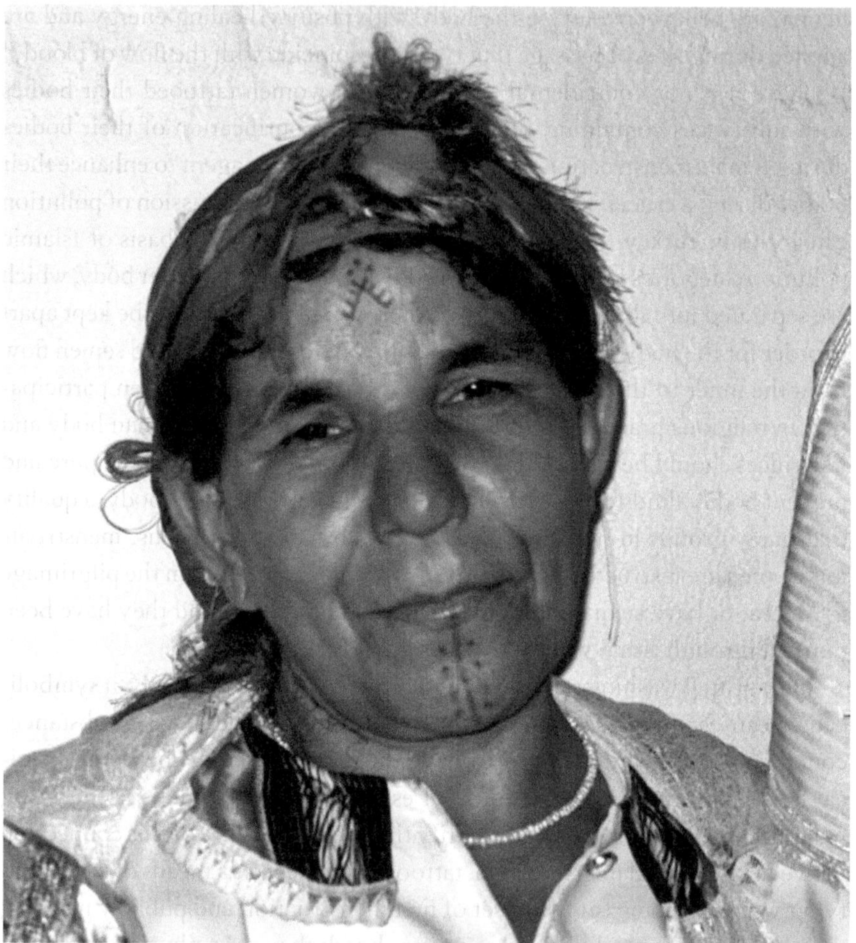

Figure 2.5. An Ait Khabbash woman's tattoos, 1997.

two straight, diagonal lines that crossed each other at the top, creating two v-shapes or chevrons, with three straight lines that radiated from the sides of the larger bottom one and three small dots that hovered above the entire composition (Fig. 2.5). This tattoo style allowed a woman to be identified as Ait Khabbash. Variation between Amazigh groups is demonstrated in Figure 2.6, which shows an Amazigh woman from the High Atlas Mountains who has a chin tattoo that distinguishes her as a member of her particular ethnic group, the Ait Haddidou. In addition, Amazigh women often designed personalized tattoos, tattooing airplanes, wristwatches, crosses, or weaver's combs on their wrists and upper arms.

As among most Amazigh groups, there is a basic relationship between Ait

Khabbash textile patterns and tattoo designs. For example, triangle and chevron patterns are common to both tattoos and contemporary textiles, suggesting that women's weavings may be borrowing from ancestral tattoo designs. Several women said that the chevron motif used for forehead tattoos looked like the two chevrons created by the wooden supports called *tirsal* used in Ait Khabbash tent construction (Fig. 2.7), reflecting the intimate connection be-

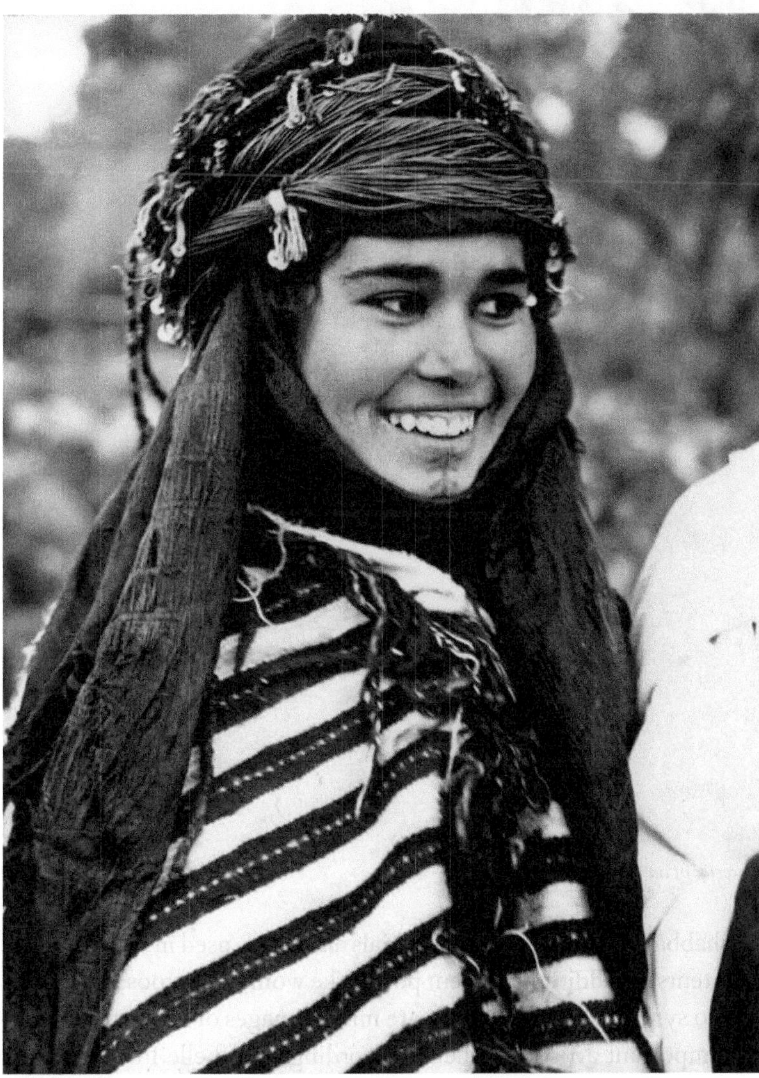

Figure 2.6. Colonial photograph of an Amazigh woman from the High Atlas Mountains near Imilchil. Photo courtesy of the National Anthropological Archives, 1968. Smithsonian Institution /04072400.

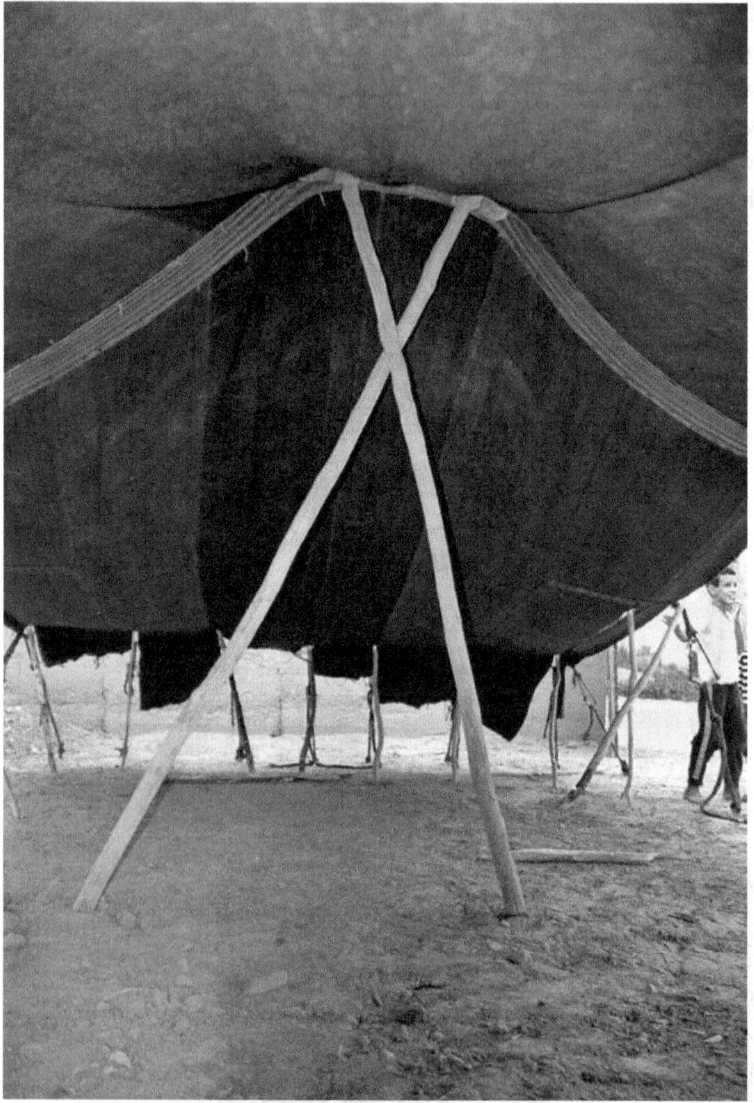

Figure 2.7. Interior of an Ait Khabbash tent, 1999.

tween Ait Khabbash women and the materials and forms used in the construction of these tents. In addition, the tent poles, like women's tattoos, divide the space into two symmetrical halves that are mirror images of each other. Symmetry is an important artistic aesthetic; according to Labelle Prussin (1995: 189), the symmetry typical of African nomadic art is a metaphor for the anthropometry of the human body that is also projected onto their built environment. Tattoos, like nomadic tents, were visual reminders of women's creative powers and reflected a nomadic aesthetic. In this way, tattoos created a correlation between women's bodies and Ait Khabbash identity, enhancing their social status by publicly and permanently reflecting the importance of women in the continuation of group identity.

Tattoos served both an expressive and social function among the Ait Khabbash. Although the practice of tattooing has almost disappeared, the artistic forms and symbolism formerly expressed by tattoos have been transferred to the embroidered head coverings worn by women, demonstrating the living and dynamic nature of Ait Khabbash arts. The media that women use have changed, but their art still serves as a public expression of their social status and group identity. At the time when religious teachings were discouraging female tattooing, women began to alter the style of the head coverings. For several generations prior to the 1970s, Ait Khabbash women had worn long sparsely decorated head coverings made from indigo-dyed cotton cloth as modesty garments (Fig. 1.18). Women told me that in the 1970s, coinciding with the disappearance of tattoos, they began to embroider elaborate vegetal motifs on their indigo head coverings (Fig. 2.8), demonstrating not only their artistic creativity but their negotiation between Islamic beliefs and indigenous definitions of women as the carriers of Ait Khabbash identity.

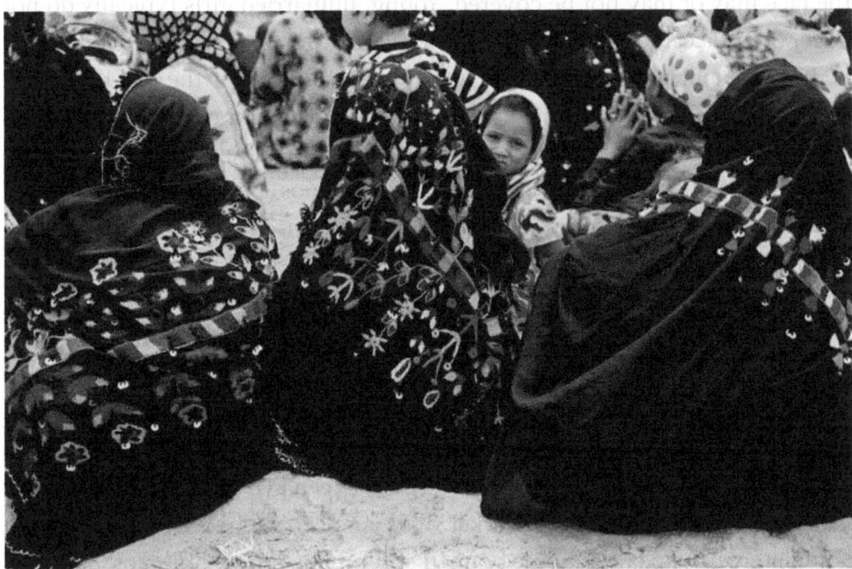

Figure 2.8. Rear view of Ait Khabbash women's embroidered head coverings, 2000.

The "veil" with which an Ait Khabbash woman covers herself is called a *tahruyt*, embroidered with brightly colored motifs and sequins and draped over her head and wrapped around her body.[26] Although the Ait Atta (to which the Ait Khabbash belong) are one of the few Amazigh groups in Morocco in which women commonly wear a head and body covering, each subgroup of the Ait Atta has its own style of covering, made from indigo-dyed cloth. The brightly colored embroidered designs and sequins of the Ait Khabbash covering thus distinguish it from the others. One Ait Khabbash woman described her head covering as her "passport," meaning that it allows her to be recognized immediately as Ait Khabbash.

The *tahruyt* is made from two lengths of cloth joined selvedge to selvedge to construct an almost square piece of cloth. The finished size of a typical *tahruyt* is seventy inches long and sixty-four inches wide. The two pieces are attached using a multicolored joining stitch, producing a single multicolored band of wool yarn about an inch wide called the *tanammast*. Women place one of the selvedge edges over the center of their heads: the *tanammast* runs horizontally across the middle of their back, and the right side of the head covering is wrapped over their left shoulder. Two edges of the *tahruyt* are adorned with multicolored and black tassels and metallic sequins, so the tasseled edge comes back around over the head and sequins frame the woman's forehead. There are different methods of wrapping the head covering once it is on the body so that the face may or may not be covered. Young, unmarried girls typically do not cover their faces, something generally reserved for married women (Fig. 2.9).

It is difficult to determine the antiquity and origin of the Ait Khabbash *tahruyt*, and early photographs of its use are practically nonexistent. Indigo was cultivated near Zagora, an area southwest of the Tafilalet oasis, from as early as the sixteenth century until as late as the 1960s (Balfour-Paul 1997: 205). One of the earliest ethnographic accounts of indigo-dyed cloth being used by women in southeastern Morocco comes from Walter Harris (1895: 289), who traveled to the Tafilalet in the late nineteenth century. He writes that women wore indigo-blue dyed cotton or wool of local manufacture but also states that most of the indigo cloth was imported from London or Bombay. Women I spoke with verified his comments and added that indigo cloth was commonly used to make women's daily clothing as well as their head coverings until the 1980s, when black cotton and polyester, less expensive than indigo cloth, became readily available in the market. This is not to suggest that indigo cloth completely disappeared. Some women still prefer indigo cloth and continue to wear it today.

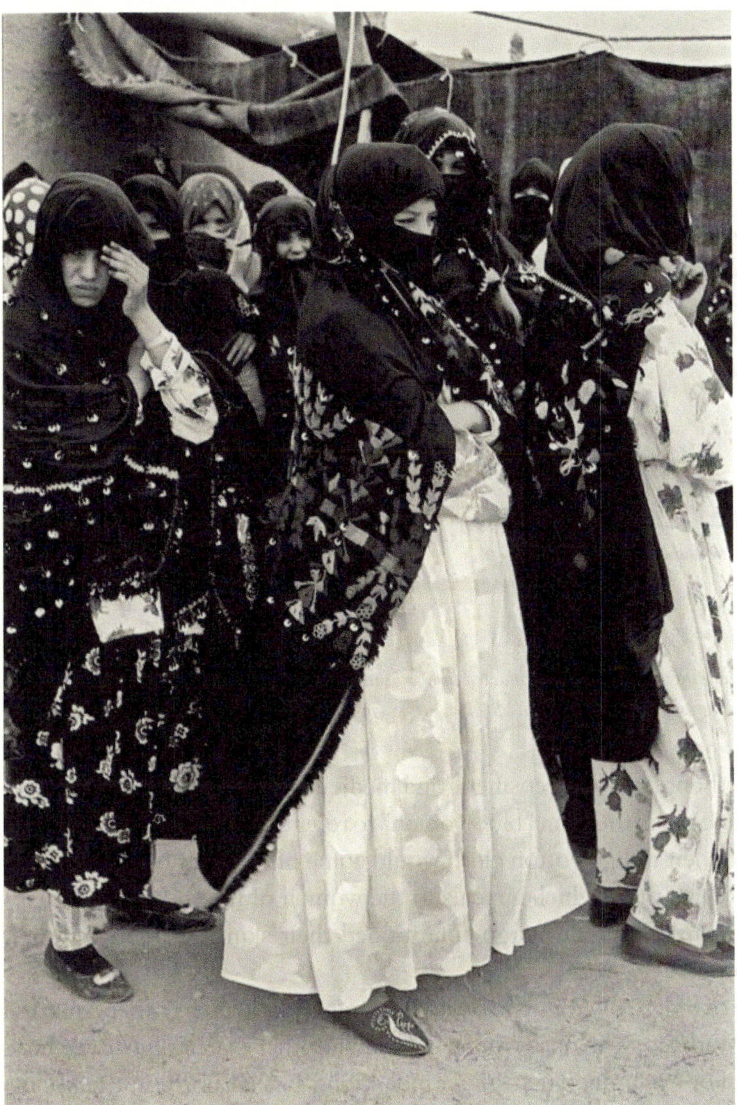

Figure 2.9. *A group of Ait Khabbash women in Hafira, 2000.*

In some of the earliest-known photographs of women in southeastern Morocco, taken between 1934 and 1939 by Jean Besancenot, a woman wears an indigo-dyed head covering decorated with only the simple joining stitch of the *tanammast* (Fig. 1.18). The use of indigo-dyed coverings was common among Ait Atta living throughout southern Morocco, as shown in the colonial-era photograph in Figure 2.10, taken near the town of Tinghir. The use of

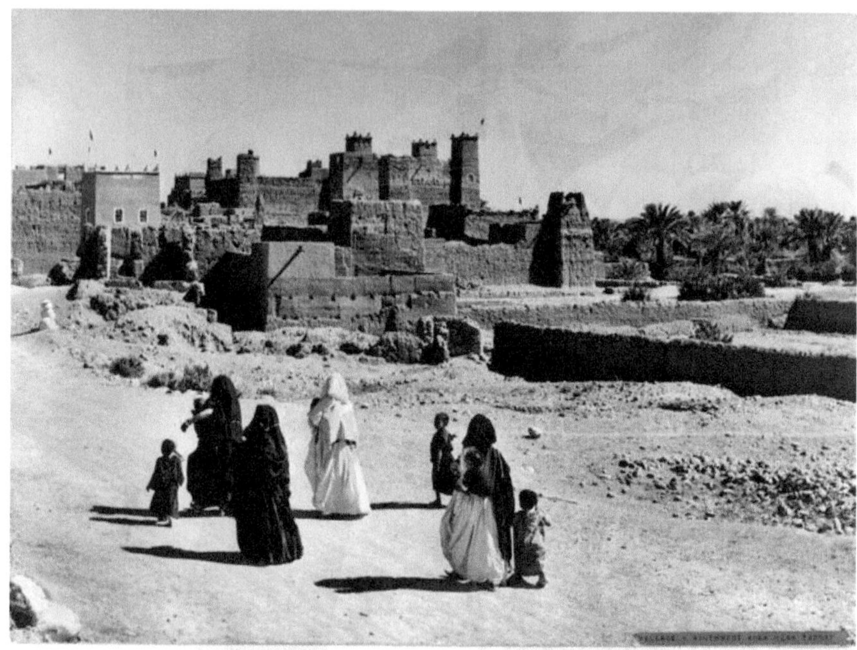

Figure 2.10. Ait Atta women wear embroidered indigo head coverings near the town of Tinghir. Photo courtesy of the National Anthropological Archives, 1930–1959. Smithsonian Institution/04072500.

indigo was thought to have cosmetic and medicinal benefits. In fact, Besance-not (1990: 160) used the term "blue women" to refer to Ait Atta women because the color of their indigo cotton cloth would come off on their bodies, "giving the skin a bluish tinge which appeals to the women of the south." Ait Khabbash women told me that indigo conditioned their skin and improved their complexions.

The use of indigo distinguishes Ait Atta women from many other Amazigh groups in Morocco, who once wore wool shawls rather than indigo-dyed head coverings. For example, Amazigh women living farther north in the Middle and High Atlas mountain ranges of Morocco often wore heavy wool shawls to protect them during their cold, snowy winters. South of the Atlas Mountains the climate becomes drastically hotter and drier, making it practical for women to wear some type of covering to protect them against the harsh sun and sandstorms common to the Sahara. Because of this, indigo-dyed cotton coverings, like those worn by the Ait Khabbash, are ubiquitous throughout the Saharan regions of Africa. Their practical element makes them the preferred covering of Arab and Amazigh women living south of the Atlas Mountains and in the Saharan regions.[27] For instance, the Kel Tamacheq, popularly referred to as Tuareg, an Amazigh group living in the desert regions of Niger, Algeria, Burkina Faso, and Mali, commonly wear indigo-dyed head coverings and clothing (Fig. 2.11). Hassaniya Arab women living throughout Mauritania and northern Senegal also cover themselves with indigo head coverings (Du Puigaudeau 1970: 13).

Ait Khabbash women wore simply decorated indigo-dyed head cover-

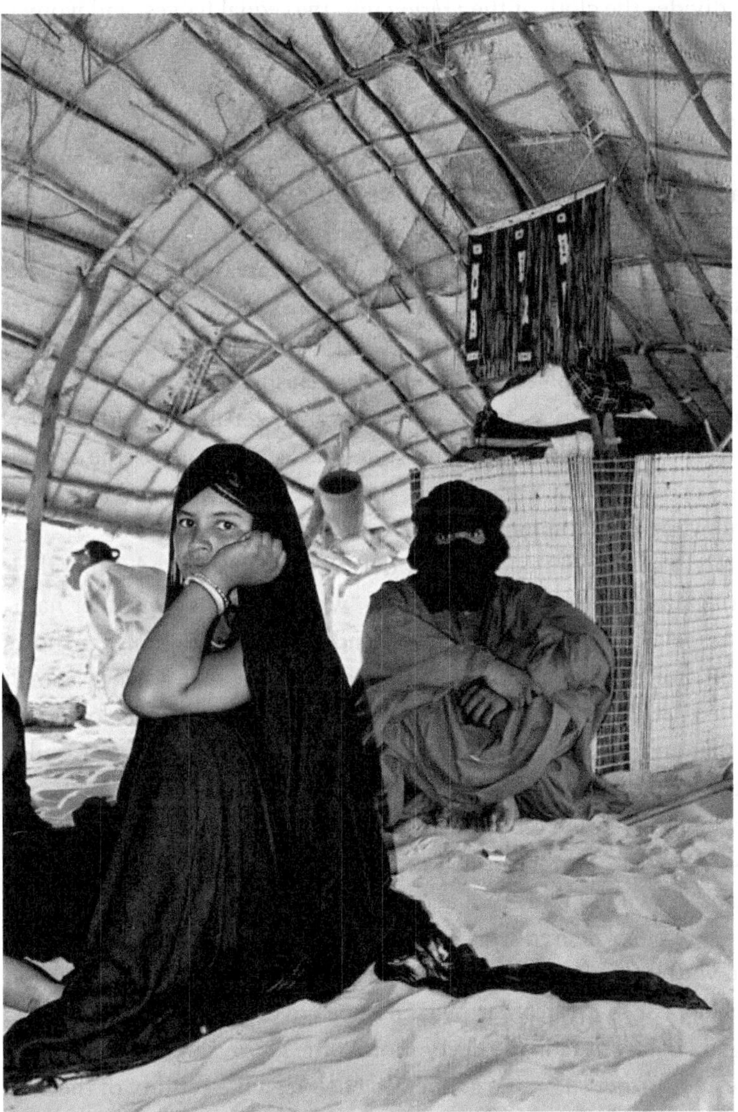

Figure 2.11. Interior of a Tuareg tent, Timbuktu, 2004.

ings that were similar to those of other Saharan groups for several generations. Today, however, Ait Khabbash women embroider various motifs on the
taḥruyt, treating it as a blank canvas ready to be embroidered with colored
lines, curves, and zigzags (Fig. 2.9). Women also attach multicolored and black
wool tassels with sequins to the lateral ends of the cloth. The *tanammast* or
central band is crucial to the composition of the *taḥruyt,* forming a ground
line for the embroidered motifs, which appear to rise up or grow out of it. The
tanammast divides the cloth of the *taḥruyt* into two equal halves, and women
align their patterns symmetrically so that the motifs are always balanced bilat-
erally: the designs on the right and left sides of the *tanammast* serve as mirror
images of each other (Fig. 2.8).

As with motifs used in weaving, these embroidered motifs associate women
with the natural world. For instance, many motifs relate to pigeons, such as the
neon green zigzag designs embroidered on the border of the *taḥruyt* featured
in Figure 2.12, said to resemble pigeon prints. Women are frequently compared
to pigeons in Ait Khabbash riddles and poems, as in a line from a wedding
song comparing the bride to a pigeon: *Zwur i wdar-inew a yatbir umlil,* "Be
in front of me, oh white pigeon." The Ait Khabbash associate pigeons with
beauty, good fortune, purity, and most importantly fertility.[28] Additionally,
women frequently told me that women's styles of clothing, such as the women
in Figure 2.9 dressed in a white skirt and dark blue *taḥruyt,* resembled a type
of black and white bird commonly found in southeastern Morocco.

The women I spoke with consistently described the motifs adorning their
head coverings as "flowers," "bird tracks," "wheat," "trees," or other natural objects associated with fertility, plenty, and prosperity. Figure 2.12 shows
the most common motif found on the Ait Khabbash head covering: a small
triangle called *takhbasht,* meaning "claws," which women told me looks like
the marks that animal claws make on the ground. The triangle motif is also
similar to the shape created by the *tirsal* or wooden element used in tent construction, which was earlier reflected in Ait Khabbash tattoo motifs (Fig. 2.7).
Little trees (*tisekla*) are also frequently represented in many different forms, as
in the designs shown in Figures 2.8 and 2.9. Flower motifs—clear references
to fertility—are embroidered with curvilinear stitches, outlined in one color
and filled in with its complementary color (Fig. 2.8). In sum, the embroidered
motifs often appear to create a fertile landscape covered with vegetation.

Once again, colors used in the decoration of the *taḥruyt* are also associated
with nature and further suggest a connection between the fertility of the land
and the fertility of women. Women purchase previously dyed wool yarn in

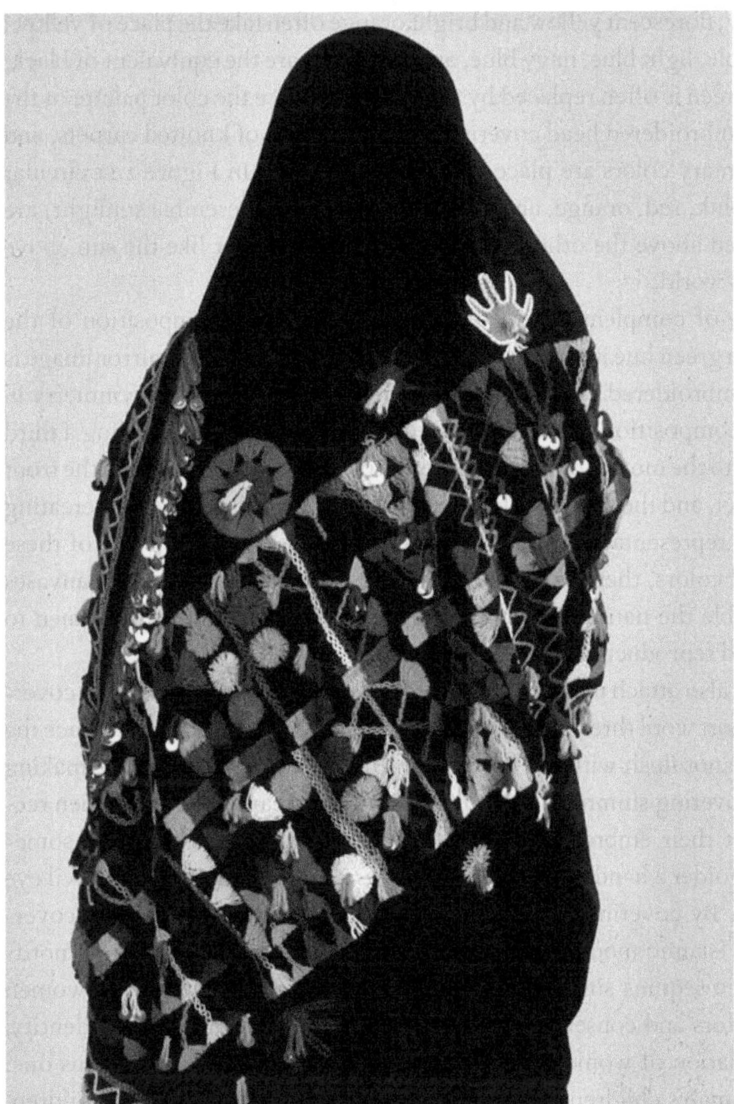

Figure 2.12. Rear view of an Ait Khabbash embroidered head covering.

the market and use this in their embroidery. Colors are divided into light and dark hues. Although purple, bright blue, pink, neon green, and other colors are embroidered on the indigo or black cloth, these colors fall within the Ait Khabbash basic color palette of red, green, yellow, and black. As previously discussed for knotted carpets, the color palette has greatly expanded in recent years, including new versions of the light hues. Hot pink and red are used interchangeably; florescent yellow and bright orange often take the place of yellow; bright purple, light blue, navy blue, and neon blue are the equivalent of black; and dark green is often replaced by neon green. Hence the color palette of the women's embroidered head coverings resembles that of knotted carpets, and complementary colors are placed next to each other. In Figure 2.12 circular motifs in pink, red, orange, and yellow (colors said to resemble sunlight) are embroidered above the other motifs and appear to hover like the sun above the natural world.

The use of complementary colors also balances the composition of the *tahruyt*. If a green hue is used to create a motif, for instance, its mirror image is typically embroidered in a red hue. Women's use of balance and symmetry in the visual composition of the *tahruyt* can also be interpreted as adding a third dimension to the motifs: one side of an embroidered image represents the front of the object, and the mirror reflection represents its back, effectively creating a flattened representation of a three-dimensional entity. By the use of these shapes and colors, therefore, women's bodies are transformed into canvases that resemble the natural world and its plentifulness, connecting women to fertility and reproduction.

Women also attach metallic sequins to the entire surface of the head covering with short wool threads, adding a dynamic energy to the *tahruyt*. Since the sequins are not flush with the textile, they move when women walk, making the head covering shimmer in the bright North African sunlight. Women recognize that their embroidered head coverings attract attention and sometimes embroider a hand motif, called a *khamsa*, to protect against the evil eye (Fig. 2.12). By covering the form of the body underneath, the head covering fulfills Islamic modesty requirements, while its brightly colored motifs and metallic sequins simultaneously attract attention to the role of women as the creators and conservers of Ait Khabbash survival and ethnic identity. This association of women, ethnic identity, and fertility is a conscious one: when a woman's children begin to get married and have their own children, her perceived loss of sexuality and fertility is marked by wearing head coverings embroidered with only minimal amounts of decoration. The elder women in Figure 2.13 told me that it was no longer appropriate for them to wear the colorfully embroidered head coverings that they had worn thirty years ago.

While many Ait Khabbash women still wear the *tahruyt*, the types of head coverings worn have begun to diversify as their lifestyles have become more varied. Since the Ait Khabbash settled in villages and towns in the Tafilalet oasis, young married women no longer work outdoors, fetching firewood and

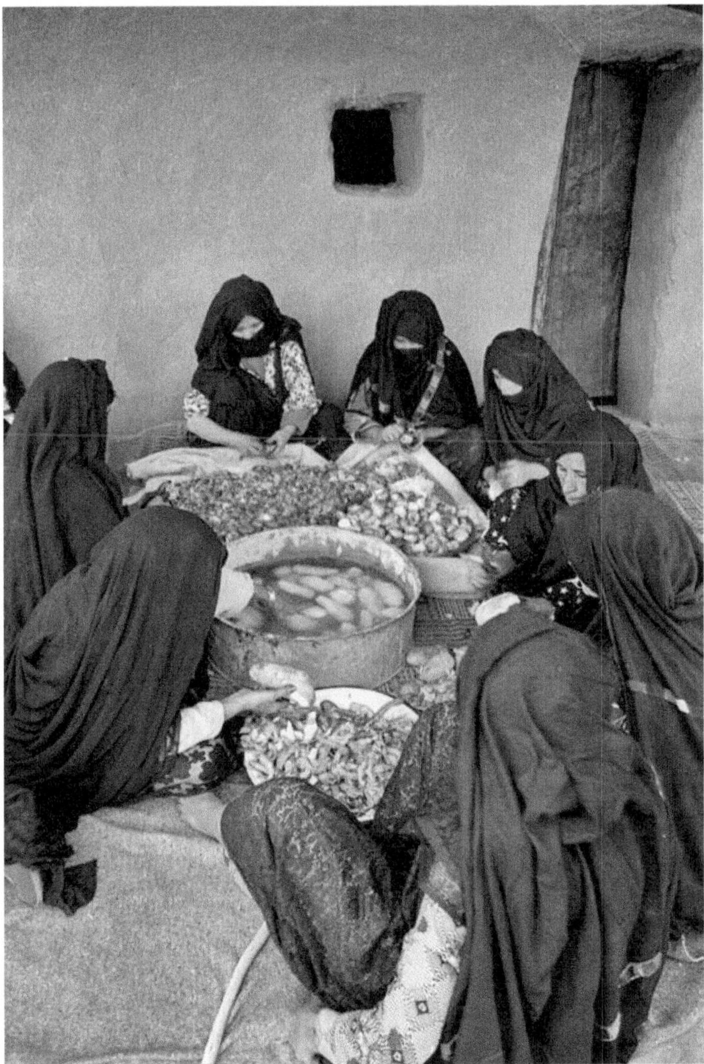

Figure 2.13. Ait Khabbash elders, assisting in the preparation of a wedding meal, wear indigo-dyed head coverings with little embroidery, 2000.

water from great distances and herding livestock. Instead they stay home while their husbands perform wage labor in the towns of Rissani and Erfoud; this allows women to wear the *jellaba*,[29] a polyester hooded gown that is more comfortable than the *taḥruyt* but not practical for manual labor (Fig. 2.14). Women often hold onto their nomadic ideals, however, raising sheep and goats on the roofs of their new concrete houses and searching the surrounding desert

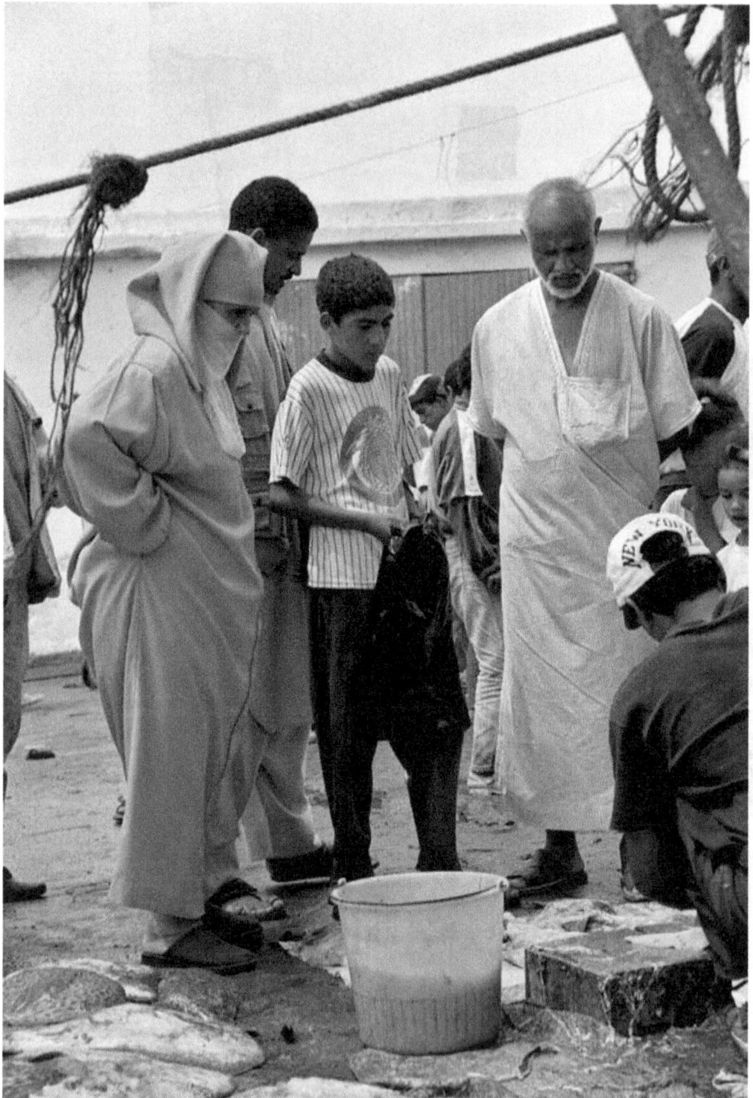

Figure 2.14. A woman wearing a jellaba *in Essaouira, 2000.*

for animal fodder or cultivating small patches of alfalfa while still wearing
the *taḥruyt*. Many Ait Khabbash men who joined the Moroccan military were
stationed in the Western Sahara and brought their wives and sisters colorful
head coverings called *mleḥfat* (singular *mleḥfa*) from the area (Fig. 2.15). These
long, colorful pieces of cloth are considered more prestigious due to their cost
and their importation from afar; a woman wearing a *mleḥfa* also signals to

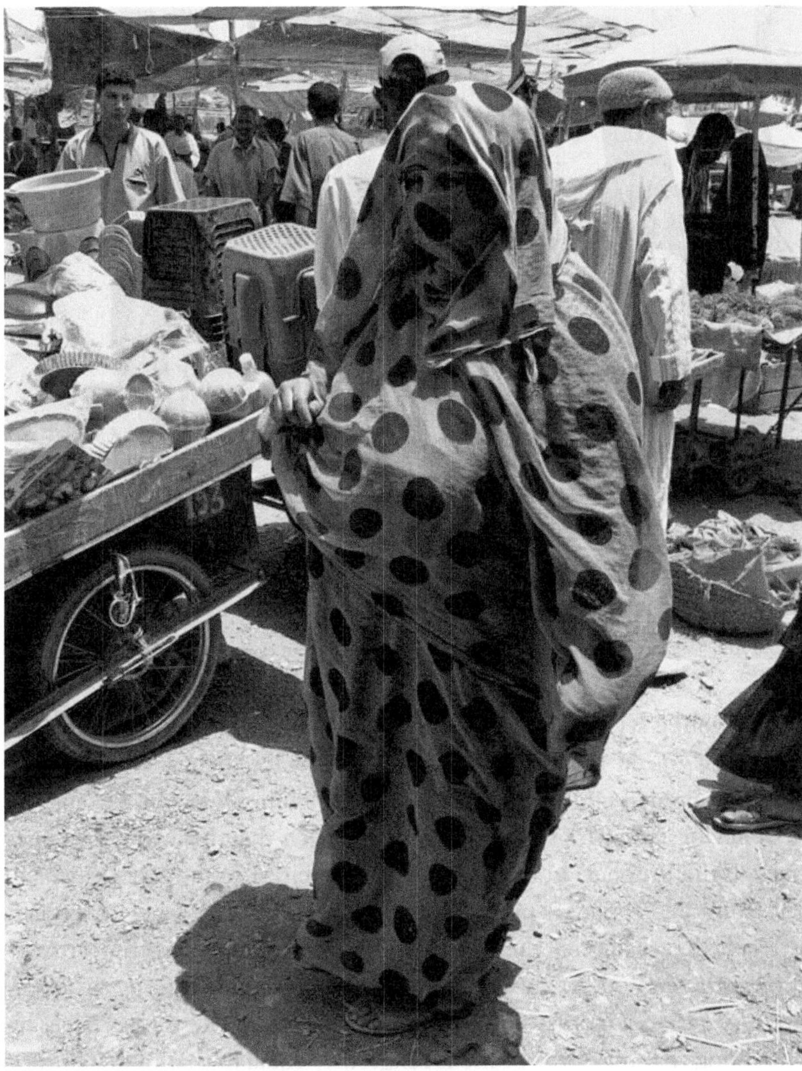

Figure 2.15. A woman in Rissani wearing a colorful outer covering called a mleḥfa, *2004. Photo by Addi Ouadderrou.*

others that she has a relative in the Moroccan military, a respectable job with good pay.

Some women reject the brightly embroidered *taḥruyt* in favor of the undecorated black head covering worn by Arab women in the Tafilalet oasis. Arab women drape themselves in long pieces of black cotton fabric, called *liẓour* (singular *liẓar*), typically leaving a small opening to see through (Fig. 2.16).

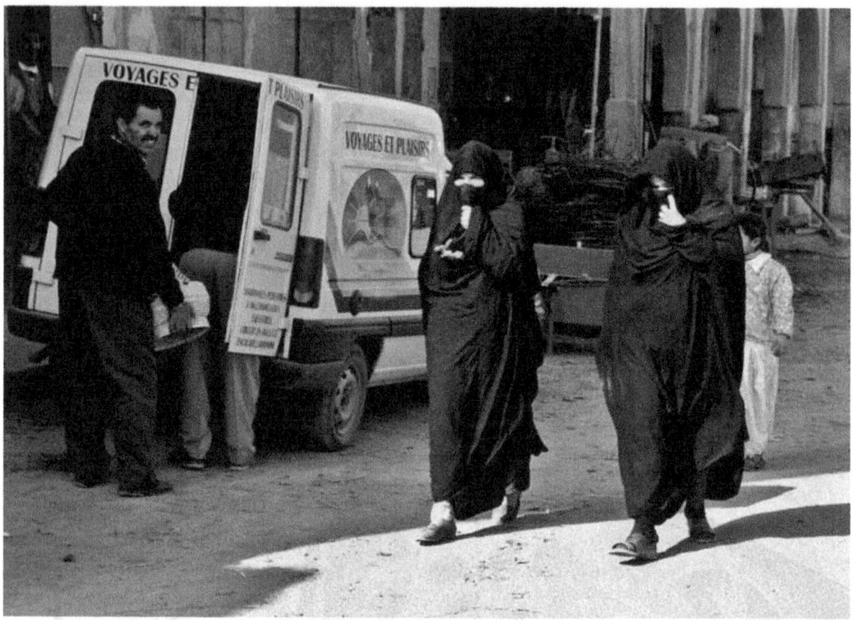

Figure 2.16. Arab women in Rissani wearing undecorated black lizour, *2004.*

This conservative style of covering among Arabs is influenced by the large numbers of *shurfa* in the Tafilalet oasis. *Shurfa* trace their ancestry to the Prophet Muhammad and his followers, priding themselves in their conservative behavior and strict style of covering, which they believe reflects the practices of the Prophet. In the Tafilalet, as in the rest of the Muslim world, descent from the Prophet is prestigious and inspires a high level of respect. Some people thus claim that the colorful Ait Khabbash head covering attracts attention and is immodest. The adoption of the Arab head covering as a Muslim modesty garment increases their religious standing in the oasis society by demonstrating that their way of life is religiously equal to that of the *shurfa*.

In addition, for the first time large numbers of Ait Khabbash girls are attending high school and view both the Arab *lizar* and the Amazigh *taḥruyt* as old-fashioned, wearing the hooded gown or *jellaba* instead.[30] Girls also wear the *hijab*, a general term for Islamic women's modest clothing that is loose and covers their arms and legs. The *hijab* commonly includes a headscarf, long-sleeved shirt, and long skirt or pants. Some girls do not cover their heads and wear short-sleeved shirts and pants to school, although this is still relatively rare. Increased educational opportunities for women mean that gender identity is becoming more variable and complex, as reflected in their styles of dress.

Adorning the body is often a political act, and Ait Khabbash women have used dress to negotiate the tension between contemporary modesty requirements and the source of their power: their connection to female fertility. The following chapter addresses these issues in its discussion of *aḥidous* performances.

THREE

Dance Performances

NEGOTIATING GENDER AND SOCIAL CHANGE

Another important art form of the Ait Khabbash is *ahidous,* a collective performance at weddings and other celebrations that incorporates oral poetry. Although *ahidous* performances are common to many Amazigh groups in central and southern Morocco, each group has its particular rhythms, dance steps, clothing styles, and song techniques, thus making Ait Khabbash *ahidous* an important indicator of their group identity.[1] Despite the inclusive nature of these *ahidous* performances, in which large numbers of both men and women participate, they are also strictly monitored by the society to project cultural values regarding acceptable male and female behaviors. The gender symbolism of these performances demonstrates the centrality of women and concepts of female fertility in the perpetuation of their culture.

Ahidous performances are carefully planned and choreographed events that combine visual, kinetic, and aural elements that engage the entire community in making music and dancing together. The performances are always initiated by adult men, who gather into a straight line, standing shoulder to shoulder, and play a distinctive *ahidous* rhythm on the *allun,* or frame drum, continuing for several minutes until some women join them. Draping their indigo-dyed embroidered head coverings (*tahruyt*) over their upper bodies so that their faces cannot be seen, the women form a parallel line facing the line of men, holding hands under their head coverings (Fig. 3.1). Ait Khabbash *ahidous* performances differ from those of some other Amazigh groups, such as Imazighen in the High Atlas, where men and women stand next to each other in the same line.

Once the lines are formed, the men begin to sing *ahidous* songs, singing a single phrase or *izli,* which is then repeated in call-and-response fashion by the women, with a wordless melodic phrase known as *tamawait* sung between

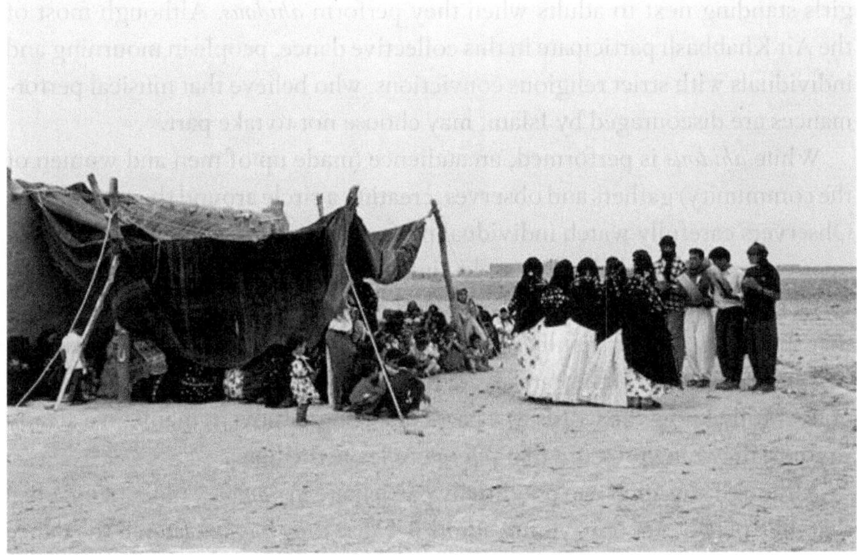

Figure 3.1. An aḥidous *performance in Hafira in front of the bride's tent.*

one *iẕli* and the next. Although improvisation is common in other areas of Morocco, the songs performed during Ait Khabbash *aḥidous* are rarely improvised. During my time in Morocco, I observed *aḥidous* performances on numerous occasions. They were most common at weddings and naming ceremonies, although *aḥidous* was sometimes performed during less formal occasions, such as celebrating a full moon or relatives visiting from afar. The greater the number of people who participate in playing *aḥidous*, the more successful it is considered by the participants; and it is not uncommon to see a hundred men and women performing *aḥidous* at the same time.[2]

Also unlike the practice in other areas of Morocco, where professional musicians are often hired to play at weddings and other celebrations, any adult who wishes to join serves as both musician/singer and dancer.[3] The concept of the professional musician, dancer, and singer does not exist among the Ait Khabbash, who, unlike their Arab neighbors, never hire professional musicians to perform at special events. Since no special instruction is required to play *aḥidous*, learning is informal and ongoing. Ait Khabbash do not say that they dance *aḥidous* or sing *aḥidous*, but the verb *aɣ*, "play," is used in Tamazight. Children hear and feel the rhythms of *aḥidous* from the time they are infants tied onto their mother's backs, picking up the steps and rhythms of *aḥidous* and later imitating their adult relatives. It is common to see small boys and girls standing next to adults when they perform *aḥidous*. Although most of the Ait Khabbash participate in this collective dance, people in mourning and individuals with strict religious convictions, who believe that musical performances are discouraged by Islam, may choose not to take part.

While *aḥidous* is performed, an audience (made up of men and women of the community) gathers and observes, creating a circle around the performers. Observers carefully watch individual performers, not hesitating to comment upon each performer's dancing style, singing voice, and style of dress. The performers themselves also carefully watch their fellow participants, recognizing that the audience is carefully critiquing both their collective and individual performance styles. If they are aware that one of their fellow performers does not yet fully know the words to a particular song or how to maintain a steady rhythm, they may pressure that person to leave the line.

Although any adult can potentially participate in *aḥidous*, older people feel that they play better than young adults because they have mastered the dance steps, the drum rhythms, and the singing styles typical of this art form. As one fifty-year-old man in Rissani described it, the skill required to play *aḥidous* comes with experience:

> The young do not have the patience to play *aḥidous* like us. The young people move too quickly and do not know the old songs. When we play, the young sit down and watch.

In fact, certain older men and women hold local reputations for their exceptional singing voices and are referred to as *bu wḥidous* for a man or *mm uḥidous* for a woman, meaning "person of *aḥidous*."

In addition, single women who are unmarried and/or divorced play *aḥidous* more than married women. Although women's faces are covered while playing *aḥidous*, the community is aware of each individual's identity. For example, during a wedding, which is typically held outdoors, men and women sit in segregated areas, often across from each other, watching *aḥidous* performances. When a single girl stands up to play *aḥidous*, all of the women, and even some men, see her face, allowing for public exposure. After her identity is known, both women and men listen to her singing voice and watch her dancing style. Since many women actively search for potential wives for their unmarried adult sons, single girls who play *aḥidous* increase their chances of finding a mate. This does not mean that married women do not play *aḥidous*; but they limit their participation to special occasions, such as the marriage of a close relative. Both the performance styles and the clothing worn during *ahidous* are subject to social critique and carefully appraised by observers, especially by the groups of women who gather and watch.[4]

When playing *ahidous*, women are expected to wear white *ihruyn* (singular *ahruy*: draped garments). White is believed to be a celebratory color, marking the importance of the ceremonial occasions when *ahidous* is typically performed. The *ahruy* is made from a piece of white fabric twelve yards long. The cloth is first folded lengthwise and draped over the body and customarily held together at the shoulders by two silver pins, called fibulae or *tiseynas* (Fig. 3.2). Today the fabric is simply knotted at the shoulders and belted around the waist. Both Arab and Amazigh women throughout Morocco commonly wore this draped garment. Figure 3.2 pictures a woman from the Anti-Atlas region of Morocco wearing a dark blue indigo-dyed *ahruy*. The derivation of the *ahruy* is unclear, but several scholars suggest that it has an ancient Greek or Roman origin (Besancenot 1990: 154). Harris (1895: 161), a late-nineteenth-century traveler to the Tafilalet oasis, recorded seeing women in this garment. My conversations with women supported earlier accounts indicating that until the 1960s or 1970s Ait Khabbash women often wore two draped garments at the same time, a white cotton *ahruy* covered with a second made from indigo-dyed fabric; or they wore a single indigo-dyed *ahruy* (as in Fig. 1.9) that was more practical for daily wear, because it did not as readily show dirt. During weddings and other festive occasions, however, women would reverse the sequence, wearing the indigo fabric inside and the white outside or just a single white *ahruy*. According to women, these two layers of cloth were used for modesty purposes, in order to cover the body. Ait Khabbash women, in contrast with the practice today, did not wear dresses, modern underwear, or *serwal* (long cotton leggings) under their *ihruyn*. During one conversation I had with two elderly women who were recounting their youth, one laughingly confirmed that women would be completely nude under their *ihruyn*. "Everything was hanging out back then," she explained. She then turned to her friend and asked, "Are you wearing underwear, Fadma?" When Fadma answered in the affirmative, she joked, "What's next, Fadma? Are you going to start wearing bras now, too?"

In the 1960s and 1970s Ait Khabbash women started to wear long-sleeved ankle-length cotton and polyester dresses under their *ihruyn* and began to make their *ihruyn* from a single layer of black lace or netlike fabric that revealed the colors and motifs of their dresses (Fig. 3.3). Since the 1990s young women have viewed the black lace *ihruyn* as old-fashioned, associating it with

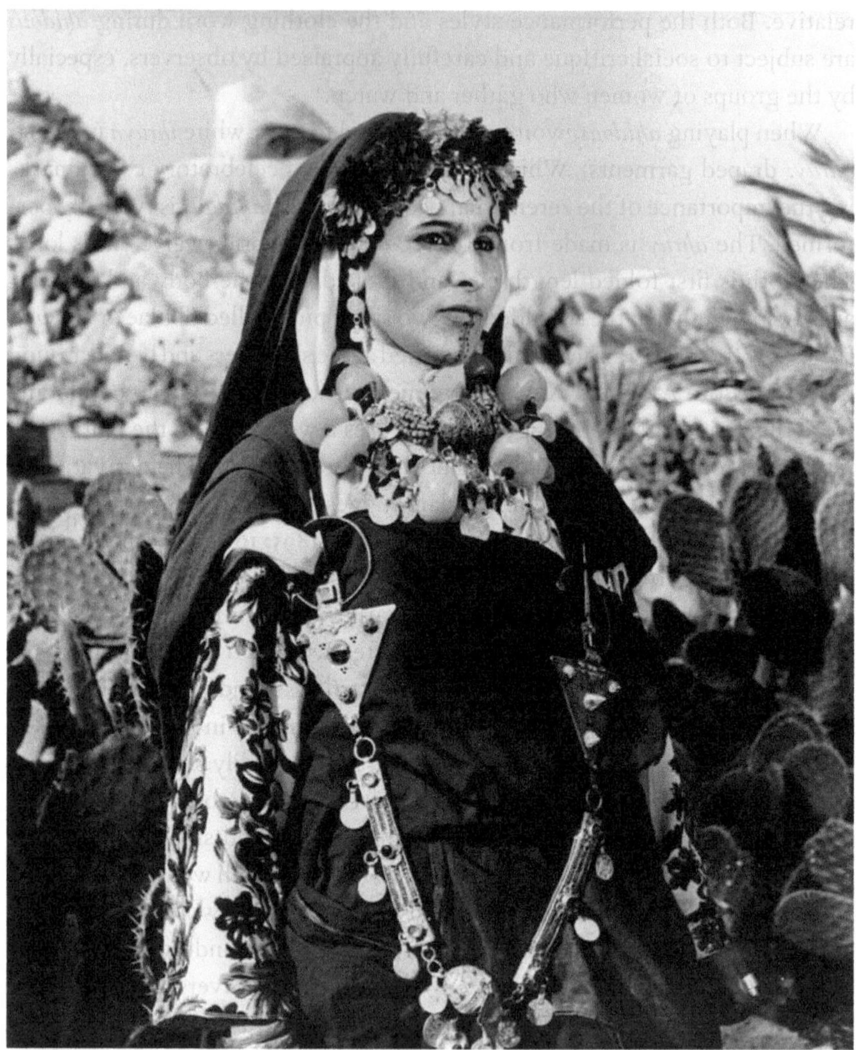

Figure 3.2. An Amazigh woman from the Anti-Atlas region wears an indigo-dyed aḥruy.
Photo courtesy of the National Anthropological Archives, 1930–1959. Smithsonian Institution/
04066400.

elderly women upholding ancestral norms. Instead these women wear a more
modern version of the *aḥruy* called a *jaltita* (plural *jaltitat*), a full skirt with an
elastic waist made out of the same brightly colored lace or netlike material as
the *aḥruy* worn over their dresses. Regardless of these recent changes, women
continue to wear *iḥruyn* during ceremonial occasions, such as weddings.

   During *aḥidous, iḥruyn* or *jaltitat,* preferably white, are obligatory dress for

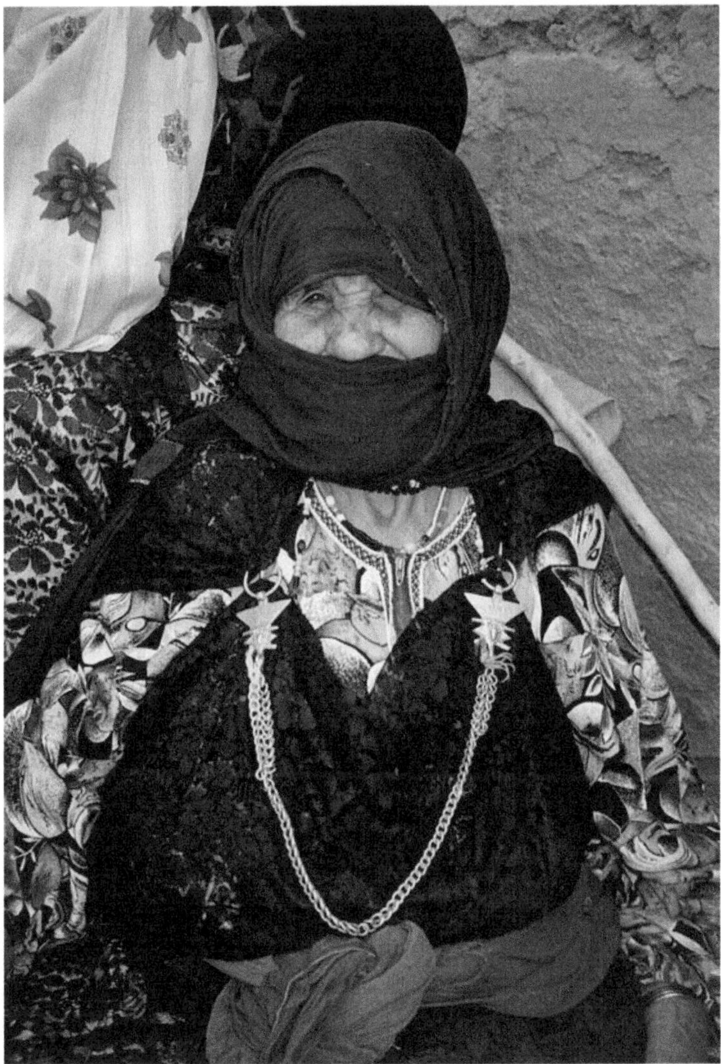

Figure 3.3. An Ait Khabbash woman in Hafira wearing a contemporary black aḥruy *pinned together at the shoulders by fibulae, 1999.*

women, who also wear thick wool or silk belts with long tassels that fall to the sides of their waists. As mentioned, women also drape their embroidered head coverings over their heads and shoulders to cover their faces. Clothing is considered an important element of the performance; if a woman wishes to play *aḥidous* but does not have the appropriate clothing, she borrows it from others. I often saw women who had finished playing *aḥidous* quickly stepping

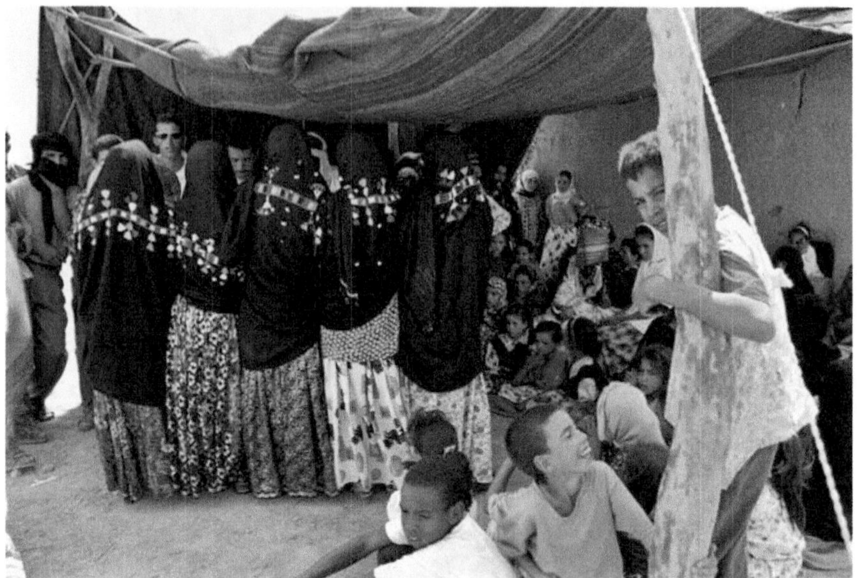

Figure 3.4. Rear view of Ait Khabbash women in Hafira performing aḥidous *at the bridal tent, 1999.*

out of their white *jaltitat* and handing them to others who did not have their own. Women also would lend a particularly well-embroidered head covering to *aḥidous* performers. During *aḥidous,* the head covering is positioned so that its embroidered central band (*tanammast*) runs horizontally along their backs (Fig. 3.4). If the dancers' head coverings are not positioned correctly, a woman in the audience may approach and adjust them in mid-performance without the dancers missing a beat.

The clothing worn by men and women during *aḥidous* further reinforces the gender roles discussed previously.[5] Men who play *aḥidous* typically wear the clothing typical of an adult male, the woven wool or solid white *tajellabiyt* (hooded gown) and white turban (Fig. 3.5); in recent years men's dress has become increasingly informal, however, and it is common to see men wearing machine-made pants, shirts, and even baseball caps. While men's hooded gowns do not emphasize their physical forms (instead hiding them under the vertical, columnar shape of the *tajellabiyt*), women's clothing calls attention to the procreative powers of the female body. The vertical lines and simplicity of the men's *tajellabiyt* contrast with the horizontal, three-dimensional visual effect of the embroidery of the women's head coverings (running horizontally across their backs) and with the multiple colors and varying patterns and motifs that usually segment the women's bodies. Individual sections of the body

are marked by distinct patterns and color differences. Their indigo head coverings overlap their white skirts at their hips and waists, drawing the eye to that
part of their bodies. The thick belt tied around their waists and their full skirts
accentuate the horizontal, rounded aspects of their bodies, visually suggesting the ample figures associated with women who have given birth to many
children. Married women are proud if their bodies become fleshy and stout
as they age, thereby demonstrating their reproductive abilities and increasing
their status in a society that honors the generative powers of the female body.
Clothing styles worn by women emphasize this feminine ideal rather than individual reality, however, as most women who play *ahidous* are unmarried or
divorced and thus unlikely to have had many children.

The Ait Khabbash are the only group among the Ait Atta in which women
cover their faces while playing *ahidous*. Mireille Morin-Barde's book *Coiffures*

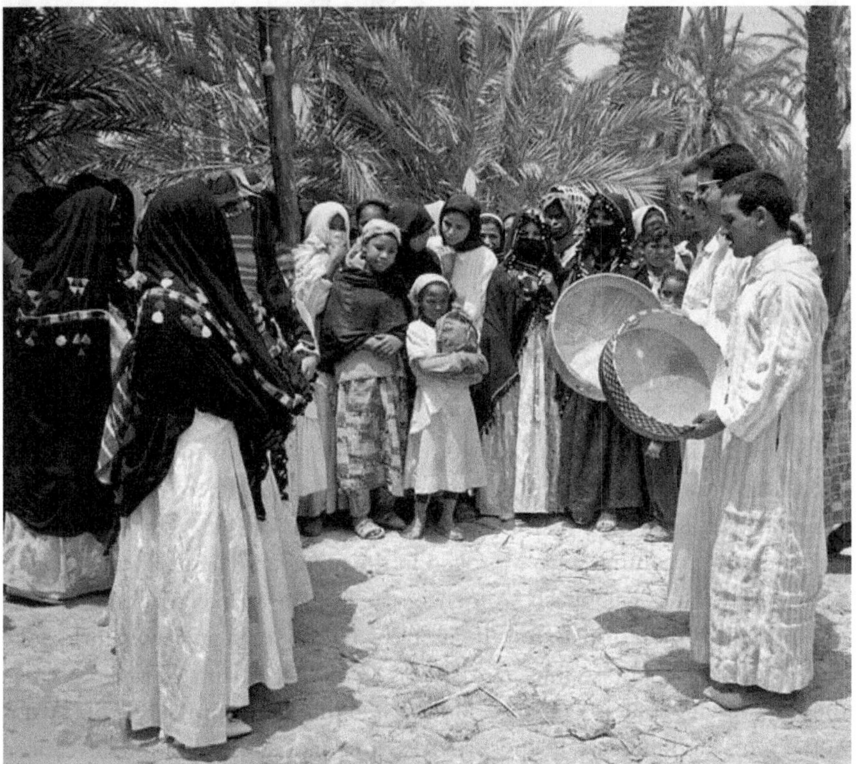

Figure 3.5. Men and women face each other while performing ahidous. *Women conceal their faces
with their embroidered head coverings. Men face them, singing and marking the rhythm on their
drums, 1996. Photo by Addi Ouadderrou.*

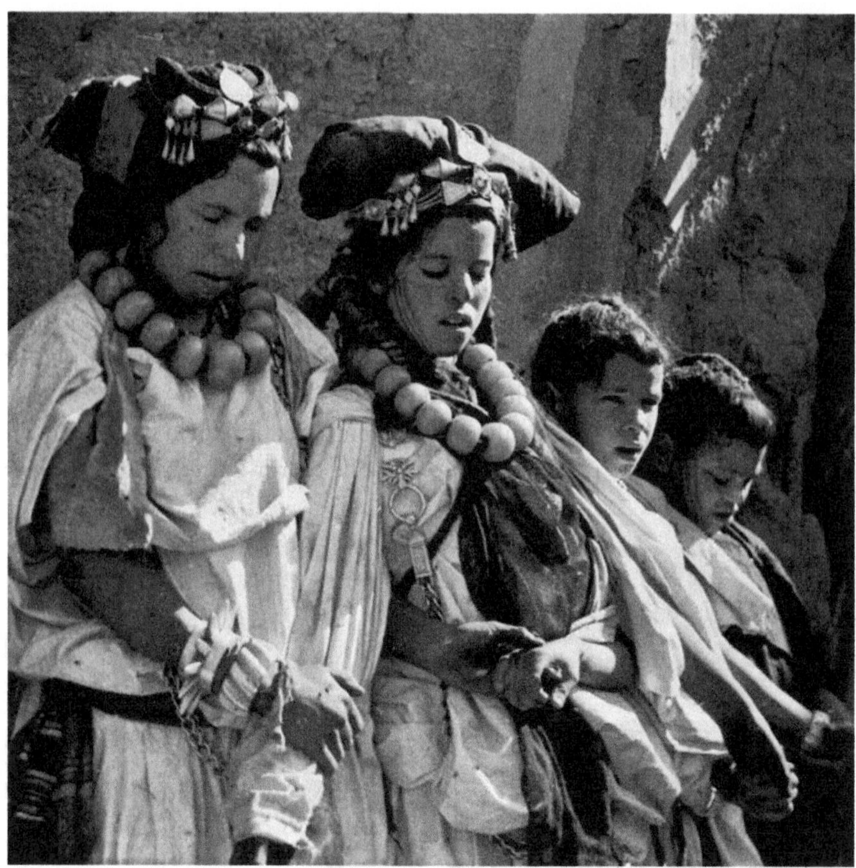

Figure 3.6. The bride, wearing a hornlike headdress, performs aḥidous *with her sister-in-law and two young girls. Photo by Mireille Morin-Barde, 1950–1952 © Édisud.*

féminines du Maroc features a photograph taken between 1950 and 1952 that shows Ait Atta women playing *aḥidous* with their faces uncovered (Fig. 3.6). Since the Ait Khabbash had lived in the heartland of Ait Atta territory before moving to southeastern Morocco in the nineteenth century, the *aḥidous* performed by Ait Khabbash women in the past most likely resembled that photographed by Morin-Barde. Indeed, the elderly men and women I spoke with confirmed that previous generations of the Ait Khabbash had not worn the *taḥruyt* while playing *aḥidous*. Most stated that social pressure from Arabs in the 1960s and increased exposure to Islamic modesty requirements caused their previously nomadic ancestors to modify *aḥidous* to include the head covering as a physical barrier between unrelated men and women facing each other during the performance. Thus women's dress during *aḥidous* allows them to fulfill local modesty requirements while also visually reinforcing their connection to fertility and the source of their societal power.

Nonetheless, the Ait Khabbash women's adoption of the head covering during *ahidous* has not eliminated criticism of their participation on the part of non-Amazigh inhabitants of the Tafilalet oasis. Many of them characterized *ahidous* to me as shameful, because it allows unrelated men and women to stand close to each other. They did not necessarily object to the public performance of poetry, since Arab men and women also perform oral poetry together, called *mzougi*. They were not Tamazight speakers, however, and — unable to understand the lyrics of Ait Khabbash songs — were under the false impression that the songs include explicit sexual remarks. Specifically, many Arab men and women told me that they believed that the songs sung during Ait Khabbash *ahidous* performances are risqué love songs where men and women communicate promises to meet later in the evening. They did not understand that, even though *ahidous* performances do involve men and women facing each other in parallel lines, the words and movements of the participants are closely governed by Ait Khabbash social restrictions that carefully monitor encounters between unrelated men and women (as discussed below).

Ait Khabbash perform three different styles of *ahidous*, each with its own style of dancing, drumming, and singing: *uatta, uâalwan,* and a new form of *ahidous* called *hiwawi.* Most of Ait Khabbash sung poetry can be performed using any of these three playing styles. According to the Ait Khabbash the oldest style of *ahidous* is *uatta* (a term derived from the name of the Ait Atta, from whom they are descended), which is played more slowly and methodically than the other forms of *ahidous.* Men start the *ahidous* by drumming a slow steady beat on their *allun* (frame drums), holding their drums vertically near their faces and using both hands to create the rhythm. The men and women standing in parallel lines begin by slowly swaying from side to side in time with the drumming. Once the pace of the song is established, the men begin to sing a line of song while women respond by repeating the song. The group then performs a step called *tawada,* meaning "march," which is done in place. As the beat of the drum quickens, the two rows of dancers slowly march backward and forward, each line advancing in turn while the other simultaneously moves backward until the performance ends. There is no special phrase of drumming that marks the end of a performance, which simply concludes when some of the performers choose to leave the dance area.

A second and more complex type of performance style is *uâalwan,* named for the Ait Alwan, a subgroup of the Ait Khabbash. *Uâalwan* begins with men and women slowly stepping from side to side and forward and backward while singing a song, gradually rotating counterclockwise as a group while the men drum more quickly and add to their steps a forward lunge, alternating between the left and right foot. The group then performs the signature *uâalwan* dance step, in which dancers step forward, crossing one foot with the other, and then step backward.

The Ait Khabbash consider the *uatta* and *uâalwan* the oldest and purest forms of *aḥidous,* claiming that they have remained unchanged for centuries. *Hiwawi,* in contrast, is a new form of *aḥidous* that has been introduced in just the last few decades. The word *hiwawi* comes from the word *ahwawi,* meaning "fickle" or "impetuous" in Tamazight. This is perhaps an indication that the Ait Khabbash consider the songs sung during *hiwawi* to be superficially trendy songs that lack the poetic metaphor of the other styles. The dancing that accompanies *hiwawi* occurs at a fast pace. Since *hiwawi* is very popular, there usually are not enough drums for all of the male players, so the other men clap their hands or beat on the back of a metal pan to the same rhythm. To the faster pace of *hiwawi,* dancers take small quick steps to the left. While also moving forward and backward, both lines rotate counterclockwise. If a large number of women are playing *hiwawi,* they may break into two or three groups, each rotating around the others in a counterclockwise or clockwise direction. I was told this dance step was an imitation of a form of *aḥidous* practiced in the High Atlas, suggesting that it incorporates influences from several different Amazigh groups.

Although these dance steps are much quicker than those in the older styles of *aḥidous,* social conventions still strictly control the extent of female body movements. Regardless of the type of *aḥidous* performed, one of the most striking traits of female dancing is the static quality of their upper bodies. Women hold hands and stand in a tight line with little space between the dancers, taking very small and contained steps and being careful not to move their bodies too much during *aḥidous.* Observers criticize women who bounce up and down or take wide steps during *aḥidous.* Even though women hold their upper bodies as stiffly as possible, their full skirts and belt tassels still swing back and forth to the rhythm of the dance, emphasizing the swinging action of their hips. Women told me this back-and-forth movement of their lower bodies is called *ssand,* "to shake," in Tamazight, which literally means "to churn milk." It refers to the act of quickly swinging a skin bag back and forth from a tripod in order to separate milk from butter, an action once performed by Ait Khabbash women practically every day, further connecting them to concepts of fertility.

In contrast, men's dancing style is not restricted by social conventions and is much more active. Men dance with their bodies bent forward slightly from the hips, bending their knees while they step forward and backward, and the steps they take have a wider amplitude than those of women. Only the men are allowed to play the *allun,* or frame drum, during *ahidous* in public and thereby control the start and pace of the dancing.[6] Thus the dancing style of men reflects the active and energetic social behavior expected of them, and its careful precision at the same time expresses their dignity and composure.

Women living in more rural areas outside the oasis, however, tend to perform larger steps with greater vertical amplitude, more resembling the large strides taken by the men, which is undoubtedly more consistent with *ahidous* performed by the Ait Khabbash in the past. The more restrained dance steps performed by women living in the heavily populated and ethnically diverse areas within the Tafilalet oasis suggest that they represent a compromise between older styles of *ahidous* and more recent attempts to regulate contact between men and women and to place modesty restrictions upon the public performance of dance and song by women.

Despite social restrictions that have caused women to wear head coverings and reduce the amplitude of their dance steps, the performance of *ahidous* creates a feeling of social solidarity among all of the Ait Khabbash. Since they are the only Amazigh group living in this part of southeastern Morocco, performing *ahidous* in Tamazight defines this community in opposition to non-Tamazight speakers in the region. Songs are never written but are passed orally from generation to generation. Some of the words used in the songs are no longer used in daily life; their exact meanings have been lost, which gives the songs an almost sacred status, generating a sense of affinity with the past. *Ahidous* performances thus function as metaphors for the integrity of the community, as aesthetic expressions of ethnic identity. Many Ait Khabbash told me that making a promise in Tamazight guarantees that it will be kept. The Tamazight expression *awal awal,* meaning "word word," refers to a promise as well as to an honest and honorable action or person. If men begin an *ahidous* song by singing a phrase in Arabic, this can be interpreted as an insult to the family who organized the celebration, disgracing them by suggesting that they are not "real" Imazighen.

During *ahidous* performances, any song from the Ait Khabbash repertoire can be played according to any of the three performance styles. Since each performance style has its own particular rhythm, the melody of the song is modified to fit the performance. Most Ait Khabbash *ahidous* songs consist of the repetition of a single phrase (*izli*), with men singing it in unison and women repeating the same phrase in a call-and-response fashion. Repetition of this single phrase, with the insertion of a wordless melody (*tamawait*) between each of the call-and-response sequences, continues in this manner until the conclusion of the performance.

Songs performed during *ahidous* are especially rich in visual imagery and use visual metaphors to express Ait Khabbash values and beliefs. As noted earlier, *ahidous* is most commonly performed during Ait Khabbash three-day weddings. The day on which each particular song is performed is strictly assigned and controlled by social convention, its content corresponding to the events that occur on that day of the wedding. For example, the *izlan n wass amezwaru* or "songs of the first day" are sung after the bride has arrived at the groom's house for the wedding to welcome and wish her well in her new home. Each one of these phrases constitutes an individual song associated with the first day:

> *Tagwerramt ad-teg tunza tambarekt.*
> [Bride, we wish that you shall be blessed.]

> *A Rasul Allah ksat-asen i wegdud a Rasul Allah.*
> [Oh Prophet, protect the marriage, oh Prophet.]

> *G-asen a Rebbi i wulawen aydda ran.*
> [God, grant their hearts what they want.]

Another song commonly performed at Ait Khabbash weddings contains the wish that the bride will be protected from jealousy:

> *A yawudj ak izzrey i gar allen.*
> [Oh bride, God protect you from the evil eye.]

Ahidous is also played on the afternoon of the first day in anticipation of the consummation of the marriage that evening. These two examples are individual songs that use metaphor and poetic language to refer to female fertility and the impending sexual intercourse between the bride and the groom:

> *Allah yâawn a yatbir d-yiwin mensiwt.*
> [Greetings, pigeon who came to spend the night.]

> *Ger ixalifn a yalmu n ssaâidin.*
> [Oh grass of happy people, give new shoots.]

The first of these songs illustrates the strong metaphorical association in Ait Khabbash culture between women and pigeons; both are associated with fertility. The second uses the phrase "grass of happy people" to refer metaphorically to the bride and the phrase "give new shoots" as a wish for future offspring, thereby referring to the role of women as the protective guardians and progenitors of Ait Khabbash ethnic identity.

Songs thus allow Ait Khabbash to refer publicly to subject matter that would be considered inappropriate in a more conversational context, particularly the topic of female virginity. The Ait Khabbash bride is expected to be a virgin and to shed hymeneal blood during her first sexual encounter; according to tradition, this occurs with the bride fully dressed, causing blood to flow onto her white dress. The bride continues to wear the white dress stained with this blood during the rest of the three-day wedding ceremony. The following are examples of some *ahidous* songs that may be performed on the second day of the marriage, metaphorically referring to that bloodstain:

> *Ay hian-ek igerramen a yagdud.*
> [Oh wedding celebration, the respectability makes you look good.]

> *Igerramen iffu Ihal ṣbaḥ-kun.*
> [Oh respectability, the morning arrived, good morning.]

Because it would be considered socially unacceptable to use the word "blood" literally, they instead use the word *igerramen,* meaning "respectability" to the Ait Khabbash. This can be used to refer to a special relationship of respect that may be established between Ait Khabbash families and different Amazigh groups who vow to treat each other in a civil fashion and never to engage in aggressive acts against each other. An Ait Khabbash bride proves her respectability by having remained a virgin until marriage, and when the Ait Khabbash hear the word *igerramen* sung in *ahidous,* they understand its implied meaning.

The Ait Khabbash also use metaphors based on the natural environment to refer to the bride's hymeneal blood, as in the following song:

> *Ukẓey itbirn s ayulid ur-da nezẓan.*
> [I saw pigeons by the mountain, and they are not being sold.]

The metaphor of the mountain represents the bride herself. Ait Khabbash women explained to me that a bride is proud of her virginity and, like a mountain, stands tall and majestic while she publicly displays the bloodstain that is a mark of her honor. Many stories exist about a bride using animal blood or other means to fake her virginity, and the phrase "not being sold" means that the bloodstain on the bride's clothing is genuine. When this song is performed, the bride (her face covered with a red silk cloth) usually joins the group and also dances *ahidous* (Fig. 3.5). The bride commonly performs *ahidous* during the wedding ceremony, while it is rare to see the groom join these group dances.

Most Ait Khabbash women are aware that their virginity will be publicly displayed at a wedding, and few are proven not to be virgins. Female virginity is connected to the importance attached to female reproduction and a woman's ability to have children. In addition to singing about female virginity, *ahidous* songs performed on the second day of the wedding honor female fertility and contain wishes that the bride will have many children:

> *Ad-it-t-mun aduku-nnem d-irban d-wulli.*
> [We hope your shoe goes with children and sheep.]
>
> *Adam ig wadu-nnem aseklu d'igern ifer.*
> [We hope you will be like a tree that gives leaves.]
>
> *Tga almu yuley uldjig ar iɣir.*
> [Grass and flowers have grown to her shoulders.]

In the last song, which compares the bride's body to a fertile field, women explained to me that the phrase "grass and flowers" both refers to the bride's potential fertility represented by the blood and describes the bride's jewelry and clothing.

A final example of a song from the second day contains a wish that the bride will find happiness, good luck, and many children:

> *Tiwnẓiwin saâd a Rebbi i yslan.*
> [What nice bangs, God grant happiness to the couple.]

As discussed earlier, "bangs" refers literally to a hairstyle commonly worn by Ait Khabbash women and figuratively to the bride's fertility. Ait Khabbash believe there is a direct correlation between the thickness of a woman's hair and her ability to have children: the thicker her hair, the more fertile she will be.

On the third and final day of the wedding celebration, songs are sung to remind the bride not to be upset when her family leaves her after the wedding and returns home. Each phrase represents a different song that expresses these mournful sentiments:

> *Ak-afey a ṣber ig msafaḍn wulawen.*
> [Oh patience, I find you when hearts say good-bye.]

> *Aḍar iɣman ad ig ameẓduɣ ad-ur uɣulen.*
> [The feet painted with henna will be an inhabitant
>   (in the groom's house) and will not return.]

"The feet painted with henna" describes the bride, whose hands and feet are dyed with henna as part of the wedding preparations; and the rest of the phrase contains wishes that her marriage will not end in divorce but that she will find happiness with her husband and his family.

The following song, also performed on the third day of the wedding, uses visual metaphors associated with fertility to refer to the bride:

> *Ihenna wsufey uley ar aḍɣar n tuga.*
> [The bees are fine and have reached the place of grass and flowers.]

In Tamazight, the word *asufey* (spelled *wsufey* in this song because the letter *a* is transformed to a *w* when two vowels are together) specifically refers to the daughter of the queen bee. The female bee leaving the queen bee's nest to begin her own hive is a metaphor for the bride leaving her mother's home to start her own family. The bees are fine, since they safely made it to the groom's house, the place of grass and flowers.

Although increasingly rare, a form of poetry sung by men has also been used during weddings to make wishes for the couple's fertility and happiness.[7] *Tageẓẓumt* can be performed on any day of the wedding preceding the performance of *aḥidous,* either as planned or spontaneously while the men are waiting for women to join them in playing *aḥidous.* The *tageẓẓumt* itself may be an original creation or an earlier well-known poem and is accompanied by a rhythmic phrase drummed on the *allun* between the lines of poetry. The verbal skills of an especially gifted poet are greatly respected and appreciated, and Ait Khabbash explained to me that in the past poets would sometimes compete to see who had the most skill at creating and singing *tageẓẓumt.* Nomadic men typically composed poems during the long hours spent following their animal herds. Changes in economic patterns have led to the decline of *tageẓẓumt,* because most Ait Khabbash men in the Tafilalet oasis hold wage-paying jobs that are time restrictive; hence they do not have the time required to compose poetry.

The following poem was sung at an Ait Khabbash wedding during the summer of 1996 by a man in his fifties living in a remote desert village, who still herded sheep. According to the format of *tageẓẓumt*, each line starts with the words *ya ya aiwa*, and the last phrase of each line is then repeated at the beginning of the next line. The poem, presented in honor of the groom, contains a wish that his new wife will have many children:

> *Ya ya aiwa, subhan Rebbi wan lwahdaiu a wadd ur yugir wadu.*
> *Ya ya aiwa urt yugir wadu rjanu yugl ẓarun nsellas i whidus.*
> *Ya ya aiwa nsellas i whidous n'asik-id a yallun s bab n lferh anbark.*
> *Ya ya aiwa s bab n lferh anbark mayd di-tiwit ak ig Rebbi amm-umda*
>   *ad ur iqqar ad ikerreẓ ad isswa.*
> *Ya ya aiwa ad ikerreẓ ad isswa i-g-k âla xir, âla xir d lmal d rbeh ad akw*
>   *ilin s lxader-nnek a mayta.*

> [*Ya ya aiwa*, praise the Lord who is the only God; nothing is greater
>   than him.
> *Ya ya aiwa*, nothing is greater than him. My desire is connected
>   to you. We heard *ahidous*.
> *Ya ya aiwa*, we heard *ahidous* and we brought you, oh drum, to the
>   host of the blessed party.
> *Ya ya aiwa*, to the host of the blessed party. Congratulations on what
>   you brought. May God make you like a lake that never dries up,
>   that cultivates and irrigates.
> *Ya ya aiwa*, it cultivates and irrigates, makes you happy. Happiness,
>   wealth, and prosperity to you. May all these things exist for you,
>   oh my brother.]

The images of fertility in this *tageẓẓumt* express the desire that the bride and groom will have many offspring; and the fourth line congratulates the groom on "what you brought," referring to the bride, who is compared to a lake that irrigates and fertilizes the land. Water, so crucial to survival in a desert region like southeastern Morocco, is often used in Ait Khabbash poetry as a metaphor for the reproductive powers of women.

Tageẓẓumt represents an older form of sung poetry in Tamazight that has declined due to changes in the economic patterns of Ait Khabbash men. *Hiwawi*, the third and newest type of *aḥidous,* is also influenced by such changes. Many of these songs are borrowed from cassettes produced in the Sous plains of southwestern Morocco and are sung in the local Amazigh language, called Tashelhit. The increased access of Ait Khabbash men to wage-paying employment has given them the financial means to acquire such cassettes, not readily available in southeastern Morocco until the last decade. The lyrics of these songs refer directly to love, beautiful women, and contemporary problems faced by the younger generation, in contrast to styles of *aḥidous* that use visual metaphors (*tikselt*) to allude to socially delicate topics. An example is the translation of a *hiwawi* song I saw and heard performed by a group of Ait Khabbash men and women in their teens and early twenties in 1996:

> *Acki-med a tiferxin an mun s-dar lhenna.*
> *Acki-med a teferxin mk-aɣ i-gadda wawal.*
> *Acki-med a tiferxin neẓra ẓẓin ar i-ɣemma.*
> *Acki-med a tiferxin cuf tiddi cuf lhenna.*
> *Acki-med a tiferxin a lhenna mak-iẓẓenẓan?*
> *Acki-med a tiferxin yan wawal i-bbey miya.*
> *Acki-med a tiferxin atbir i-bbey tawenẓa.*

> [Come, girls, let's go together to the henna party.
> Come, girls, if we have the same ideas.
> Come, girls, we know the beauty is putting henna on her hands.
> Come, girls, look at the girl's shape, look at the henna.
> Come, girls, henna, who sells you?
> Come, girls, one word cuts one hundred.
> Come, girls, the pigeon cut her bangs.]

On this occasion the *hiwawi* was still performed in Tamazight, but with the addition of some Moroccan Arabic words. When I played a recording I had made of this song to elderly Ait Khabbash men and women, they found it too straightforward and candid, claiming that it lacked the subtle poetic language and the complex use of visual metaphors found in *uatta* and *uâalwan.* Each line began with the phrase "Come, girls," seemingly reinforcing their stereotype that *hiwawi* lyrics are overtly flirtatious. Many Ait Khabbash elders found it socially and religiously improper for the song to refer directly to a woman as "the beauty" and to draw attention to a woman's body with the phrase "look at the girl's shape."

Although older Ait Khabbash men and women find it morally and socially inappropriate, *hiwawi* is the most popular form of *ahidous* performed at weddings today. It is common to see lines of twenty or more young men performing with an equally large number of young women. The songs, rhythms, and playing styles of *hiwawi* are constantly changing and evolving, giving this hybrid performance style a dynamic quality. *Hiwawi* songs not only contain fewer poetic metaphors but are often improvised by the performers.

Thus *ahidous* performances are yet another example of how Ait Khabbash forms of artistic expression are changing to fit current realities. Young men and women are beginning to object to the social and religious restrictions that prohibit contact between unrelated men and women and to the arranged marriages that result. *Hiwawi* performances allow them to express their frustrations publicly in a way that they could not in everyday conversations with their elders.[8]

Yet regardless of recent changes in *ahidous* performances, they remain a central aesthetic expression of Ait Khabbash identity, continuing to stand as an important symbolic enactment of what it means to be Ait Khabbash. The songs, the style of dress, and even the dance steps demonstrate not only acceptable gender roles but the integral association of female fertility, art, and ethnic identity within Ait Khabbash society. They provide yet another means for women to negotiate the complex social and religious issues influencing their society. Despite the recent transformations in *ahidous* performance styles, in Ait Khabbash weddings women's decorated bodies continue to serve as public symbols of identity and the propagation of the group into the future. This centrality to their ongoing survival as a people is perhaps best seen in the adornment of the bride in Ait Khabbash weddings, which, as the following chapter shows, has barely changed since the transition of the Ait Khabbash from a nomadic to sedentary existence in the 1950s and 1960s.

FOUR

Women as Public Symbols of Identity

THE ADORNMENT OF THE BRIDE AND GROOM

it Khabbash women celebrate weddings with a fervor that matches the scorching heat of the summer wedding season. They spend hours sitting with the bride in a tent constructed specifically for the occasion and for three days chant songs, beat drums, and dance, re-creating the marriage ceremony passed down from their Amazigh ancestors. The control that Ait Khabbash women exercise over weddings is another way in which they preserve the cultural distinctiveness of their group despite other societal influences that have changed their daily lives. As discussed in previous chapters, the carpets, tents, and dress styles of the Ait Khabbash that previously reinforced ethnic identity in southeastern Morocco have given way during the last few decades to the influence of the workplace, schools, and the mosque, which now shape people's style of dress and other forms of aesthetic expression more than do their ethnic affiliations.

In Ait Khabbash weddings, however, the communal celebration and adornment of the bride and the groom have barely changed over time. During these weddings, Ait Khabbash women unfold a now infrequently used nomadic tent made by earlier women to serve as a temporary home for the bride. They carefully dress the bride in the red scarf, white clothing, wool belt, and silver jewelry that their ancestors wore on a daily basis, and they chant the songs of their mothers and grandmothers while henna is applied to the bride's hands and feet and sing for the groom as he is dressed in a similar red scarf and white clothing. While life continues to evolve for the Ait Khabbash, weddings allow them to express their distinctiveness and maintain their sense of ethnic identity.

This chapter describes the process of dressing the bride and groom as well as other activities in preparation for the three-day wedding ceremony to demonstrate once again that women, rather than men, are responsible for maintaining the artistic symbols of Ait Khabbash Berber ethnic identity and to explore the implications of this. It argues not only that women manage weddings but that the bride's decorated body serves as the public symbol of what it means to be Ait Khabbash, confounding the public/private dichotomy used by many scholars to describe gender roles in North Africa and elsewhere.

Both the bride and the groom are dressed in specialized ceremonies in their separate homes to mark their change in status. Most scholars describe the Moroccan bride as silently secluded in a private space, passively allowing herself to be dressed by other women, while the groom plays an active public role.[1] During wedding preparations, the Ait Khabbash Berber bride is dressed in public and sits on public display while the groom is dressed under the cover of a white cloth and then restricted to a small tent or house located on the periphery of the wedding celebration, limiting his public participation. Yet this association of women with the public realm does not mean that women hold a powerful position in Ait Khabbash society. Rather, the place constructed for women due to their association with the public expression of ethnic identity can be stifling, restricting women to idealized gender roles and limiting their life options.[2] This chapter demonstrates that the adornment of the bride is based on an engendered aesthetic that draws from ideas of containment and fertility.[3]

Constructing the Bridal Tent

Ait Khabbash women control ceremonial life, actively creating most of the art forms used at weddings, while men play a largely peripheral role. Women are also instrumental in arranging marriages, searching for brides for their sons.[4] Typically an unmarried man's mother, older sisters, and aunts actively ask their friends and family to recommend eligible girls. In the past, marriages were commonly arranged by women without the bride and groom's consent. Today the prospective bride and groom typically meet in a gathering arranged by their mothers and agree or do not agree to the proposed marriage. Once the choice is fixed, the mother of the groom visits the bride's family with gifts of tea, henna, and meat, and a date is set for the marriage.

The wedding itself is also the affair of women. Often the number of women present is more than triple the number of men, and (as we shall see) the men who do participate take on some of the roles typically associated with women in daily life. In order to prepare for the actual three-day wedding, the groom chooses three men (called *isnain*) to take over a customary responsibility of women by setting up the bride's tent a short distance from the groom's home before leaving to fetch the bride for the wedding. Almost all the events of the three-day wedding ceremony take place in and around the large bridal tent (see Fig. 3.1). The tent serves as an important symbol of Ait Khabbash history and ethnic identity.[5] When the bride arrives at the groom's home, she and her female family members spend the entire three-day wedding ceremony in the tent, in contrast to Arab weddings in the Tafilalet oasis, which are held almost entirely indoors.

Although the women in the groom's family do not construct the tent, they sing songs to accompany the work of the three *isnain,* who are close friends and/or relatives of the groom. Although Ait Khabbash men are typically not in contact with unmarried or unrelated women, the *isnain* are trusted with the mission of traveling with the bride from her father's to the groom's house or tent.

The word *isnain* comes from the Tamazight verb *nei,* which means "to mount"; in the past the *isnain* would mount camels, horses, or mules and travel several days until they reached the bride's family tent. Today the groom's family typically rents a van complete with a driver who will drive the *isnain* to the bride's home. Before leaving to carry the bride to her soon-to-be husband's house, they are dressed in white *tajellabiyts* and white turbans, clothing that marks the importance of their mission and associates them with purity and goodness. Reflecting their nomadic roots, men who perform the task of the *isnain* are expected to be trustworthy, honorable, and capable of the physical hardship of traveling great distances. They wear kohl or antimony on their eyes, a form of makeup otherwise worn by women to protect their eyes from the glare of the sun while traveling across the landscape and to denote their ceremonial status.

The *isnain* are responsible for packing and loading the bride on a mule or camel, much as women would load and unload a nomadic tent as they moved from place to place. Prussin (1995: 188), in her discussion of the African nomadic aesthetic, argues that the action of disassembling and loading a nomadic tent results in the inversion of space. In other words, the nomadic tent is literally turned inside out when it is loaded onto a pack animal; and, when it is reassembled, it is transformed back into a volumetric structure. This inversion of space, Prussin (1995: 18) states, is a feature of African nomadic marriage ceremonies, where nomadic tents can be turned inside out or ridgepoles may be planted upside down for the duration of the wedding. I interpret the construction of the bridal tent by Ait Khabbash men and the role that men play in transporting the bride to the groom's camp or home as representing an inversion of norms that fits Prussin's description of African nomadic weddings. In this case, gender roles are reversed, and this role reversal is acknowledged by Ait Khabbash women through song.

Women's call-and-response songs are performed in Tamazight and accompany almost all events at a wedding.[6] These songs (called *izlan*) are especially rich in visual imagery and use visual metaphors to express the cultural values and beliefs of the Ait Khabbash. These songs are performed sitting down and may continue for an hour or more; they are always performed in public and announce to the community that a wedding is taking place. In unison, one group sings a single line of a song (called *izli*) that is repeated several times before the group moves to the next line of the song. Since the *izlan* performed during weddings are never improvised, the ability to sing them requires a certain amount of cultural knowledge and considerable memorization of numerous lines of each song. Thus older women, who are more familiar with the *izlan*, lead the song and are answered by the younger women. Particular songs are associated with specific events, and each song involves visual images that pertain to the particular event. For example, while the *isnain* are constructing the bride's tent, the women sing the following song:

1. *An-zzur Rebbi i zwur-ay.*
2. *An âeqqed i wexyam tigusin.*
3. *Ad ur d-yawiy yiḍ agusif.*
4. *Taɣ-aɣ tasa-nnek a yibrurey.*
5. *Amm uxiam igan itriran.*
6. *A yma-new da-kes-s-aɣ ulli.*
7. *Iṭs n uzal ak-em iɣwan.*
8. *Annayɣ amedlu yaɣ s-iɣir.*
9. *Annayɣ-k a leâlam ik-d asif.*
10. *Ad wteɣ ayejdim ad-d gulun.*
11. *Arraw n ugellid a lbaca.*
12. *Ad awen-n-hdu tigziwin.*

[1. With God's help we start.
2. We pound the stakes for the tent.
3. We hope the night does not bring rain.
4. Our liver is worried about you, hail.

5. Hey you, whose tent is full of holes.
6. Oh my brother, I take sheep to graze.
7. Taking a nap during the day is what you like.
8. I see fog moving toward the mountain.
9. I see the sign coming by the river.
10. I sit down to wait for them to arrive.
11. People of the king and the pasha.
12. We offer beautiful young girls to you.]

Women reported to me that this song allowed them to tease the *isnain*. When they sing "We pound the stakes for the tent," they are actually referring to the men doing a woman's job; later in the song, they further mock the men by referring to them as lazy. The teasing continues in lines 6 and 7, when women sing about taking the sheep to graze while their male relatives are sleeping, a public recognition of the importance of women's labor to the group, suggesting that men do little work. Line 8, "I see fog moving toward the mountain," refers to the arrival of the *isnain* and the bride, whose white clothing is symbolized by the fog at the "mountain," the groom's home. It is unusual for unrelated men and women to travel together, representing another inversion of social norms. In addition, women express their desire for good weather by hoping that rain does not come and spoil the event and the worry of their livers, believed to be the seat of sentiment, that hail may come.

The physical differences between the bride's tent and the tents formerly used in daily life reflect its ceremonial significance. The bride's tent is much taller than the nomadic tent (shown in Fig. 4.1) and typically takes a square or rectangular shape with a flat roof, distinguishing it from the nomadic tent's sloping roof. One of the wedding tent's sides (the front) remains open during the wedding festivities, so that the wedding spectators can view the bride and her family (Fig. 3.1).

Women's Work and Weddings

Although women are relieved from physically constructing the bridal tent, their labor is crucial to the wedding's success. Women work together to perform the practical aspects of weddings, further illustrating the concept of *adwal*, "cooperation." Despite the work involved in the marriage of a friend or relative, women generally love to attend weddings, which relieve them from

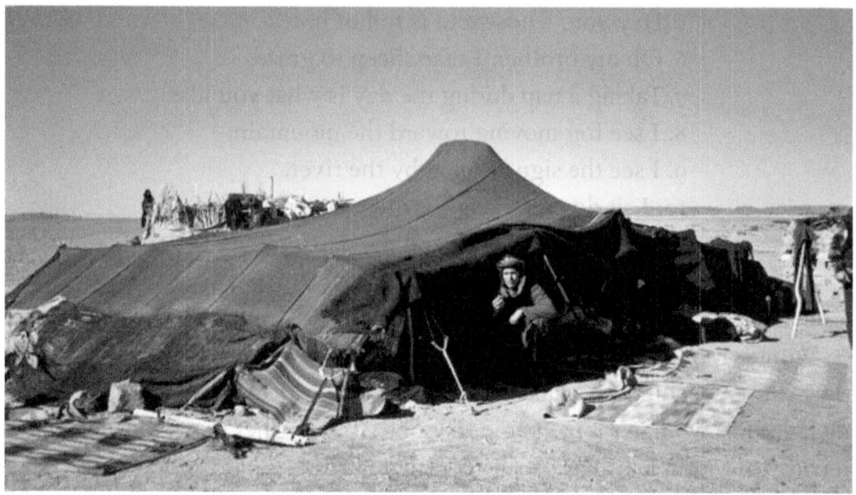

Figure 4.1. An Ait Khabbash nomadic tent near Erfoud, 2004.

the drudgery of everyday housework. As Fatima, an Ait Khabbash woman in Rissani, explained,

> Weddings mean I don't have to sweep every morning; I don't have to make lunch; I don't have to make bread for at least four days. But if one of your relatives or close friends has a wedding, this means work. Everyone has to help. But this work can be fun. There are many people to talk with, and you see relatives that you never see.

Women from the groom's family share the tasks of cooking, cleaning, and baking for the wedding participants and guests, gathering together in the open air near the bride or groom's home to spend numerous hours on wedding preparations. The women may spend several days grinding wheat into flour to make vast quantities of couscous by hand. (Although families living near a miller often have their wheat ground for them, hand grinding is still common in remote areas of southeastern Morocco.) They may also distribute flour to other households in the area, asking neighboring women to bake ten or more loaves of bread each day of the wedding to relieve them of some of their chores. These loaves are intended for the numerous wedding guests.

Using stone hand mills, Ait Khabbash women grind grain to make flour. They begin in the afternoon and may continue through the night and into the morning. The act of grinding enough grain to support the entire wedding party can take more than twelve hours and requires considerable communal effort. The groom's family may borrow ten or more hand mills; and as many as five women may sit around each hand mill, helping each other turn the handle so the grain can be ground. If five women work together, one woman pours grain through a hole in the top of the grinder, two women turn the handle 180 degrees, and the other two complete the rotation.

Once the grinding has begun and the women achieve a steady work rhythm, they sing communal songs to pass the time. Publicly announcing the upcoming wedding, the women sing the following song:

1. *Nezzur Rebbi i zwur-ay.*
2. *Ah-imt a tiwetmin idda yitri s-afella.*
3. *Ah-imt a tiwetmin its ayd issiyin lâar.*
4. *Timzadin yat tuḥel yat tqqen idikan n uskmud.*
5. *Timzadin yat tuḥel yat tsellem g ẑâefran i teddu.*
6. *A ymanu gant-ak awnul awi-d tirggiyin yuf-ak.*
7. *Yiweyi wzwu ticicin.*
8. *Arim-d ddehn ara rriḥan.*
9. *An-kkes i wedlal anayur.*
10. *Lberkukc an-qqed agerḍ iny-i.*
11. *A lal n uzreg ara-d tiyni.*
12. *Talbabaṭ ur-id icuccan.*
13. *Yummer-i bab n yirden yummer-i.*
14. *Yummer-i ad key udi s-uâmur.*
15. *Lluz iâta yur-ney i giy-t-id i krad ileyman.*
16. *Sey-i zzeâfran meqqar iyla g imkitta meya.*
17. *Zreâ imarin a bu tjuja i kin i luḍa.*
18. *Asra g iḥtal umeksa makw-n iggaren a yikerwan?*
19. *Lḥidj wenna-t inewan abrid n lxir ayennay.*
20. *Azzel-d a targwa n waman azzel-d a targwa n uyyu.*
21. *I k-as yat tselhamt i k-as iyyis i wsbaḥiy.*
22. *I k-as yat tegzimt iffeyn akal.*
23. *Zwarn-id izamarn ulli gan tawenza ddan s-aman.*
24. *Ad iyâawen yay-id afus.*
25. *Seg dadey s-imal i niy-d iyyis yagg-en zar-i yeyr-i.*
26. *Yyer-i ima s-yan umeḥdar.*
27. *Uggiy-d akzey axam n ima.*
28. *Uggiy-d akzey axam s-ikḍif.*

29. *Uggiɣ-d akẓeɣ axam s-iyyis.*
30. *A yiqerbulla n tegmarin n uẓaɣar.*
31. *A yiḥelbab n tiyḍin yiwey wasif.*
32. *Rar-imt-id irir-inew a tibesbasin.*
33. *Rar-imt-id irir-inew a tibeḥbaḥin.*
34. *Muhammad Mulay Ali ili-d ɣur-i.*
35. *Muhammad Mulay Ali awa ster ɣuf-i.*

[1. We start with the help of God.
2. Come on, women, the morning twilight is rising.
3. Come on, women, it's shameful to be sleepy.
4. Grinders, one is tired, the other is putting on shoes of old, hairless goat skin.
5. Grinders, one is tired, the other forfeited saffron and left.
6. Oh my brother, they did not do a good job for you, it is better if you bring *tirggiyin*.[7]
7. The wind took my *ticicin* (platter made of palm leaves).
8. Bring us oil and bring perfumed herbs.
9. To clean the dust from our hair.
10. Soup to soothe our throats.
11. Oh owner of the grinder, bring us dates.
12. Soft dates, not dry ones.
13. The owner of the wheat allowed me.
14. He allowed me large quantities of *udi* (fermented butter).
15. We have so many almonds that we carried them on three camels.
16. Buy me saffron, even if it's expensive and costs more than 100 rials (a form of currency).
17. Sow piles of grain, owner of two work animals, and give them to the vast field.
18. When the shepherd comes back, who will separate you lambs?
19. The one who thinks about taking the pilgrimage, that's a good thing.
20. Flow, canal of water; flow, canal of milk.
21. God gave the cavalier a wool cape and a horse.
22. And gave him a young, beautiful girl who just left the ground (grew up).
23. The line of rams arrived at the water before the ewe and looked like bangs.

24. God help me and give me a hand.

25. Next year he will visit and invite me.

26. My brother will invite me to the birth of his new baby.

27. I went and I recognized my brother's tent.

28. I went and I recognized the tent with the carpet.

29. I went and I recognized the tent with the horse.

30. Oh, you are like horses' hooves from Azayar (a region
    famous for horses).

31. Oh, you are like a pack of female dogs taken by the river.

32. Answer my song, hoarse women.

33. Answer my song, women with laryngitis.

34. Muhammad, Mulay Ali, come to me.

35. Muhammad, Mulay Ali, give me your blessing.]

Visual images in these *izlan* reveal Ait Khabbash conceptions of identity and gender, most obviously in the metaphoric references to fertility. Women told me that fermented butter (line 14), almonds (line 15), grain (line 17), canals of water and milk (line 20), a wool cape (line 21), and the line of rams that looked like bangs (line 23) were all metaphors for the fertility of the land and the reproductive potential of the married couple and were also specific references to items associated with women. In lines 25–26, women sing about their brother inviting them to celebrate the birth of his new child, referring to the groom. In lines 27–29, the horse and carpet near the groom's tent predict a successful marriage and prosperous future. Horses are animals of great prestige throughout Morocco, but they are especially valuable in southeastern Morocco, where Saharan climatic conditions make it difficult and impractical to own one. Reinforcing the Ait Khabbash's dependence on women's labor, the mention of carpets and a wool cape (prestige items created by women) self-valorizes the importance of women's economic contribution to Ait Khabbash society.

As discussed by the Moroccan scholar Fatima Mernissi (1989: 5), most Moroccan women see themselves as participating actively in the economic life of the family, and Ait Khabbash women are no exception. While Ait Khabbash nomadic men herded the livestock, women milked the animals when they returned to the tent at the end of the day. In line 18 women ask, "When the shepherd comes back, who will separate you lambs?"; this suggests that the groom is the wealthy owner of a large number of livestock. That phrase also refers to nomadic women's separating of lambs from their mothers so the ewes can be milked, once again praising women's work, enhancing their position in the community. The women sing that their efforts at grinding grain should be rewarded, asking the groom to bring them saffron, which is very expensive and used by women to paint designs on their faces, and *rrihan,* a perfumed herb applied to the hair. Line 10, "Soup to soothe our throats," refers to the soup that Ait Khabbash typically consume for breakfast and thus suggests that the women have worked throughout the night into the morning.

As demonstrated in this song, Ait Khabbash women are proud of their abilities to support their families economically. This song is a public self-recognition of their social and physical strength, reinforcing Fatima Mernissi's claims that Moroccan women do not fit into what she calls the "pervasive male discourse" propagated by the Moroccan media and public policies based on the idea that men economically support women. Rather, Mernissi (1989: 5) suggests, Moroccan women see themselves "as a race of giants doing daily battle," caring for themselves and their families. The Ait Khabbash wedding songs demonstrate that these women, too, do not view themselves as economically dependent on men but recognize that their labor is essential to the financial well-being of their families. The strong ties of women to each other also provide them with powerful supportive relationships that benefit themselves, their children, and the entire society.

Dressing the Bride

As the women from the groom's family continue to prepare for the wedding, the *isnain* travel to the bride's house, carrying gifts from the groom. An Ait Khabbash man is expected to buy his bride the jewelry and clothing that she will wear as a married woman, which she returns to her husband if divorce occurs. This is in sharp contrast to Arabs in the region: an Arab bride's family provides her with a dowry that includes gold jewelry, a bedroom set, tables, sofas, and cooking utensils that she keeps in the event of a divorce. Fatouh, an Ait Khabbash friend from Mezguida, explained what she believed to be one of the key differences between Arab and Berber marriage practices:

> At our weddings, the groom buys the bride her jewelry and she wears it after the wedding. He also buys her clothes, and today he even buys a bed and armoire for their bedroom. We are not like the Filala [Arabs from the Tafilalet oasis], where the bride's father buys her a bed, armoire, dishes, and much gold jewelry. He buys her everything and she takes it to her husband's house. If she does not bring a lot of things, her mother-in-law will

make trouble for her. It's terrible. This is why Filala and Ait Khabbash rarely marry. We refuse to buy our daughters all these things because it's not our way. Filala hate to have daughters because they are expensive. Our way is much better. We do not have to pay men to marry us.

When the *isnain* arrive, women friends and relatives of the bride greet them by performing songs in their honor. After their arrival, the *isnain* would have remained seated on their horses, but today they sit on top of the van they have driven as they wait for the women to begin singing. The *isnain* then lower the bride's gifts one by one, as they hear each item referenced in the women's song. As the gifts are lowered, they are placed on a tray carried on a woman's head (Fig. 4.2) while the women sing:

1. *Bismi neẓẓur-k a Rebbi.*
2. *Neẓẓur-k t-ẓwur-m i lumur.*
3. *Muhammad, Mulay Âli.*
4. *Ad iẓwur ig-aɣ ameksa.*
5. *Awi-d a sidi Rebbi lxir*
6. *Ad-d-ig am ugusif ẓar-i.*
7. *A yisnain d-iẓwaren ulli,*
8. *Hag-g-iwt an-ẓẓeg akwn-sili.*
9. *Neẓẓeg yan idiri isul yan.*
10. *Mraḥba s-wudmawen n yelli.*
11. *Ariw-d ikebran mellulnin.*
12. *Ariw-d iẓbian d-tiseɣnas.*
13. *Ariw-d iḥeẓẓuma n leḥrir.*
14. *Ariw-d sebbaṭ n ufasiɣ.*
15. *Ariw-d lluban n ufasiɣ.*
16. *Ariw-d aɣdda diɣ kullu.*
17. *Akwn iâeẓẓa Mulana.*
18. *Ariw-d aserdun ariw-d ikḍif.*
19. *Akwn iâeẓẓa Mulana.*

[1. We start with the name of God.
2. God guide us and help with our things.
3. Muhammad, Mulay Ali.
4. God leads us and is our guardian.
5. Oh God, bring blessings
6. To me like a downpour.

7. Oh *isnain* who came before the sheep returned,

8. Wait until we milk so we can be free for you.

9. We milked half and still have half to milk.

10. Welcome to the faces who came for my daughter.

11. Give us white *iḥruyn* (draped garments).

12. Give us bracelets and fibulae.

13. Give us belts of silk.

14. Give us shoes of Fez.[8]

15. Give us amber of Fez.

16. Give us everything else.

17. May God give you glory and power.

18. Give us the mule and carpet.

19. God gives you glory and power.]

Like many women's songs, after first calling upon God, this song begins by affirming the importance of women's labor. Lines 7–10 refer to flocks of sheep and their abundance of milk, symbols of fertility that suggest the bride's

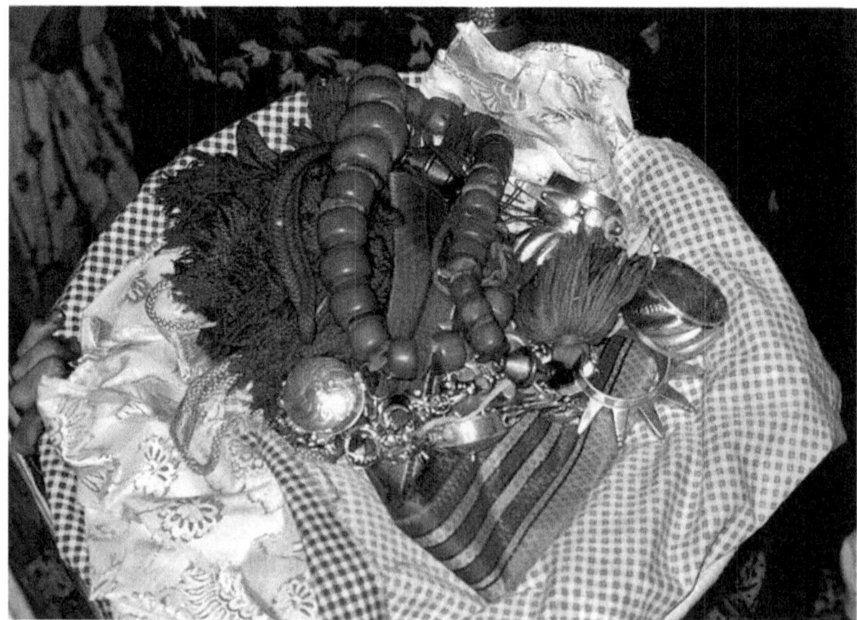

Figure 4.2. The bride's fibulae, silver bracelets, amber necklace, red headdress, and tassels are placed on a platter and presented to the bride by the groom's representatives, 1999. Photo by Addi Ouadderrou.

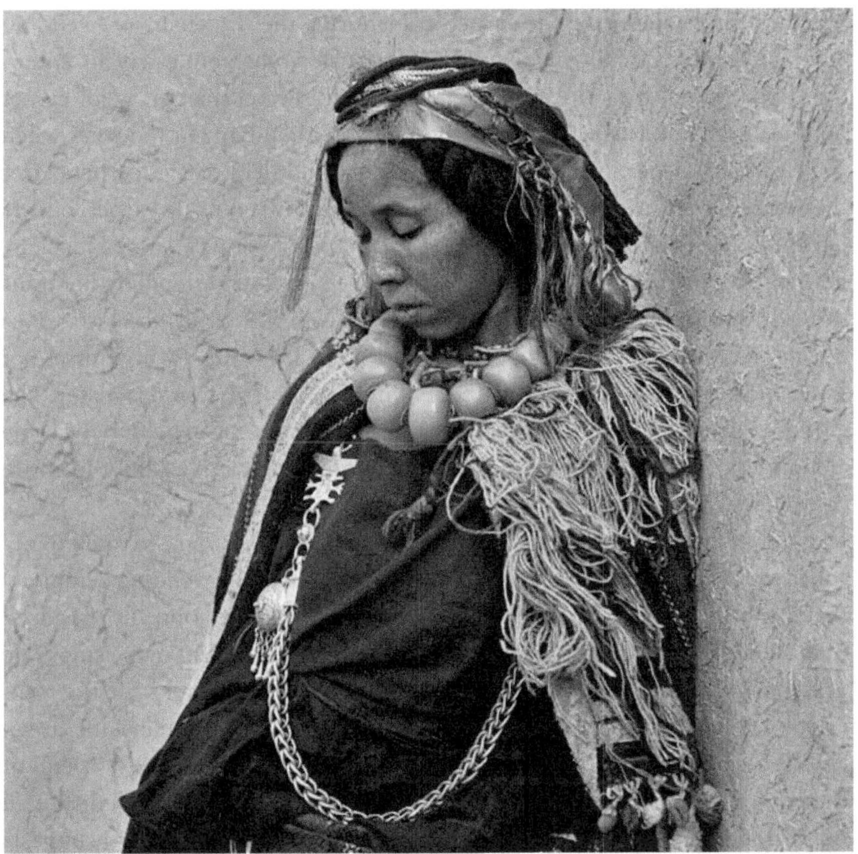

Figure 4.3. This colonial photograph of an Ait Khabbash woman depicts the style of dress commonly worn in the past. Photo by Jean Besancenot, 1934–1939. Image courtesy of the Institut du Monde Arabe, Paris.

family is wealthy. Lines 11–16 and 18 refer to the gifts that the groom has sent for the bride. In line 12, women ask the *isnain* to give them *izbian*, the heavy, thick silver bracelets worn by married women, and *tiseynas* or fibulae, large silver pins with a thick silver chain draped between them, such as those worn by the woman in Figure 4.3. The belts referred to in line 13 are long, thin belts made of red silk fabric imported from the city of Fez (and slightly visible in Fig. 4.3).[9] Although this belt is given as a gift to the bride, during the wedding ceremony she actually wears a wool belt made by her mother. Wool is linked to fertility, symbolizing that the bride will soon become a mother herself.

The *isnain* typically bring a red carpet to the bride's home that is then taken with her to her husband's home. The color red suggests virginal blood, menstruation, and childbirth. The carpets used during the Ait Khabbash wedding ceremony were typically made by Ait Khabbash women but today are sometimes purchased in the local market. The bride sits on this red wool carpet both at her home and when she arrives at the bridal tent. In the past, when traveling across the desert for days, the bride would sleep on this carpet. After the *isnain* have lowered the gifts, the bride sits down on this carpet, covers her entire upper body with a cloth, and wears one of her new silver bracelets, marking her entrance into a liminal or in-between state and signaling her transition from virginal girl to married woman. From this point, the bride does not show her face to anyone but her husband and the woman who dresses her every morning until the wedding ceremony is complete, four days later. The clothing given to the bride by her husband is hung on a string behind the bride along with the clothing from her family, giving her relatives and the entire community a chance to evaluate their wealth.

Later in the evening the bride is dressed at her family's home in a ceremony called *asqimu*. The dressing of the bride is so crucial to the wedding ceremony that a special term is used for the one woman who carries out this ritualized duty: *tamaccaṭ,* meaning "the woman who brushes," a fitting name since one of the primary responsibilities of the *tamaccaṭ* is to brush and style the typically long hair of the bride. The *tamaccaṭ* must be a married woman with grown children who has never been divorced. Typically a relative or close friend of the bride's family, she is never paid for her services but rather considers it an honor and a privilege to perform the services of *tamaccaṭ,* because it suggests that she is recognized as having extensive cultural knowledge.

The bride is dressed outside and in public, and the public nature of this role in the wedding can also increase the anxiety of young brides. Expected to be virgins, they are nervous about their first sexual encounter and the prospect of leaving their families for an uncertain future with their new husbands. To help the bride during this time, she is given emotional support by her female elders, who share their cultural knowledge and life experience. Once the young girl is dressed in her bridal clothing, the elder women circle her and collectively perform a solemn song in Tamazight. No musical instruments, clapping of the hands, or dancing accompany this song. The women sit motionless while singing, reflecting the seriousness of the occasion. The song begins when the *tamaccaṭ* removes the previous covering that the bride has worn since the arrival of the *isnain,* instead covering only her face with a small cloth and allowing her hair to hang down her back (Fig. 4.4).

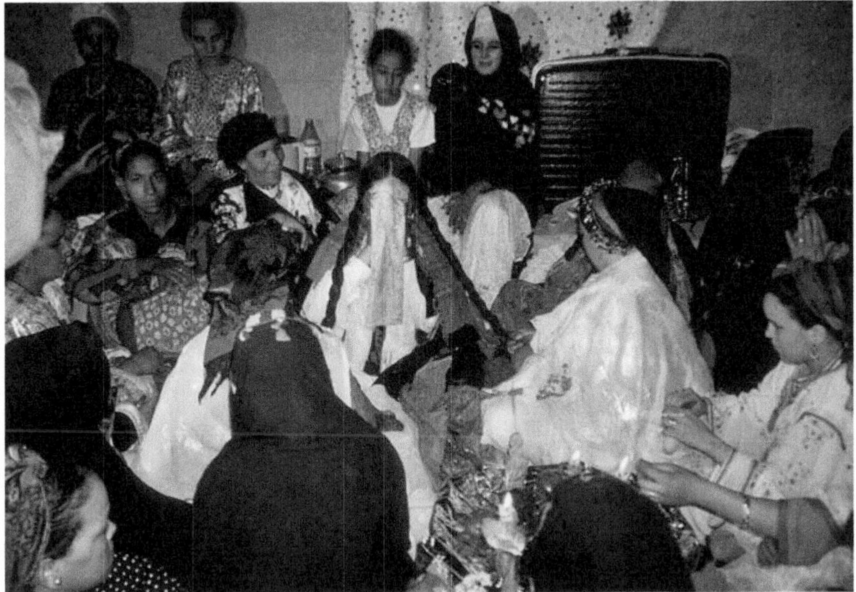

Figure 4.4. A bride's hair is braided before her headdress is applied, 1997.

The song begins by praising God and refers to the bride as the Prophet's daughter:

> *Yelli ẓẓureɣ ẓar-m Rebbi.*
> *Yellis n nnabi a yelli.*
>
> [My daughter, God be with you.
> Daughter of the Prophet, hey, my daughter.]

Young unmarried girls hearing this song gather some distance away from the bridal tent, distancing themselves from the bride physically as well as psychologically. One young Ait Khabbash girl explained that hearing this song often makes her feel nervous and sad,[10] since it makes her think about when she too must be married and leave her family. She, like other girls, equates the song with marriage and sex, a sensitive topic for a virginal girl, and this embarrasses her in front of her female relatives. Instead young girls remove themselves from the somberness of dressing the bride to engage in a celebration based on the sheer enjoyment of being relieved of the drudgery of everyday housework, passing their time singing and dancing with scarves around their hips

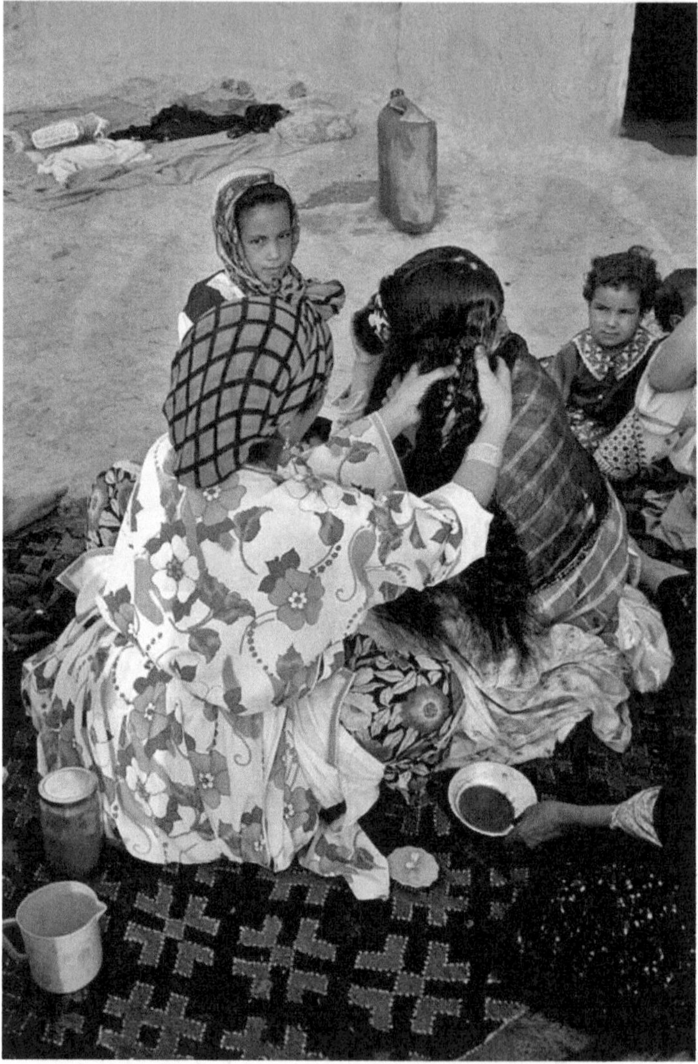

Figure 4.5. An Ait Khabbash bride has a perfumed herb called rriḥan *brushed through her hair, 2000.*

to the rhythms created by other girls on the *allun* (frame drum), enhanced by rhythmically hitting tea glasses on a metal tray or clapping their hands.

Meanwhile, in the bridal tent the *tamaccaṭ* brushes a perfumed herb called *rriḥan* through the bride's hair (Fig. 4.5). Great importance is attached to the styling of the bride's hair. Women told me that the thickness and the length of the bride's hair are seen as a direct reflection of her fertility. Women comment on this during a wedding, because they believe that the more abundant her hair, the more children the couple will have. It is also believed that the very brush used to style the bride's hair absorbs the essence of her reproductive power; if a woman sees the brush used to style her hair during her wedding, it can induce pregnancy. Thus brides who do not want to get pregnant immediately after their marriages, possibly fearing divorce, ask their mothers to hide their brush until they are ready to start having children, giving them a sense of control over their reproductive abilities.[11]

After *rriḥan* is applied to the bride's hair, the bowl containing the mixture is passed around the room so that female guests may put a small smudge under their noses and continue to smell the herb throughout the wedding ceremony. Scents are yet another important aspect of the Ait Khabbash aesthetic system. To the Ait Khabbash, pleasant-smelling substances appease not only humans but also the spirit world, pacifying the *jnoun* and protecting people from their disfavor and harm.[12]

After the bride's hair is brushed and tied into two braids, the women's song continues:

> *Les-imt ikebran mellulnin.*
> *Ger s-uderbal aγ leḥrir.*
> *K-imt-as i liẓur ayenna trit.*
>
> [Wear white *iḥruyn* (draped garments).
> Throw old clothes away and put on silk.
> Choose the clothes that you want.]

The women's instructions to the bride to throw away her old clothes refer to her changing status from unmarried virgin to married woman. During this part of the ceremony, the bride stands as the *aḥruy* (the draped garment discussed in Chapter Three) is wrapped around her body, its white color symbolizing purity and blessings. The bride literally throws away her old clothing, which in most cases, I observed, consisted of old skirts and faded T-shirts. Their mothers essentially treat teenaged girls as wives-in-training, requiring them to do most of the housework and cooking and making it impractical for them to wear nice new clothes. To dress an unmarried girl nicely might signal to the community that she is frivolous, possibly even promiscuous, and unprepared to take on arduous household chores typical of Ait Khabbash women. Over the back and sometimes front of the white *aḥruy,* a red cloth with yellow vertical and horizontal stripes (called *tamxeẓniyt*) and a thin, sheer black cloth

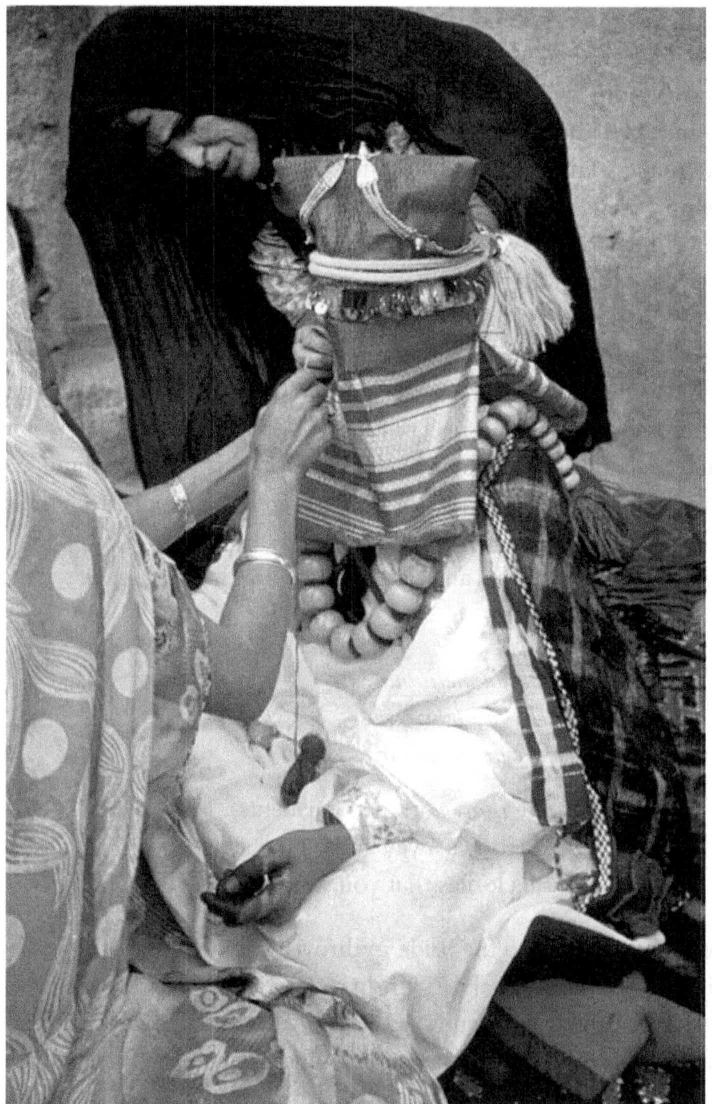

Figure 4.6. A bride's headdress in Merzouga is sewn over her head, 1997.

(called *tawkayt*) are placed (Fig. 4.6). Both the *tamxezniyt* and the *tawkayt* are reminiscent of the *tabarda*, meaning "saddle," a cloth that Berber women commonly wore attached to their shoulders and draped over their upper backs (Fig. 4.7). Although *tabarda* are rarely seen today, all Ait Khabbash women once wore embroidered *tabarda* to protect their daily clothing from staining by henna and other herbs commonly worn in their hair.

The bride is now dressed in clothing that marks her new role as a wife and her entry into the groom's family, which the song now praises:

> *Nka-kem i widda kem-ilan.*
> *Arraw n igeldan ak-em ilan.*
>
> [We gave you to those to whom you belong.
> You belong to the sons of the rulers.]

The phrase "sons of the rulers" in the second line refers to the groom, suggesting that he comes from a prestigious family.

The next several lines of song describe the following steps in the bride's adornment by the *tamaccaṭ* and may be repeated several times until the particular action that they are singing about is completed. The first of these lines is sung as the *tamaccaṭ* covers the bride's head with a headdress called *aâbroq:*

> *Yuley ukenbuc iyef iẓil.*
> [*Aâbroq* tops the head and looks nice.]

After a rectangular thin pad (*igorran*) is tied to the top of her head, the bride's head is covered with a rectangular red silk cloth with yellow stripes called *tasebniyt n uâbroq* (Fig. 4.6),[13] which the *tamaccaṭ* secures by sewing its sides shut. The fabric over the bride's eyes is then rubbed with water to allow her to see through the cloth. Once the basic shape of the headdress has been created, the *tamaccaṭ* covers it with additional tassels and jewelry. First she ties a small band embroidered with sequins (called *tacheddat n muẓun*) around the head, simulating bangs. This is the preferred hairstyle of Ait Khabbash women because of its association with female fertility, as discussed earlier.

Then the *tamaccaṭ* wraps a *taboqest* (a green cord with thick tassels on its end) around the top of the *aâbroq*, creating hornlike projections at the top of the headdress (Fig. 4.8).[14] She tops the *aâbroq* with a silver chain and pendant called *isensirn* (the plural of the word *asenser*, meaning "chain": the *isensirn* consists of a series of pendants connected by chains). This headdress is removed at the end of the wedding ceremony; in the past, however, the woman would have worn a red scarf, tassels, and *isensirn* on a daily basis, marking her marital status (Fig. 4.3). While the origin of this headdress is unknown, it is interesting to note that colonial-era photographs of Jewish women from the 1930s show them wearing similar headdresses with hornlike projections (Fig. 4.9).

The bride wears this headdress over her face during the entire three-day wedding ceremony, removing it while she is with her husband and returning each morning to the *tamaccaṭ*, who redresses her in the *aâbroq*. The Ait Khabbash adornment of the bride's head is analogous to the act of dressing the head in many other African societies, which commonly consider the head to be the site of intelligence and culture. In *Crowning Achievements*, for instance, Mary Jo Arnoldi (1995: 13–14) writes that Africans "use hats and hair styles to express and explore shared and deeply held cultural beliefs and values towards ethnicity, gender, life stages, status and authority, occupation, and social decorum." The headdress worn by the Ait Khabbash bride does all of these things and more, publicly demonstrating the bride's liminal status and serving as an important symbol of Ait Khabbash identity. Because wedding guests and female members of the community do not see the bride's face until the last day of the wedding, the *aâbroq* diminishes the bride's individuality, transforming her instead into a symbol of her group.

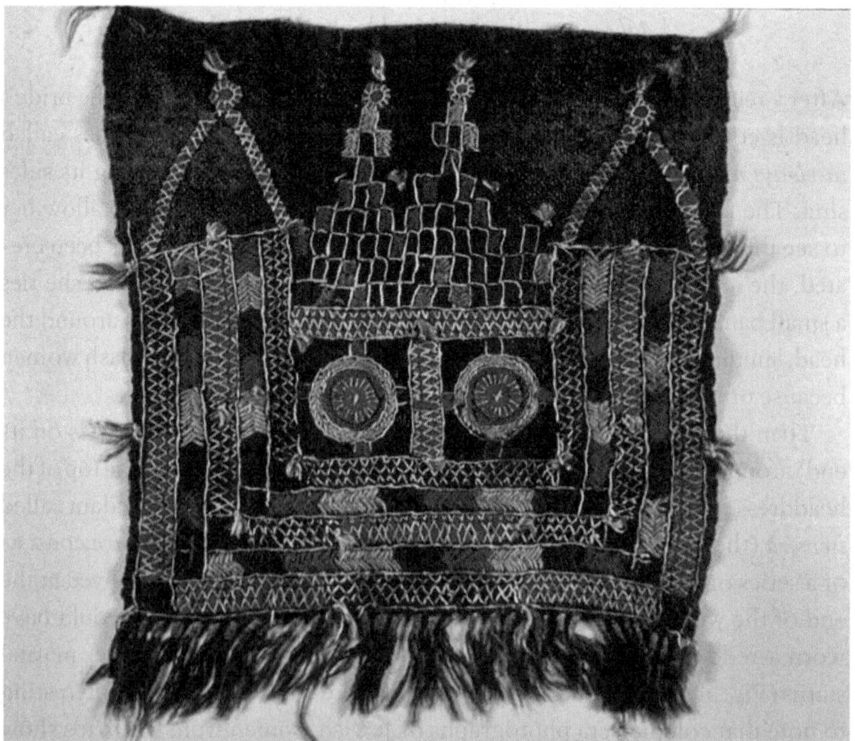

Figure 4.7. An Amaẓigh woman's embroidered back panel, early twentieth century, from the collection of the Minneapolis Institute of Arts, the Ethel Morrison Van Derlip Fund.

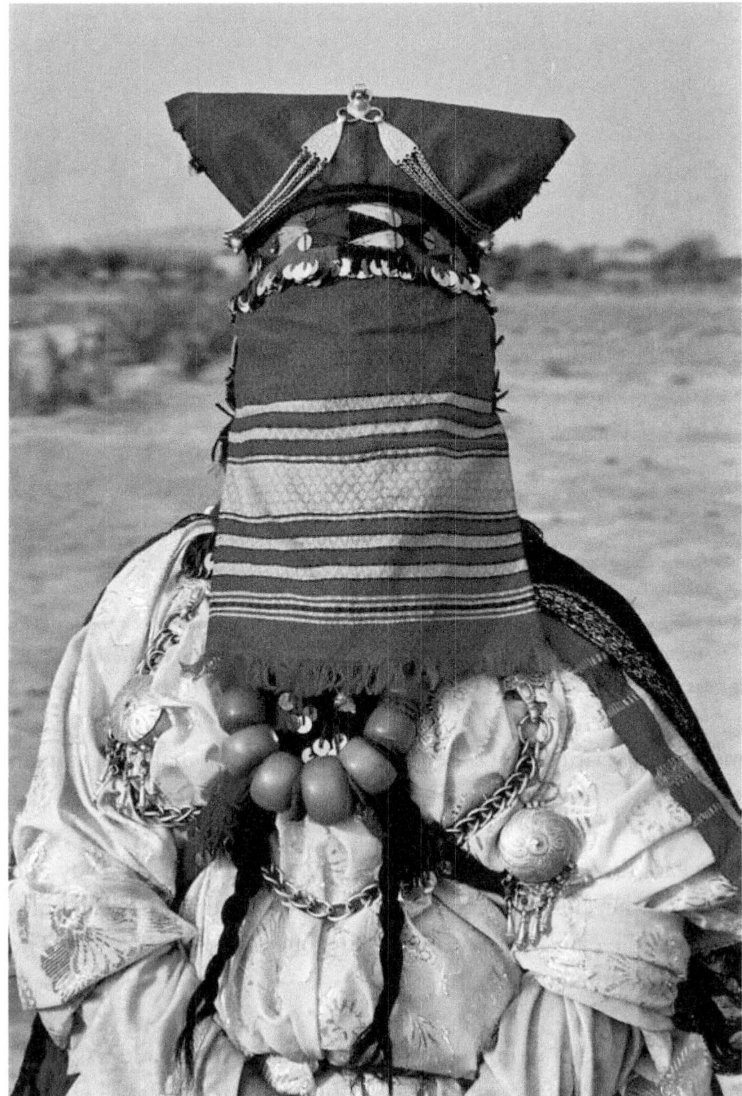

Figure 4.8. A fully dressed Ait Khabbash bride in Hafira, 2000.

At the weddings that I attended, women discussed with me the meaning and practical functions of the bride's headdress. All attention is centered on the bride during the wedding ceremony, as people scrutinize how her clothes drape around her body, the length and thickness of her braids, and even the shape and texture of her hands. The bride's headdress, they told me, provides her with a mechanism by which she can distance herself psychologically from

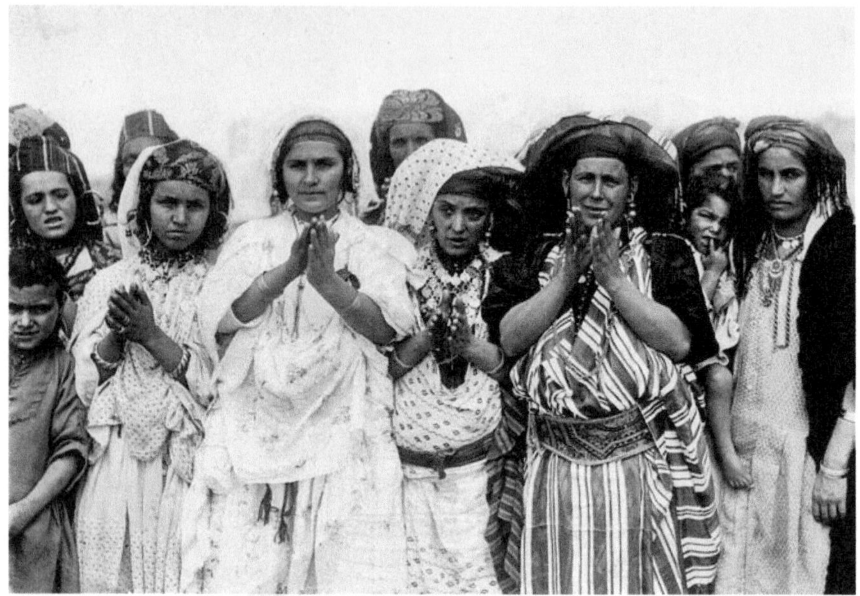

Figure 4.9. Jewish women from the Tafilalet. Two wear hornlike headdresses reminiscent of those of Ait Khabbash brides. Photo by Germaine Laoust Chantréaux, 1930s. Image courtesy of the Maison Méditerranéenne des Sciences de l'Homme, Fonds Roux, Aix-en-Provence.

the sometimes hurtful critiques of other women. As one Ait Khabbash woman explained:

> The bride wears the *aâbroq* because she is shy. She is from far away and maybe never saw her husband and he never saw her. She pokes small holes in her *aâbroq* so she can see her surroundings but no one can see her. The *aâbroq* makes her more comfortable.

The same Ait Khabbash woman also described how the headdress helps the bride hide all emotion from viewers. "If she seems too happy," she explained, "people are suspicious. Why is she so happy to be married? Maybe she had a boyfriend and likes men." Conversely, if the bride expresses sadness at her wedding, the woman explained, "People will say that she is unhappy to be married and maybe they will divorce quickly." Furthermore, the bride's headdress is intended to protect both her and her viewers from jealousy and the evil eye. It is believed not only that other women, especially the mothers of unmarried daughters, are likely to be jealous of the bride but also that the gaze of the bride has the power to steal the beauty or outer physical essence of other women. The headdress also covers the bride's facial orifices, openings that are vulnerable to invasion by the *jnoun* that prey on people passing through important life phases.

The *aâbroq* can also be viewed as a metaphor for the female-constructed nomadic tent and a reflection of an African nomadic aesthetic. Labelle Prussin first made this connection between nomadic marriage practices and women's tent construction in her book *African Nomadic Architecture* (1995). Prussin writes that female-dominated African nomadic arts are based on the aesthetics of the tent, an enclosed, bounded space associated with female fertility and containment. She also interprets the aesthetics of nomadic marriage ceremonies as being based on the desire by nomads to create an enclosed, concentrated space to counter the expansive, open space that is part of the nomads' physical realm. Therefore, the nomadic bride is often placed in a palanquin, defined by Prussin (1995: 47) as a saddle with a framework built above it that can support a canopy-like enclosure. Prussin (1995: 195) analyzes the symbolic nature of the palanquin as a "closed container within which the protected bride can move through the dangerous, unknown, infinite space to her new domicile."

Although the Ait Khabbash bride is not placed in an actual palanquin, her body is contained and enclosed by the red headdress and many layers of cloth and tassels wrapped around her body. As the bride travels from her father's to her husband's home, her headdress serves as a closed container to protect her from the exterior world. Hence my analysis of the bride's headdress builds upon Prussin's discussion and argues that the headdress reinforces acceptable gender behavior as dictated by the control of female fertility and reproduction necessary to ensure the continuation of the Ait Khabbash lineage and culture; the act of binding the bride's head symbolizes the physical control of female sexuality. The headdress's red color, reminiscent of hymeneal blood, menstrual blood, and the blood of childbirth, denotes female reproduction.[15] The *aâbroq* also contains other colors associated with female fertility: green tassels wrapped around the top and yellow and black horizontal stripes near the bottom. Thus while the *aâbroq* is a celebration of the bride's sexuality and fertility and symbolizes the pivotal role that women play in nomadic cultures, it also represents the control necessary for the maintenance of a distinct Ait Khabbash ethnic identity.

As evident from the following lines of the song, the bride's sexuality is further bound and contained by the additional layers of bulky jewelry in which the *tamaccaṭ* dresses her:

> *Qen-d a âeẓẓa taɣuni.*
> *Qqen-d a âeẓẓa tiseɣnas.*
>
> [Oh my dear, get the leash.
> Oh my dear, get the *tiseɣnas*.]

Women explained that the word "leash" in this song is also used to describe the rope tied around a goat or sheep's neck and refers to the bride's large necklace with more than thirty amber beads, called *taẓra n lluban* (Fig. 4.8). Beginning with the Phoenicians, amber from the Baltic regions of Eastern Europe has been traded all over the Mediterranean world for centuries. The honey-colored amber, a lightweight material made from fossilized pinesap, is relatively rare and expensive, so the Ait Khabbash sometimes wear necklaces made from less expensive copal, ambroid, bakelite, or casein beads. Copal, a semifossilized amber found in many areas of the world (including the west coast of Africa), could easily have been traded across the trans-Saharan trade routes into Morocco. Ambroid, formed by melting amber pebbles and pressing them together into larger pieces, is another less expensive substitute. Imazighen also wear necklaces of beads made of bakelite, a hard plastic invented in Europe in 1909, and cloudy yellow beads made from casein, an inexpensive manufactured substance produced from milk.[16] Amber is valued by the Ait Khabbash for its protective and healing qualities. An herb seller in the market of Rissani, for instance, once offered to grind an amber bead he was holding to make medicinal incense for me.

The two *tiseɣnas* (commonly called fibulae or brooches) that attach the *aḥruy* at the bride's shoulders are made of silver, another material believed to have beneficial properties. Amazigh groups throughout North Africa commonly wear fibulae; each group has its own shape, style, and size, making them an important symbol of ethnic identity. The *tiseɣnas* can be divided into three distinct sections: two pins, two pendants, and a chain (Fig. 4.3). Some scholars have suggested that the pins of the *tiseɣnas* are meant to protect the bride against the evil eye, symbolically having the ability to burst or pop the eye (Bynon 1984: 147).[17] Women also told me that in the past women were known to have used pointed tips of the *tiseɣnas* as weapons to protect them during warfare. The triangular pendant is referred to as *tadmert* (from the Tamazight *admer*, which means "chest," referring to the location where the pendant is worn). Attached to the bottom of each pendant is a large silver chain that drapes between them. Ait Khabbash women attach to the chain two small round boxes with bulging carved lids called *lamriat* (meaning "shiny boxes"); five smaller pendants dangle from each box (Fig. 4.3). Women use the *lamriat* to hold perfumed herbs.

The design of the *tiseynas* reflects the aesthetic of symmetry and movement that is a feature of Ait Khabbash arts more generally. The two sides of the *tiseynas* are mirror images of one another, echoing the symmetry of the human body. As the wearer walks, the chain moves to the rhythm of her body and the *lamriat* swing back and forth, suggesting an analogy to women's breasts that is furthered by their rounded, conical shape and placement over the chest and the five small pendants intensifying their kinetic energy. Through these references to the human body, the *tiseynas* are yet another way in which Ait Khabbash women carry symbols of group identity on their bodies and draw attention to the importance of female sexuality for the propagation and continuation of that group.

Scholars have frequently noted that the triangular shape of the fibula's pendant, one of the most common motifs found in Amazigh art, represents a stylized hand or eye motif, intended to protect women from the evil eye.[18] The triangle motif is also featured in the silver bracelets worn by married women and brides. Of the two styles of cast silver bracelets worn by Ait Khabbash brides, the most extraordinary is the one called *iẓbian n iqerroin*, "bracelets of animal horns," which are made of a series of triangular pointed projections and worn on each wrist. Figure 1.9, a photograph from the 1950s, shows an Ait Atta woman wearing these silver bracelets. Each *aẓbiy n iqerroin* (the singular form) is a very heavy, solidly cast bracelet with twelve triangular-shaped points that radiate from its central band. *Iẓbian n iqerroin* are usually not worn alone but with other bracelets called *iẓbian n masmod*, "flat bracelets." Between the two bracelets is a thin circle of leather to prevent the wearer's skin from being pinched. Until the 1970s a married woman continued to wear these heavy bracelets on a daily basis, even while setting up tents, milking ewes and goats, and grinding grain. These bracelets could be used as weapons to protect women from outsiders and sometimes unintentionally inflicted harm on "insiders" as well; one woman showed me a scar on her head where her mother, who had been angry with her, had hit her on the head with an *aẓbiy n iqerroin* harder than intended.

Further binding and containing the bride's body is the wool belt wrapped around her waist. The bride stands while the *tamaccaṭ* lifts the folds of her white *aḥruy*, wrapping the long braided belt called a *tasmert* around the bride's waist several times (Fig. 4.10) while the women sing:

Tubedda beddant-am liam.
Heẓẓem iḥeẓẓuma n leḥrir.

[Stand up, the days stand up for you.
Put on silk belts.]

Although the song calls for the bride to wear a silk belt, today women typically make belts out of wool for their young daughters in anticipation of their eventual weddings. The belt is created out of dyed red, green, yellow, and black fibers, colors typical of Ait Khabbash art; at the ends it has a fringe of purple, blue, yellow, pink, and green strands of wool (named *ibirran*) that hang down behind her, swinging when she moves (Fig. 1.11).

This binding and tying of the bride's waist, the area where female reproductive organs are located, is another example of the way in which the bride's dress serves as a metaphor for the control of female reproduction; this is further supported by the belt being made of wool, an Ait Khabbash symbol of fertility.

Significantly, the wool belt is given to the bride by her mother and not by her future husband, as it is the bride's family that is responsible for monitoring her behavior and ensuring that she remains a virgin until marriage. The belt is bound and tied around her waist for the first time on the eve of her wedding night, when her virginity is to be demonstrated and her family's reputation and honor upheld or destroyed.[19] Married women continue to wear wool or silk belts around their waists.

The final stage in the dressing of the bride is the application of henna to the bride's hands and feet as the women sing these lines:

Ara-d afus n iffus, ara-d afus s-iyman.
Ara-d aḍar n iffus, ara-d aḍar s-iyman.

[Give your right hand, give your hand to be decorated.
Give your right foot, give your foot to be decorated.]

The application of henna is an elaborate form of body adornment that has become one of the central features of almost all Moroccan wedding ceremonies. In many areas henna is applied by a professional *neggafa* (makeup artist), who may spend as many as eight hours elaborately decorating the bride's hands and feet with henna.[20] During Ait Khabbash weddings, henna plays a less central role in the bride's adornment and usually takes less than fifteen minutes to

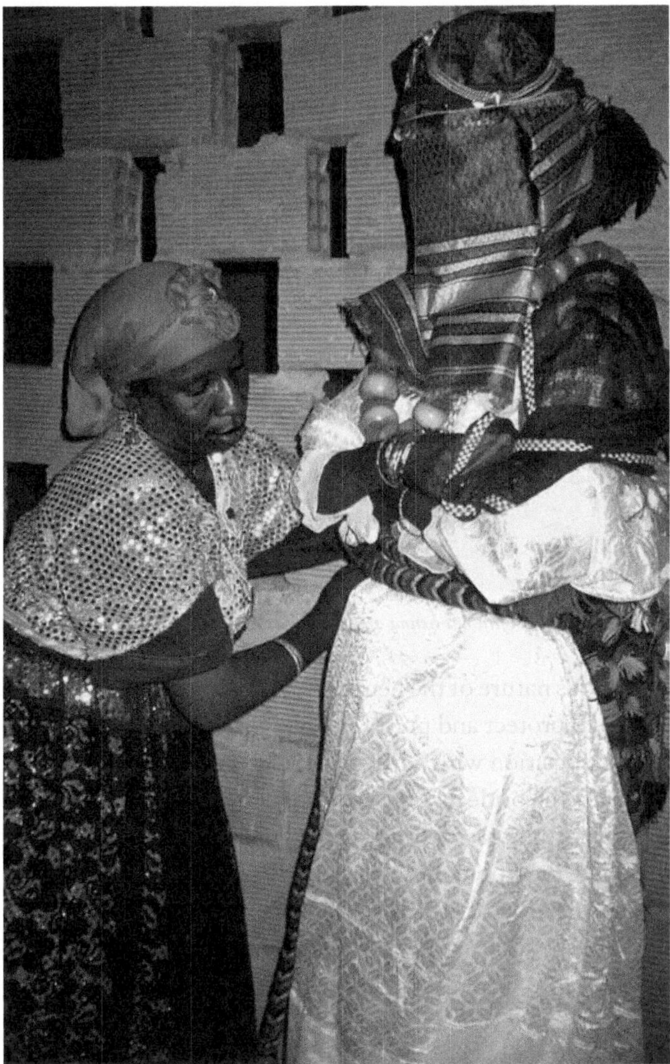

Figure 4.10. An Ait Khabbash bride in Rissani has a wool belt, a symbol of fertility, wrapped around her waist, 1997.

apply. The *tamaccaṭ* uses her index finger to smear henna on the palms and tops of the bride's extended hands, continuing it several inches beyond the wrist (Fig. 4.11). The tops and bottoms of the bride's feet are also decorated up to her ankles. Her hands and feet are then covered with a white cloth in order to allow the henna to dry and dye the skin a deep red color.

Among the Ait Khabbash, the actual henna designs are considered less im-

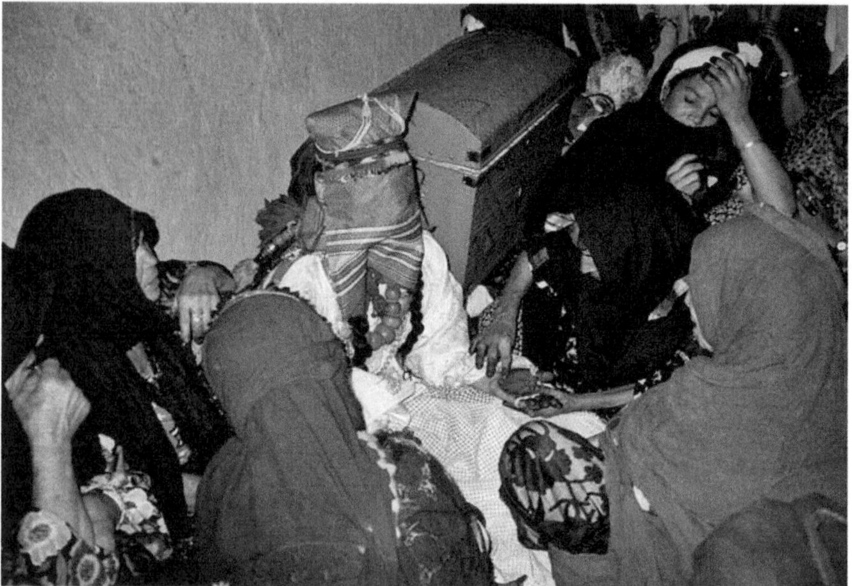

Figure 4.11. An Ait Khabbash bride in Hafira has henna applied to her hands, 1999.

portant than the auspicious nature of the henna itself. As discussed in Chapter Two, henna is believed to protect and purify the body during rites of passage ceremonies due to its association with "divine blessing" (*baraka*). The *baraka* of henna further protects the bride against the danger of the evil eye and the *jnoun* that prey on people as they pass through crucial moments of the life cycle.

While henna is applied, the women continue to sing for the bride. The words they sing call for the protection of the bride from the spiritual as well as the human world:

> *Tisent am iẓẓian a yelli.*
> *Tisent am ibrurin wala.*
>
> [Salt stays on you, my daughter.
> The salt that is on you makes you look beautiful.]

The mention of salt refers to the need to protect the bride from dangerous *jnoun,* who are also called *wida tsentel tisent,* meaning "those who are hidden by salt" (referring to the idea that salt protects against them).

The conclusion of the song is often met with tears on the part of the bride's family, allowing women to express sentimental emotions not typically manifested in public:

Yelli-new yelli a ta qqim g lman.
A talli segmiɣ tuɣul tẓery-i.
A tamaccaṭ-inew a taneẓdamt-inew.
A tamaccaṭ-inew, a tanagamt-inew.
Udjir-am amareg a mma-new.
A baba ya baba qqim g lman.
Yaɣi wmareg yaɣ ait mam.
Willi-ɣ d-itddalet s-ikḍif.
Yaɣi wmareg yaɣ ikerwan.
Ad ur titkkat-em ula tergem-t-tit.
Terwa ur terwi tuɣul-id yelli.
Amm imurig a mma n tislit.

[My daughter, stay in peace.
The one that I raised and left me.
Oh my brusher, oh my wood collector.
Oh my brusher, oh my water fetcher.
Oh mother, I will miss you.
Oh father, oh father, stay in peace.
Your brothers and I will miss you.
Those with whom you were covered by the
    same carpet.
The sheep and I will miss you.
Don't hit her or insult her.
If she is good, fine. If she is not, my daughter
    comes back to me.
Oh, the bride's mother with tears.]

In most areas of North Africa, women normally hide emotions of love and remorse except during the recitation of poetry or in private situations.[21] Thus wedding songs are socially acceptable outlets for Ait Khabbash women to express their sentiments of grief at the marriage of a female family member. As previously discussed, women spend many hours of the day with their unmarried daughters, making the marriage of a daughter particularly difficult for mothers, because it typically results in long periods of separation. Transportation between different areas is difficult and tedious, and a new bride may be separated from her family for a long time before she sees them again.

The song recognizes and addresses the difficult situation encountered by a new bride. Women of the bride's family ask that her husband's family treat their daughter justly and fairly when they sing, "Don't hit her or insult her. If she is good, fine. If she is not, my daughter comes back to me." Women ask for their daughters to be sent home if they misbehave rather than be treated harshly by her husband's family. Women told me that they are often fearful that their daughters will be mistreated when they marry. New brides are the lowest members in the family hierarchy and are responsible for cooking, cleaning, and taking care of their husband's family. Mothers-in-law often overburden their daughters-in-law with work in order to keep them busy so that their sons do not have the opportunity to bond with their new wives. Some women fear that, if their sons become emotionally attached to their wives, their wives may easily control them and may pressure them to break away from the extended family structure. The disintegration of the extended family means that women may lose an important source of financial support in their old age.[22]

After the bride is dressed, she gets ready to leave her parents' house. In the past, travel was done by camel or mule, requiring the bride and the *isnain* to travel many hours or days before reaching the groom. Typically the bride arrives at the groom's house at sunrise, a time when the *jnoun,* who are most active at night, are less likely to cause trouble. Concerns about sexual modesty prevent the bride's father from attending the wedding at the groom's home, since sexual intercourse between his daughter and her husband (in a desire to demonstrate the bride's virginity) becomes a topic of public conversation.

Dressing the Groom

Although the process of adorning the groom is not as complex or deeply symbolic as dressing the bride, women from the groom's family also sing for the groom as he is dressed. They are not able to see the actual ceremony in which he is dressed by a small group of men from his family, however, because a large white cloth is draped behind him to create a visual barrier between the groom and the women (Fig. 4.12).

While the groom is being dressed, he sits on his mother's lap, although the white cloth draped around the groom's back also blocks her view of the ceremony. When I asked women why they were not allowed to see the groom, they said it was not for modesty reasons but to protect him from *imkuraren.*[23] Most people did not want to talk to me about *imkuraren,* saying that I did not need to learn about evil things. One Ait Khabbash man suggested that I "spend [my] time learning about important things, not superstitions." After I kept insisting, my mother-in-law finally relented and explained that *imkuraren*

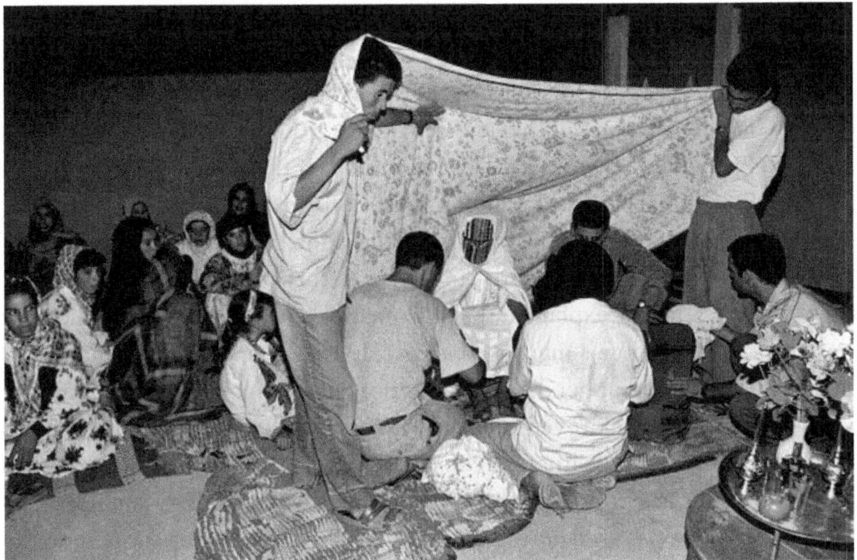

Figure 4.12. An Ait Khabbash groom in Hafira is dressed, 1999.

refers to the use of certain incantations, plant materials, and other objects to influence people to act in certain ways for good or evil purposes. Women practice *imkuraren* more than men, she explained, recounting how she suspected that her son's first wife, unhappy in her marriage, had put herbal mixtures in their family's food with the intention of making them ill. Their suspicion of her caused so much discord in the household that he eventually divorced her, illustrating that women, who rarely have the economic and social means required to initiate divorce, can use *imkuraren* to end bad marriages.

My mother-in-law finished her story by recounting a local saying, "If two women talk together, the devil is between them"; she explained that women are often accused of plotting together against someone. I asked her if she agreed with this, and she responded in the affirmative. She felt that women commonly practiced *imkuraren,* especially at weddings. Some types of *imkuraren,* especially a type called *thiqaf,* are so powerful that they can be used to stop the bride and groom from consummating their marriage. *Thiqaf* (deriving from the Arabic word *qif,* meaning "stop") describes an action performed against a person to stop him or her from achieving something. One form of *thiqaf* is the placement of two small metal objects, such as brand-new needles or nails, on the ground some distance apart; when a victim unwittingly passes between them, the objects are later tied together with thread. The act of binding the metal objects symbolizes the action of closing or binding something. It is believed that *thiqaf* can "close up" the bride by making her hymen resistant to sexual penetration, leaving her unable to engage in sexual intercourse until the two metal pieces are untied and separated. Other remedies to such problems are available, however; at several weddings that I attended, the bride, having difficulties with sexual intercourse, notified a woman at the wedding party, who then undid *thiqaf* by walking the bride between two tall cones of Moroccan sugar (associated with purity due to their white color).

My mother-in-law explained that a woman who may secretly be jealous or resentful of the groom's marriage can use *imkuraren* and *thiqaf* to make him impotent.[24] Anger that her daughter was not chosen to marry the groom may cause a woman to seek revenge against him and his family. A woman who is unhappy in her marital situation can threaten her husband with *imkuraren* to create disorder in her household.[25] Therefore, the white cloth (a color associated with purity) is used during the dressing ceremony to stop the potentially harmful power of women by setting up a physical barrier of protection.

Although they cannot actually see the groom, the women sing a song to accompany the act of dressing him:

> *Bismi Allah Rraḥman rraḥim.*
> *Muhammad, Mulay Âli.*
> *Ad iẓwur ig-aɣ ameksa.*
> *Awi-d a sidi Rebbi lxir*
> *Ad-dig am ugusif ẓar-i.*
> *Iẓwar-ak Rebbi a memmi.*
> *Iẓwar-ak i gger-ak.*
> *Ikjem diɣ utbir timelsa.*
> *A yisli a bu leâmamat,*
> *Ara-d afus n iffus, ara-d afus s-iɣman.*
> *Ara-d aḍar n iffus, ara-d aḍar s-iɣman.*
> *A bu tkurbyin tiwrayin,*
> *Tubedda bedant-ak liam.*

> [In the name of God, the merciful and the beneficent.
> Muhammad, Mulay Ali.
> God leads us and is our guardian.
> Oh God, bring blessings
> To me like a downpour.

> God guides you, my son.
> He guides you, and he follows you.
> The pigeon enters his clothes.
> Oh groom with the turbans,
> Give your right hand, give your hand to be decorated
>   (with henna).
> Give your right foot, give your foot to be decorated
>   (with henna).
> Oh wearer of yellow shoes,
> Stand up, the days stand for you.]

While these lines are sung, the groom begins to be dressed in white clothing, a red scarf, a white *tajellabiyt* (hooded gown), and a white *asilham* (hooded cape) (Fig. 4.13).

After calling upon God, the women's song rather surprisingly refers to the groom as a pigeon, a gendered symbol associated with women (as in the motifs referred to as "pigeon's tracks" that adorn women's embroidered veils and references to the bride as a pigeon in wedding songs and *aḥidous* performances). The use of similar metaphors to describe both the bride and the groom is unusual in Morocco. Instead, scholars who write about Moroccan weddings commonly remark that the groom is symbolically transformed into a sultan or king;[26] as Henry Munson, Jr. (1993: 122) notes, this "is certainly a significant metaphor, reflecting among other things a homology between the authority of husbands and that of kings" and thus reinforcing the Moroccan definition of manhood. During Ait Khabbash weddings, however, the reference to the groom as a sultan is rarely made. The word "pigeon" praises the groom, implying that he is beautiful. My analysis also suggests that the use of this word (commonly used to refer to women) demonstrates that women, who control ceremonial life, apply feminized symbols to the groom, further illustrating that group identity is created and maintained by women.

A similar contrast can be made between the style of dress worn by the Ait Khabbash groom and the Arab groom in southeastern Morocco, who wears a white hooded gown (*jellaba*), black cape, and a curved dagger—all symbols of masculinity. The latter does not cover his face but pulls the hoods of his jellaba and cape over his head. Instead, after the Ait Khabbash groom is dressed in the white clothing, a long red silk cloth with multicolored stripes is wrapped around his head so that his entire face is covered except for his eyes.

A similar cloth is then draped over the groom's right shoulder, across his

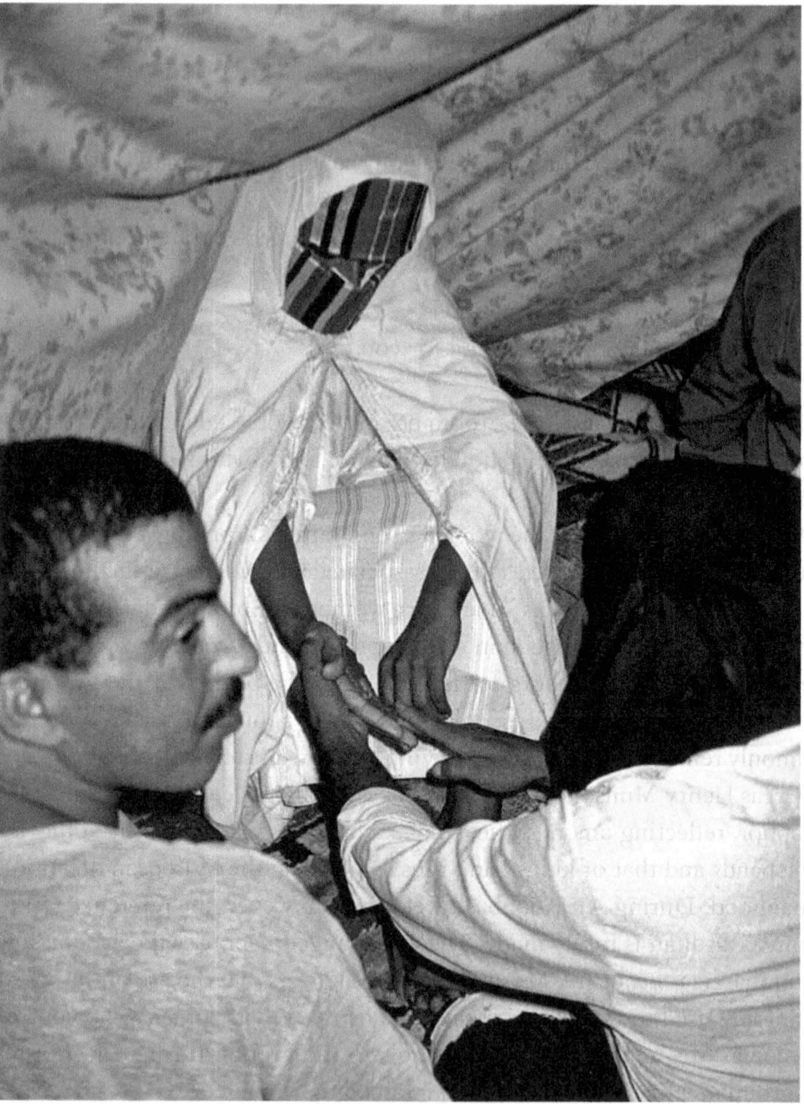

Figure 4.13. An Ait Khabbash groom has henna applied to his hands, 1999.

chest, and tied at his left hip (Fig. 4.14). A woman's silver bracelet is tied to the end of the belt. This red silk cloth and the red silk cloth over his face (sometimes partially covered by a white turban and the hood of his cape) are actually women's silk belts and are similar in color to the bride's headdress. I would argue that the use of "pigeon" (a feminine construct) to refer to the groom and his being dressed in clothing and jewelry associated with women reflect the Ait Khabbash recognition of women as models for group unity. In their song for the groom, women appear to be projecting the power of procreation associated with female symbols, such as pigeons, to the groom. Thus the red silk belt, a metaphor for the controlled sexuality and fertility of women, is at the same time a potent symbol of male reliance on women to ensure the continuation of Ait Khabbash identity into the future and a recognition that

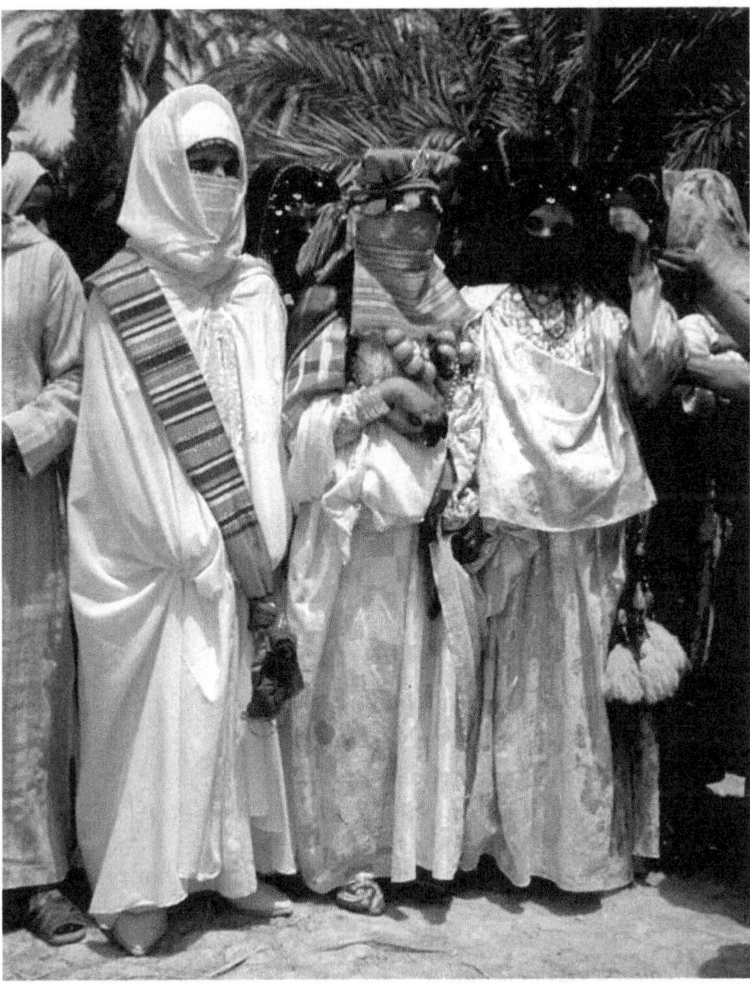

Figure 4.14. The bride, groom, and groom's mother pose for a photograph in Mezguida, 1997. (The groom's mother requested anonymity, so this photograph was altered using photo retouching software, extending the woman's head covering to conceal her lower face.)

female imagery is crucial to Ait Khabbash identity. One Ait Khabbash man also explained to me that the use of the red belt and woman's silver bracelet by the groom also suggests that men and women must work together during marriage. The groom, by wearing a woman's red belt across his chest with a silver bracelet at the end, visually pledges to support his wife during marriage. Hence the dress of the groom shows that men and women do not exist in separate spheres; rather, gender categories overlap with each other, demonstrating gender cooperation typical of Ait Khabbash society.

Next the entire palm of the groom's hand and his feet are covered with wet green henna and wrapped in pieces of white cloth. The groom then slips on his backless yellow leather shoes, which are imported from the central Moroccan city of Fez and are only worn on ceremonial occasions. The men who dress the groom place a needle in his right shoe; its pointed shape and metallic silver color are believed to protect him from evil forces such as the evil eye, *imkuraren,* and the *jnoun,* who dislike shiny metal objects. Men then outline the groom's eyes with kohl, a type of eyeliner typically used by women. On a red carpet laid on the ground, the groom faces a brazier filled with hot charcoal. Incense placed on the charcoal envelops the groom's body, perfuming him with its sweet-smelling smoke and pacifying the *jnoun,* who prey on people passing through the life cycle. After the smoke perfumes his body, the song continues:

> *Ur irḍi ad it-t-akel akal.*
> *Akel ikḍif ayd-ak it-t-waṭan.*
> *Akel ikḍif ayd-ak ik waḍu.*
> *Gimt-as ur giɣ a lemluk.*

> [He does not like to walk on the ground.
> Walk on the carpet spread out for you.
> Walk on the carpet intended for you.
> Oh angels, do things for him that I could not do.]

The women's song for the groom concludes with a metaphor referring to male fertility:

> *Memmi a yigimi n waḍil,*
> *Isilewn i weẓrur ar akal.*

> [My son, you are like a grapevine,
> That hangs down to the ground.]

Women told me that grapes, a rare and highly desired fruit in the desert climate of southeastern Morocco, are considered symbols of fertility. The groom is compared to a grapevine that does not simply bear fruit but is so heavy with an abundance of grapes that it hangs down and touches the ground, again referring to sexuality and reproduction as themes of the Ait Khabbash wedding. After the conclusion of the song and the dressing of the groom, he is removed from public to shield him from the evil eye and *thiqaf*, which the Ait Khabbash believe have the power to make him impotent.[27]

This contrasts greatly with the Arab groom in the Tafilalet oasis. The dressing of the Arab groom occurs at a large party restricted to men and accompanied by much feasting, singing, and dancing. The groom's female relatives make a brief appearance at sunrise, when they enter the party to apply henna to the groom's hands and feet. While his mother and sisters apply henna, other female relatives cross knives over his head to drive away the *jnoun* and the evil eye. The next day the Arab groom publicly tours his village on horseback, dressed in white with a black hooded cloak and carrying a sword as a demonstration of his manhood. Women from the village greet him by waving red scarves at him, trying to touch him and his horse with their scarves. This honors the groom as if he is a sultan or a king; as M. Elaine Combs-Schilling (1993:122) argues, the groom "takes on the ruler's persona, embodies his postures, affects his attitudes, adopts his authority, and becomes central and pivotal to all that transpires." Thus the Arab groom in the Tafilalet oasis plays a central, active role in the wedding, while his bride is rarely seen in public. All of the ceremonies surrounding the bride take place in the privacy of her family's house.

In contrast, the Ait Khabbash groom is hidden from public view after he is dressed. One of the *isnain* carries the groom on his back to a small tent set up at a distance from the wedding celebration, and this man will be the only person who has contact with the groom until the bride is brought to spend the night (Fig. 4.15).

The most striking difference between the participation of the bride and of the groom in the wedding ceremony is the public role played by the bride and the concealment of the groom from the public eye. Confined to the nuptial tent, he does not become a public part of the wedding ceremony until he successfully pierces the hymen of the bride. While a woman is transformed into a public symbol of Ait Khabbash identity, the groom is hidden away from sight in order to protect his reproductive abilities from outside manipulation.[28]

The roles played by the bride and the groom and the groom's reliance on

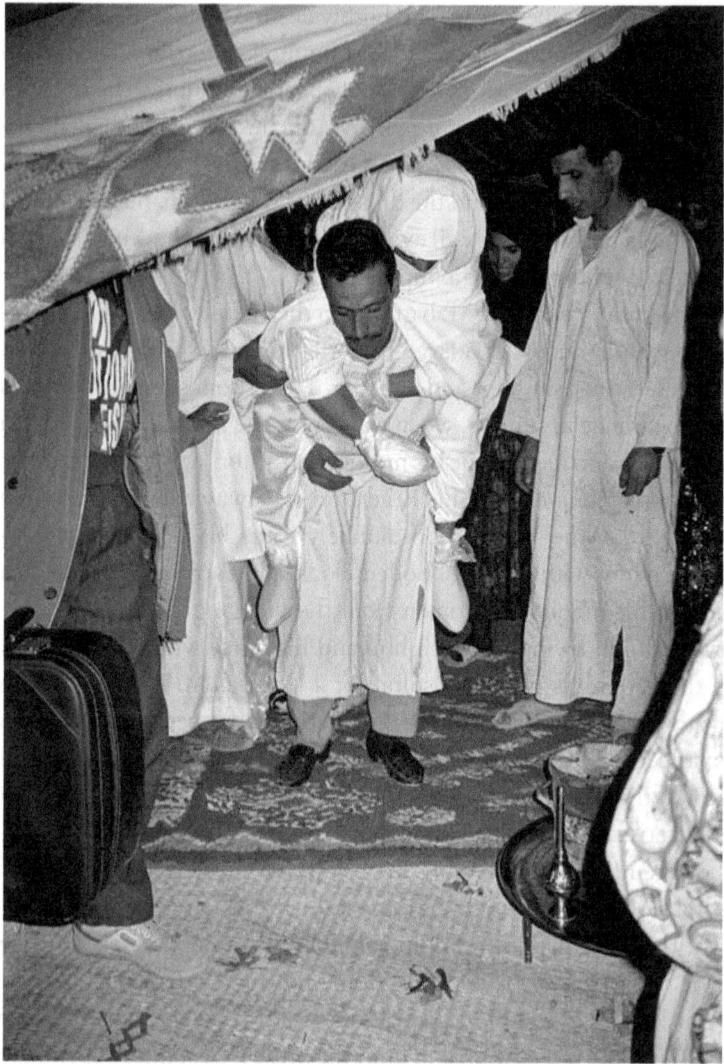

Figure 4.15. An Ait Khabbash groom in Merguida is carried to a secluded room, where he will await the bride's arrival, 1997.

female symbols of identity together argue against a simplistic public-private dichotomy. Instead they demonstrate that men and women do not occupy opposing spheres of influence: their roles in Ait Khabbash society overlap and influence each other.[29] Therefore I argue that the public and the private, treated by previous scholars as discrete categories, exist in a reciprocal relationship. While the public role of the bride reveals the complexity of gender roles and demonstrates how binary categories tend to oversimplify gender relations, it also shows that the public realm should not necessarily be equated with power. Once again we see that although women control the public visual symbols of Berber ethnic identity, a position that grants them prestige, it also restricts them to specific roles in that society. As noted by Valentine Moghadam (1994: 19), when women are defined as reproducers of a collective group, this often leads to the control of their reproduction and sexuality in the interests of maintaining boundaries between their group and others. The visual and performing arts surrounding the actual three-day wedding ceremony itself further emphasize the physical and symbolic continuation of the society through the bodies of women. This association of women, wedding arts, and identity is discussed in the next chapter.

FIVE

Performing Amazigh Gender Roles

WEDDING CEREMONIES

As a complement to the discussion of the wedding preparations in the previous chapter, this chapter concentrates on the events that occur during the actual three-day wedding ceremony. Ait Khabbash weddings are not religious ceremonies. In order to marry officially, the bride and groom sign marriage papers at the local government office without any festivities. Although they are now married, the wedding is consummated and celebrated at a later date. The celebration is a three-day event in which even the smallest details and activities reflect and maintain cultural values and social arrangements that are sacred to the Ait Khabbash and essential to their group identity. Activities center on the bride, reflecting Ait Khabbash recognition that female fertility is crucial to Ait Khabbash identity and their survival as a distinctive group. The artistic forms and symbols of this identity are controlled and maintained by women, both affirming the positive status of women and reinforcing societal restrictions placed upon them.

Ass Amezwaru: *"The First Day"*

The first day of the wedding officially starts with the arrival of the bride, her family, and the *isnain* at the bridal tent set up outside of the groom's home. Today the *isnain* generally accompany the bride to her husband's house by van or car; but to maintain their connections to their nomadic past, the van stops a short distance from the groom's house. The bride then mounts a mule, horse, or camel, which she rides the rest of the way to the bridal tent. A member of her family carries the bride from the van to her mount to prevent her feet from touching the ground and thus protect her from *thiqaf* (an action performed to stop a person from achieving something, as discussed earlier). Ait Khabbash

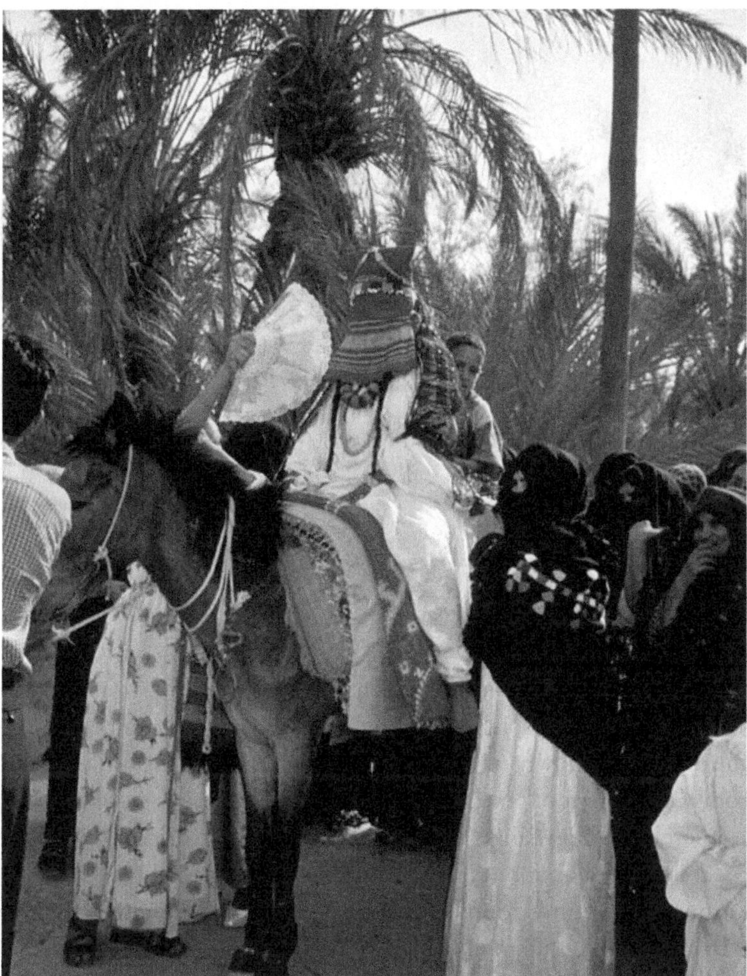

Figure 5.1. The bride's procession to the bridal tent in Mezguida, 2001. (Several women shown here requested anonymity, so this photograph was altered using photo retouching software, extending their head coverings to conceal their lower faces.)

women told me that the bride is in great danger of *thiqaf* that might prevent her from consummating her marriage. Like the bride herself, the mule that carries her to her tent is adorned in a very specific fashion: the red carpet brought from the bride's home by the *isnain* is placed on its back, and a red scarf is draped over its rear (Fig. 5.1). A small boy, who must be named Muhammad, sits behind her on the mule or camel for her journey, representing wishes for the bride's fertility and the hope that she will have many sons (Fig. 5.2).

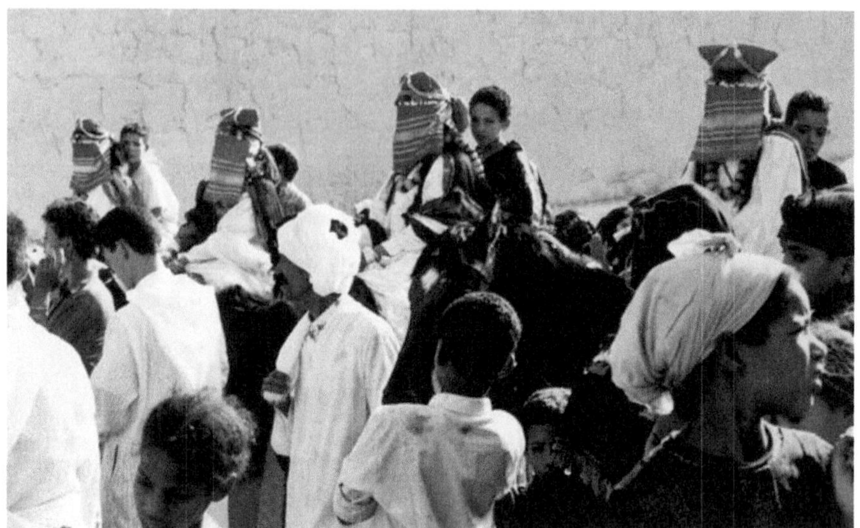

*Figure 5.2. Four Ait Khabbash brides in Mezguida ride mules to their husbands' tents in a
communal wedding, 1995. Photo by Addi Ouadderrou.*

As the bride mounts the mule or camel, she is welcomed by women from
the groom's family through song accompanied by rhythms drummed on the
allun (frame drum). As shown in Figure 5.3, women surround the bride to protect her from *thiqaf;* her mother often leads the mule, and her sisters stand on
either side (thereby also revealing the family identity of the bride, whose face
is covered). It is not uncommon for several marriages to be held on the same
occasion. Figure 5.2 pictures four Ait Khabbash brides riding mules to their
individual bridal tents, set up next to each other in a large clearing.[1]

Although the bride needs to travel only a short distance to the tent, her trip
may take more than three hours. This is because men from the groom's village,
in one of the few occasions during the wedding in which men play a public role,
engage in a game that tries to impede the bride and the *isnain* from advancing
toward the tent. The men teasingly and repeatedly block the path of the *isnain,*
allowing them to pass only after performing some embarrassing deed, such as
singing a song in the men's honor, kissing their hands, or performing a dance
(Fig. 5.3).[2] The men also jokingly try to steal items from the bride's mount,
such as the red scarf that covers its rump. In the past, guns were fired each
time the *isnain* were stopped, but people have used cap guns in the last twenty
years. This playful threat of physical violence by villagers against would-be
intruders reflects the historical importance of close local ties in constructions

of Ait Khabbash group identities. Even if the bride is from the same village as the groom, the same symbolic game-playing occurs between the *isnain* and the men of the groom's village. Women from the groom's village also participate in this ceremonial game, taking the side of the *isnain* by taunting male villagers with sarcastic playful comments in an attempt to help the *isnain* and the bride proceed.

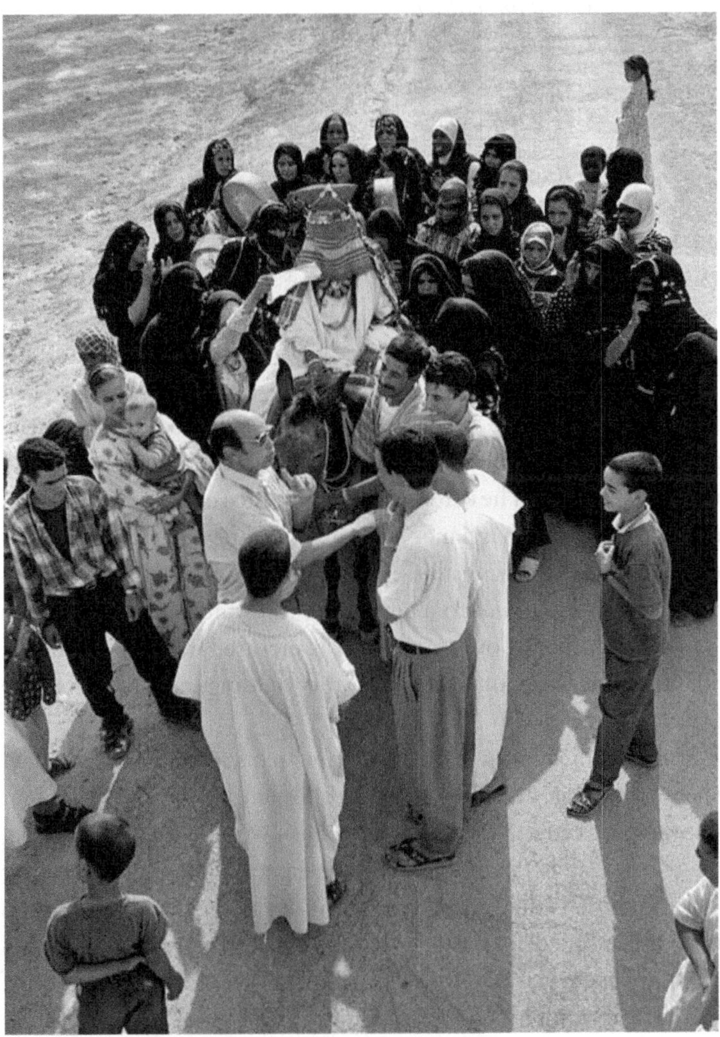

Figure 5.3. An Ait Khabbash bride is playfully stopped by men of the groom's family en route to the bridal tent, 2002. Photo by Addi Ouadderrou.

There is a contrast between men physically protecting group honor through mock warfare and women welcoming the bride as a symbol of female fertility, the source of female status. As mentioned, women from the groom's family sing joyful songs welcoming the bride and playfully urging her to proceed to the bridal tent, where they call for her to descend from the mule:

> *Geẓ-d amm lman.*
> *Geẓ-d am larbaḥ.*
> *Geẓ-d am ikḍifen.*
> *Geẓ-d am wurtan.*
> *Geẓ-d am ileyman.*
> *Geẓ-d am larbaḥ.*
>
> [Descend, you with peace.
> Descend, you with good luck.
> Descend, you with carpets.
> Descend, you with farms.
> Descend, you with camels.
> Descend, you with good luck.]

These references to the bride as someone with peace, good luck, carpets, farms, and camels equate the bride with prosperity, suggesting that her family has a certain level of prestige. The ceremonial importance of the bride's arrival demonstrates the Ait Khabbash reliance on women for the creation and maintenance of ethnic identity. During this entire event, in contrast, the groom is confined with one of his *isnain* to a small tent to await meeting his bride at nightfall. (In Fig. 5.4 the groom's small tent is pictured in the foreground, while the bridal tent, the ceremonial center of the wedding, can be seen in the distant background.)

When the bride finally arrives at the tent, in which she will be living during the three-day wedding ceremony, she and her entourage circle the tent three times counterclockwise;[3] as one Ait Khabbash woman explained to me, "We circle the tent to say hello and give it our respect." The mule, horse, or camel carrying the bride is then stopped in front of the tent, and the bride is given a bowl of milk. She drinks one sip and sprinkles the rest on the wedding guests. While Westermarck ([1914] 1972: 190) notes that the practice of offering the bride milk is intended to make her future "white" or lucky, milk is obviously also connected with fertility, further marking the association of the bride, fertility, and the propagation of Ait Khabbash ethnic identity.

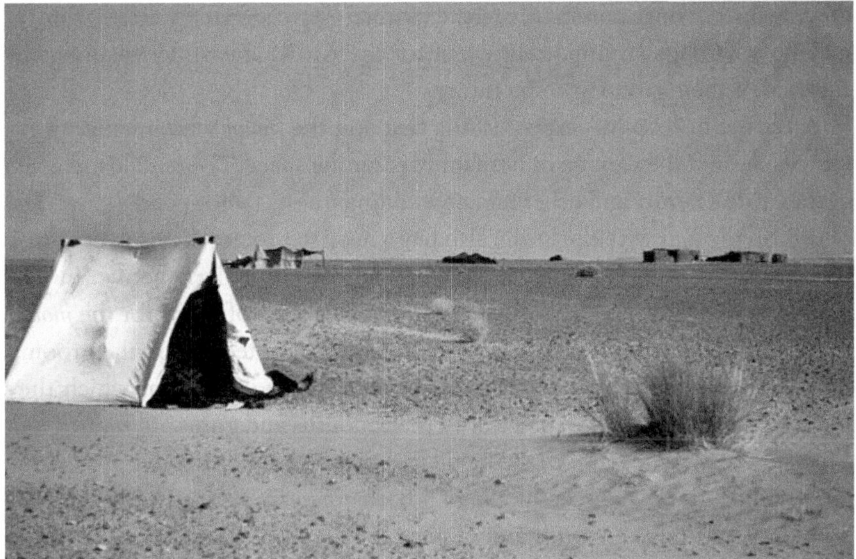

Figure 5.4. An Ait Khabbash groom's tent is isolated from the bridal tent, seen in the distant background, 1995.

The entrance of the tent (the space where the bride sprinkles milk on her wedding guests) is a site that carries symbolic significance. As previously discussed, the bride's tent differs from the tent that the Ait Khabbash once used on a daily basis not only in its boxlike shape but because it is open in the front, allowing people to congregate in this public space. That distinguishes the bridal tent as an especially vulnerable and dangerous liminal or transitional space. Women explained to me that the Ait Khabbash consider entrances to tents, villages, drains, wells, and doorways to be dangerous because of the presence of spiritual beings or *jnoun,* referred to as *ait udyar* or "inhabitants of the place" in Tamazight. The Ait Khabbash believe that these spirits inhabit both real and symbolic passageways. By circling the tent three times and sprinkling milk on its entrance to pay respect, the bride hopes to pacify them and also to purify the place from any *thiqaf.* In crossing through one of life's most significant passages, the bride and groom are considered especially vulnerable to attacks by the *jnoun.*

I would argue that the Ait Khabbash trepidation concerning passages also reflects a fear of social disorder, from which they must protect their identity. Weddings signify and reinforce social and gender norms, further protecting group identity and maintaining ethnic purity. In addition, the bride completes the transition from a potentially fertile virginal girl to a sexually active woman, making weddings an important event for the Ait Khabbash by ensuring the survival of their group into the future.

After the bride pays respect to the tent and the *jnoun* who inhabit its entrance, she and the women of her family enter the space. The female members of the bride's family and other female wedding guests (who spend a great deal of time in the tent with the bride) also feel a need to protect themselves during wedding ceremonies, a time when the *jnoun* are particularly active. In particular, body orifices are considered vulnerable points of entry for the *jnoun*, as noted by Westermarck ([1926] 1968, 2: 345). To protect them, the groom's family gives female guests a walnut root called *meswak*, from which they break off and chew a small piece until their mouths and gums are stained red. The *meswak* is believed to have medicinal powers that clean and protect the teeth against decay, but ceremonially it both creates a protective red-colored boundary around the mouth and mimics the blood that will be spilled from the bride's genital orifice. This use of *meswak*, like the covering of the bride's head, demonstrates the belief that the ideal female body is one that is closed or contained and metaphorically illustrates Ait Khabbash reliance on women to protect group honor and identity.[4]

Sweet-smelling substances are also used to protect women's bodies from attacks by the *jnoun*. The groom's family provides the women sitting in the bride's tent with a small brazier filled with burning charcoal; incense is dropped on the charcoal, creating fragrant and sweet smoke. Unmarried girls, in contrast, never perfume their bodies with incense. I interpret this as meaning that they do not attract the harmful spirits drawn to body openings, because their genital orifices have not yet been "opened." Janice Boddy (1989: 330) notes a similar practice among women in the Sudan, who use incense under their dresses "to drive away evil spirits attracted by noxious odors" and to boost feminine defenses and resist penetration by outsiders during the wedding by creating a boundary between a woman's body and the spiritual world.

After these arrival ceremonies, little else happens the first day of the wedding. The families and friends of both the bride and the groom are usually tired and often spend the day catching up on lost sleep, nervously awaiting the consummation of the wedding. After nightfall,[5] usually around nine or ten o'clock, the wife of one of the *isnain* discreetly accompanies the bride to the small tent or a distant house where the groom has remained since the previous day and where the marriage will be consummated. Before sexual intercourse, the groom frees the bride's body from the clothing and jewelry that adorn

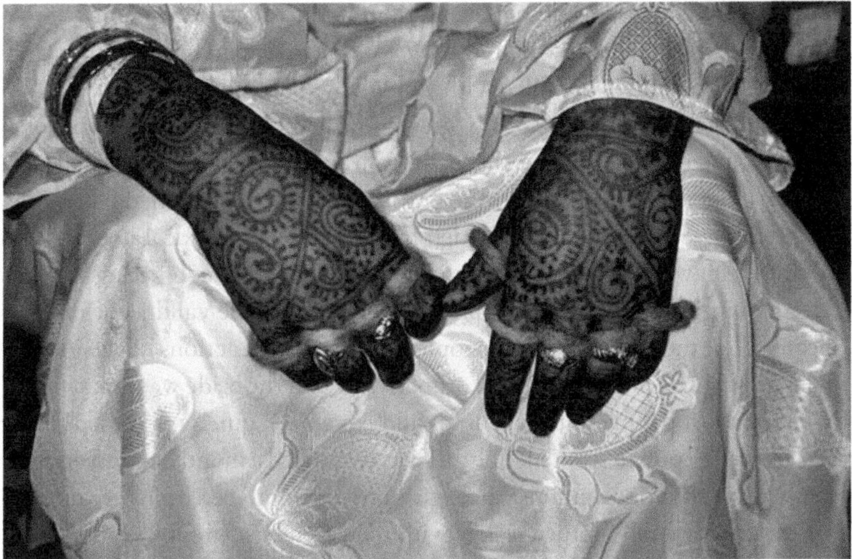

Figure 5.5. An Ait Khabbash bride's henna-adorned hands have strings wrapped around the fingers that will be untied by the groom, 1997.

her, unties her hair braids, and unwraps the belt that binds her waist. In addition, when the bride has henna applied to her hands and feet, wool thread is woven first between her fingers and then between her toes to join them together (Fig. 5.5). The Ait Khabbash bride in Figure 5.5 has had her hands adorned in a contemporary style of henna inspired by the intricate interlacing henna designs common to urban areas of Morocco. The groom must unwrap the thread, which allows him to spend time talking with his bride and makes the two feel comfortable with each other.[6] The Ait Khabbash believe that sexual intercourse "opens" the bride's body and that the blood that results from her first sexual encounter is evidence of her virginity. Because the consummation of the wedding occurs at night, the bride's virginity is not publicly witnessed and celebrated until the following morning.

Stories abound in Morocco about how hymeneal blood can be faked by the bride or by the groom if he has prior knowledge that his bride is not a virgin. If the bride does not shed blood, however, the groom is allowed to divorce her immediately after publicly exposing her failure to do so. As noted by Combs-Schilling (1989: 208), Moroccan popular culture contains many tales of girls slain due to their failure to prove their virginity, but these tales are not based on fact. I also found that these severe repercussions typically did not happen. For example, I attended a wedding celebration in Merzouga in September 1996. While I sat one afternoon watching *ahidous,* I heard a loud horn rhythmically honking. Three white vans filled with young boys passed in front of the house. On top of the first van was a fully dressed bride holding a piece of paper. I quickly found out that this was the bride from another wedding, who had been publicly chided and divorced by the groom after she did not shed blood during intercourse. Her father responded by rushing her to a local doctor, who provided him with a "certificate of virginity," swearing that his daughter was indeed a virgin. While many people wondered about the validity of the certificate, all of the fanfare caused people to question the actions of the groom, saying that he did not treat the girl properly. Even if the bride was not a virgin, the majority of people felt that she should have been quietly divorced rather than creating a public scandal. The girl was remarried a month later to another man. As this situation demonstrates, girls proven not to be virgins are not disowned; they typically return to live with their families, who try to find them new husbands as quickly as possible.

Ass an-Ammas: *"The Second Day"*

The second day of the wedding is one of the most festive days, because the bride's virginity has been proven, the marriage has been consummated, and everyone relaxes and has fun. The bride, no longer a virgin, is now a married woman. The groom has proven his virility and is no longer vulnerable to *thiqaf.* Although his seclusion is now ended, his participation in the wedding activities is still limited, and the bride remains the central figure in Ait Khabbash weddings.

DRESSING AND INSTRUCTING THE BRIDE

Early on the morning of the second day, the bride is redressed in the red headdress, white clothing, and silver jewelry she wore the previous day. Elder women once again accompany the event with songs, performing *izlan n ukrad n ṣbah,* "songs of brushing the hair in the morning," as the bride's hair is brushed and she is redressed. These songs, unlike those sung as the still virginal bride was dressed at her father's house, are now filled with instructions, teaching the newly married woman her expected role and duties in her new household. The first song begins by asking God to bless the occasion:

Bismi nezzur-k a Rebbi.
[In the name of God, we start.]

The song then again greets the bride on the morning after she has spent her first night with her husband:

Tagerramt ṣbaḥ n lixir.
Ad it-âawen-t a Mulana.
Tibermit-inew tin lefḍur.

[Good morning, bride.
You help me, my God.
My bowl is for breakfast.]

The following *izlan* describe the bride's new role in her husband's household:

Ad tcin ilusan tcey.
Ad swin ilusan swey.
Ad ssun ilusan ssuy.

[I eat after my brothers-in-law eat.
I drink after my brothers-in-law drink.
I spread out my bedding after I spread out my
      brothers-in-law's bedding.]

The song reflects the bride's new social reality. Uprooted from the family in which she grew up, she may make occasional visits home; but most of her life will be spent in this unfamiliar household. Typical of new brides in most regions of Morocco, an Ait Khabbash bride occupies an uncertain and sometimes precarious position in her husband's household until the birth of her first child and is expected to appear demure and timid in her behavior.

The women continue to sing while the bride is dressed, referring to the different articles of clothing she wears:

Tizi ossawn s-afella.
Ad it-âawen-t a Mulana.
Ad it-âawen-em i lumur.

Boubban-k assin-k a yaẓaẓa.
Boubban-k assin-k a lhenna.
Boubban-k assin-k a rriḥan.
Boubban-k assin-k a leḥrir.
Warru yeh warru yeh warru warru yeh warru.

[Rising up.
Help me, God.
God, help me with everything I do.
Carrying heavy loads.
Carrying henna.
Carrying *rriḥan* (perfume).
Carrying silk.
Rhythmic chant.]

The women I spoke with interpreted the phrase "Rising up" (sung when the bride stands up to have her belt tied) as a metaphor for the bride passing through the life cycle to become a wife with new responsibilities and challenges. The women call for God to help the bride succeed in her new household. The "heavy loads" carried by the bride are her jewelry, such as her amber necklace, silver bracelets, and fibulae. This phrase suggests that the groom's family, which purchased these for her, is wealthy; in the past, not every family could afford to buy the new bride these items of jewelry, especially the expensive amber necklace. The henna, *rriḥan* (perfume), and silk referred to in the song are items worn by the bride during the wedding ceremony, signaling her transition from a girl, not concerned with her daily appearance, to a well-dressed and perfumed woman.

The bride is dressed again in the white dress she wore the previous day, which now is stained with spots of blood after being used by the couple to soak up the bride's hymeneal blood. The bride will wear this bloodstained garment throughout the entire wedding to display her virginity to everyone present. The bloodstain also publicly announces to the entire community that her sexuality has been carefully controlled and monitored by her family and herself. Hence it ensures that any children she may bear will be Ait Khabbash and will be members of her husband's patriline and underlines women's role in ensuring the Ait Khabbash's continuation and survival. The Ait Khabbash, like many nomadic groups, base their ethnic identity on blood descent from a common ancestor; thus the virginity of a bride guarantees the purity of this bloodline.[7] As previously discussed, the importance that the community places on genealogy is demonstrated by the term "Ait Khabbash" itself, which means "people of Khabbash," tracing their ancestry to Khabbashi, a descendant of Dadda Atta and the Ait Atta. Ait Khabbash restrictions upon female sexuality and fertility, represented by the bloodstained *ahruy*, are thus a metaphor for protecting and preserving the boundaries between themselves and others and reinforce ethnic constructions. All links to the external non–Ait Khabbash world must be contained and maintained or the group will dissolve; the opened, uncontrolled female body is thereby seen as dangerous to the integrity of the society, simultaneously putting women in both a precarious and powerful position.

ASSERKED: MEN HONOR THE BRIDE

On the second day of the wedding, the *isnain* and other men perform a song in the bride's honor called *asserked,* further asserting the prestige granted to the bride in Ait Khabbash society. *Asserked* is performed in honor of the bride by the *isnain* in the bridal tent during the second and third mornings of the wedding. The *isnain,* who are often joined by other men, sing a very slow-paced song for the bride, expressing the wish that she be granted a joyous and bountiful married life (Fig. 5.6). They sit on the ground in the bridal tent while the bride sits propped up on a bench looking down at them, her bloodstained gown clearly visible. (Because the song is relatively long and can be performed for more than two hours, only a sample of the song is included here; the rest can be found in the appendix.)

The song begins by congratulating the bride on her virginity:

> *Iffu lḥal ur iffu manẓa-kmin a tislit?*
> *Iffu lḥal ur iffu manẓ-iken a yigerramen g ikḍif?*

> [Has the morning come yet or not? Where are you, bride?
> Has the morning come yet or not? Where are you, blood
>   on the carpet?]

Although the *isnain* refer to blood on the carpet, this is a metaphoric reference to the bride's bloodstained dress, since it is socially inappropriate to refer directly to her hymeneal blood.

The following lines compliment the bride by singing about her material

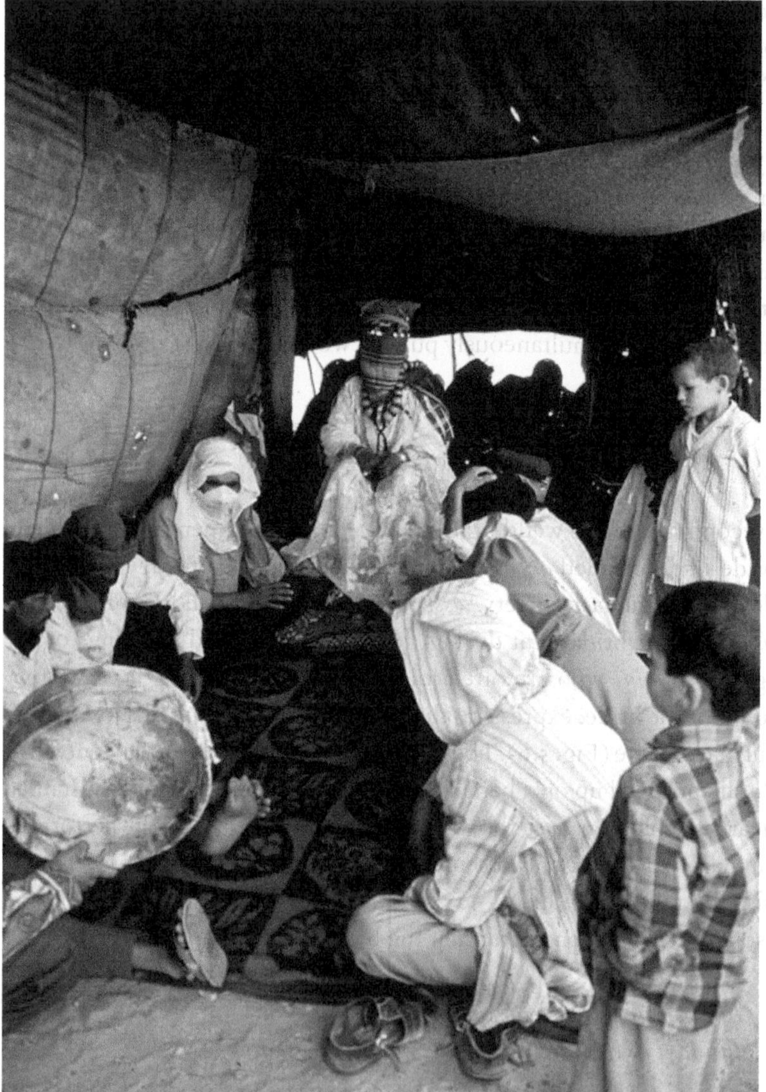

Figure 5.6. An Ait Khabbash bride sits in her bridal tent, 1996.

wealth and wishing for her good fortune by evoking imagery from their no-madic past:

> *Iffu lḥal ur iffu manẓa-kmin am wulli?*
> *Iffu lḥal ur iffu manẓa-kmin am tleγmin?*
> *Rjiγ Rebbi d Nebi ad am kin a tislit,*

Sebâa n warraw Ait iwedjan tifaliwin.
Sebâa n warraw imnayn gin kullu laciax.
Meyat naga ayd itggan rḥil-nnem.
Meya n tekdift ayd itggan usan-nnem.

[Has the morning come yet or not? Where are you,
    owner of sheep?
Has the morning come yet or not? Where are you,
    owner of camels?
I hope God and the Prophet give you, oh bride . . .
Seven sons with horses and swords . . .
Seven sons who are cavaliers and leaders . . .
100 camels to move your belongings . . .
100 carpets to be your spreads.]

The song continues by telling the bride how beautiful and how important she is by comparing her to the silk cords used to hold the daggers of Ait Khabbash men:

Tabuqest n leḥrir dda s-tt-ageln imnayen tifra.
[Cords of silk the cavaliers use to hang their *koummiyat*
    (daggers with curved blades).]

This phrase further demonstrates the male reliance on women, since, as one man explained to me, a dagger with a strong, beautiful silk cord is like a man supported by a hard-working, beautiful woman. The bride reciprocates the men's compliments by standing up and throwing powdered perfume (*rriḥan*) on them as the following is sung:

Âniγ tirwed imnayn annayγ ageḍrur tamʒem rrma a yistran.
[Maybe the cavaliers are coming. I saw the dust. Get your arrows
    ready for battle.]

This song performed by men gradually changes and is directed at the bride's mother rather than the bride, teasing her through the verses they sing. This teasing is meant as an accolade, because it suggests that the men have a close, familiar relationship with the bride's family, allowing them to joke together freely without social restriction. The men stand up and perform *aḥidous* in front of the bride, teasing her mother and asking her mother to give them almonds:

> *Âtti aḥ n bab-nnem arim-d lluẓ.*
> *Âtti ayiɣf n-ẓerri it-t-inign tadwunt say-d ibawn mek-am laḥ lluẓ.*
> *Âtti isuggurn s-taẓẓirt a taqmut n mush.*
> *Âtti amr a Rebbi tegnugit seg-bougafer irreẓ uyanbub-nnem ad ig idammen.*
> *Âtti n-ssudda laâyoub-nnem samḥ-i âadri.*

> [Oh aunt (the bride's mother), we are warning you, give us the almonds.
> Oh aunt, with a head resembling the head of a cockroach, searching for fat, go and buy fava beans if you can't afford almonds.
> Oh aunt, who is looking into a jar with a face like a cat's.
> Oh aunt, we wish that you may fall down Bougafer Mountain, break your face, and become covered in blood.
> Oh aunt, your weaknesses are clear to us, we forgive you.]

At the end of this song, the bride's mother laughingly throws almonds at the men. This song further demonstrates that much of male participation in the wedding centers around the bride. In addition to complimenting the bride and using visual imagery associated with female fertility and male bravery in warfare to flatter her, the men show their closeness to her and her family by entering into a joking relationship with her mother. This song with its vivid visual imagery reiterates the point that men are reliant on women for the preservation of Ait Khabbash identity. During their nomadic past, men preserved group honor through warfare, while women maintained group identity through childbirth and childrearing. This connection between women and fertility is the basis for their status in Ait Khabbash society, influencing their artistic production.

THE SACRIFICE

After the bride has been dressed and *asserkeḍ* has been performed, wedding guests wait in anticipation for the animal sacrifice, which many Ait Khabbash consider the most important event of the wedding. Around midday a ram or goat is sacrificed by the groom. Everyone waits to see the size of the sacrificial animal and anticipates the meat that will be served later that day. Large white rams with long horns are preferred, as white animals are believed to bring the bride and the groom good luck and a trouble-free life. Many families sacrifice black rams or goats, however, because they are more plentiful. This is the first time that the groom appears in public.

The sacrifice of the ram is an important event and tends to draw hundreds of spectators. The ram is adorned with cloth similar to the cloth worn over the faces of the bride and the groom, associating the married couple with the sacrificial victim. Prior to its sacrifice, the groom and then the bride step over the animal first with the right leg and next with the left (Fig. 5.7), which appears to mark their passage from one of life's stages to the next.

After the bride and groom step over the ram, the sacrificial animal is laid on the ground in front of the bride's tent. The bride lifts the red cloth over her face, and a thin white cloth is put in its place to enable her to witness the sacrifice. The groom then takes a knife and slits the throat of the sacrificial animal, or he may hand his knife to a friend or relative to perform the sacrifice for him. The flow of the sacrificed animal's blood is a metaphor for the blood that was spilled the previous night and that will be spilled during childbirth, ensuring the continuation of the Ait Khabbash ethnic identity and thereby symbolizing the bond that exists between the married couple and between the two families (Fig. 5.8).

This act of animal sacrifice is also reminiscent of the Feast of the Great Sacrifice performed by Muslims all over the world, reenacting the sacrifice of the Prophet Abraham, who was asked to prove his love of God by sacrificing his son. His willingness to do so bears witness to the covenant between God and his worshipers. Pleased by Abraham's faith, God then supplied him with a ram to sacrifice in place of his son. Each year Muslims all over the world ritually reenact the Great Sacrifice to proclaim their identity as Muslims and renew their faith in God.[8]

The sacrifice of an animal is a central symbol of group membership among the Ait Khabbash and also demonstrates how ethnic categories can be constructed. A man who wishes to become Ait Khabbash can become part of the group by sacrificing an animal to one of its members and expressing his intention to join the Ait Khabbash, thereby entitling that person and his family to the same rights and privileges as the rest of the group. Although this is not commonly practiced today, many Arabs in the region (especially those who were involved in the caravan trade or who regularly traveled through Ait Khabbash territory) became members of the Ait Khabbash, who were known for fiercely protecting the safety of all members of the group. As previously discussed, in the nineteenth century three non–Ait Khabbash Amazigh groups sacrificed animals to be adopted into the Ait Khabbash. Although the groups are united today, members of the four original groups are considered to be more ethnically pure. The three "adopted" groups are prohibited from inter-marrying among themselves; however, there are no social restrictions prohibiting marriages among the original four groups (Gélard 2003: 173). While

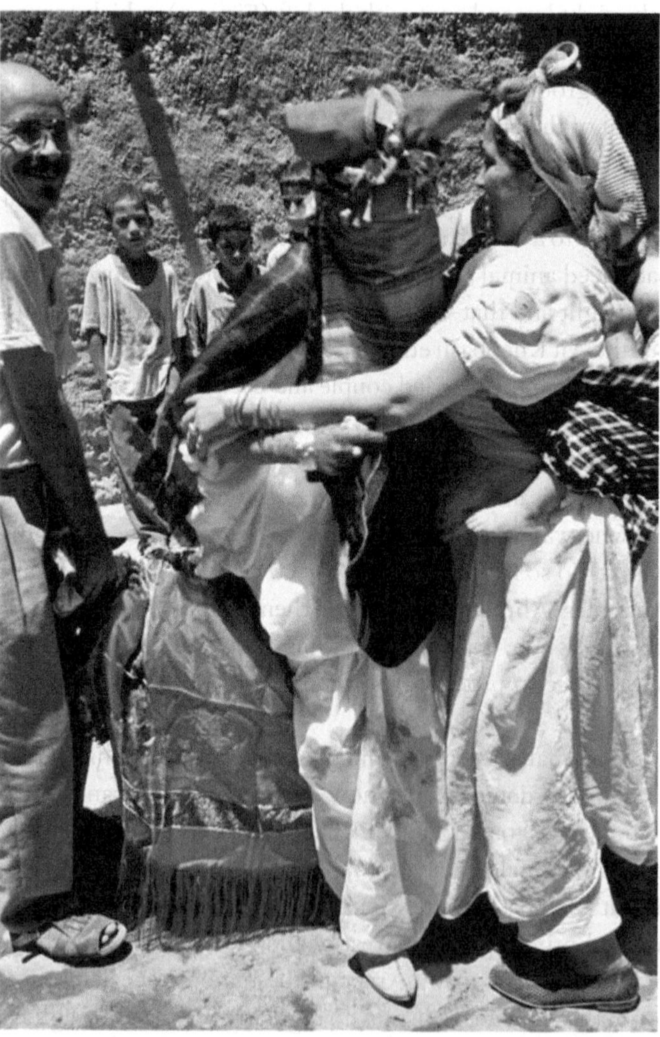

Figure 5.7. An Ait Khabbash bride in the Ziz Valley (between Erfoud and Errachidia) steps over a ram, covered with a red scarf, before its sacrifice, 1997.

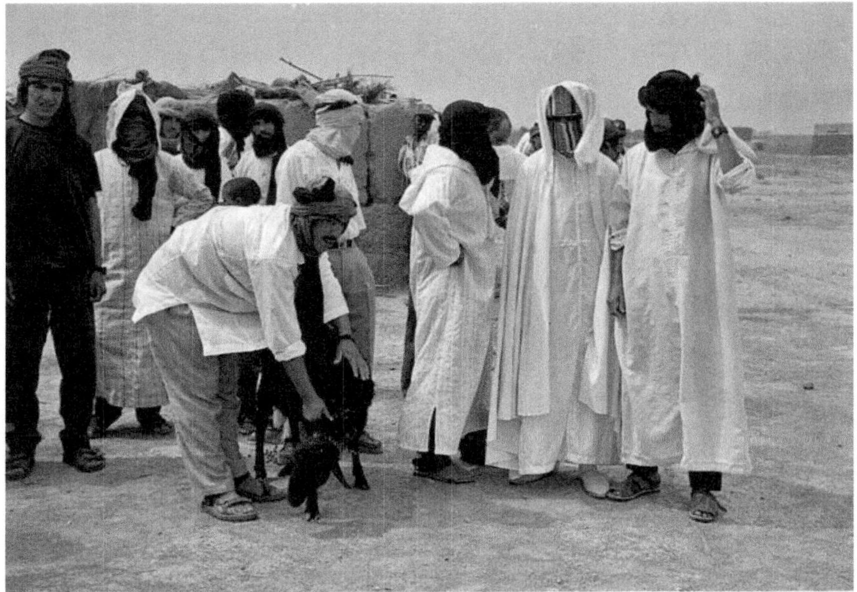

Figure 5.8. An Ait Khabbash groom in Hafira with the sacrificial ram, 1999.

this demonstrates how identity is constantly being negotiated, it also reveals that marriage is colored by the attempt to preserve the purity of the group's bloodline and by extension its ethnic purity.

Among the Ait Khabbash, blood flow is required to create a bond between families. During the wedding ceremony, the flow of the bride's virginal blood and the sacrifice of a ram adorned with a cloth similar to that worn by the bride reinforce this bond.[9]

DRESSING THE BRIDE AS A PIGEON: *TAQCICT*

After the animal sacrifice, the groom's wedding duties are finished until the evening of the third day. The groom may stay at home with his male friends or join the other wedding guests in front of the bride's tent, but the public wedding activities now center on the bride and her adornment, including dressing her in a hairstyle called *taqcict,* said to make her look as beautiful as a pigeon.

Taqcict is a hairstyle worn by the bride on the second afternoon of the wedding ceremony. In the late afternoon of the second day, the *tamaccaṭ* removes the *aâbroq,* covering only the bride's face with a red silk cloth with yellow stripes and allowing her hair to be unbraided and hang freely down her back.

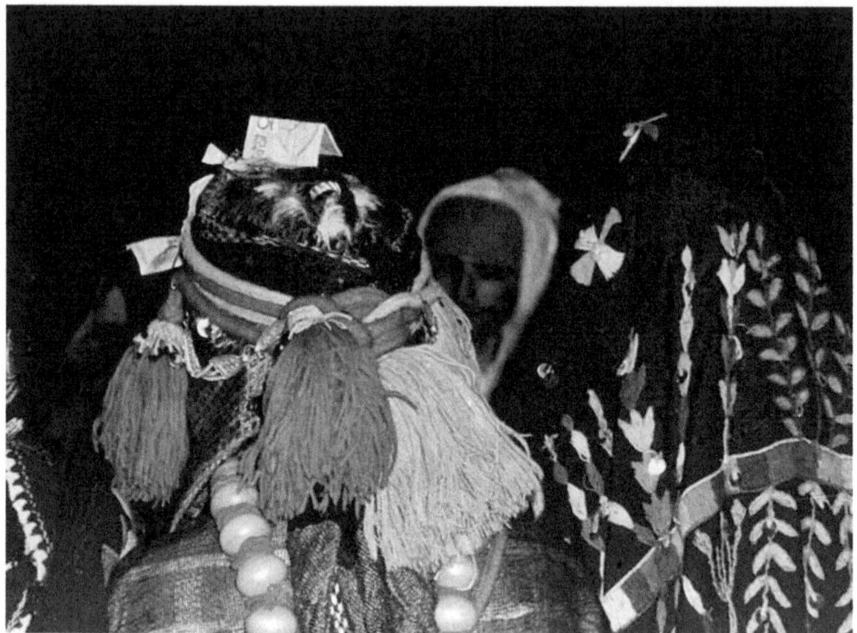

Figure 5.9. An Ait Khabbash bride's taqcict *or "pigeon" hairstyle, 1996.*

The *taboqest* ("green cord with a thick tassel") holds the red face covering in place while the bride's hair is styled in the *taqcict* hairstyle (Fig. 5.9).

The bride's hair is braided into two plaits on the right and the left, leaving some hair free in the center to be braided into a small braid to which the bride's wedding ring is attached at the top of her head. The top of the head is then adorned with two types of powder, one from pounded pomegranate skins (called *lxelxelt*) and one of ground saffron or fine powdered sugar. Smudges of these pigments are alternated until three of each adorn the very top of the head. While the hair is being styled, female relatives surround the bride and sing the following song:

> 1. *Bismi Allah rraḥman rraḥim.*
> 2. *Yelli ẓẓur-γ ẓar-m Rebbi.*
> 3. *Asra g kem-id usiγ a tiseksit,*
> 4. *An kerd adlal-nnes i Fatima.*
> 5. *Ad it-âawn-em ayenna-d usiγ.*
> 6. *A tamaccaṭ lḥarma-nnem herru.*
> 7. *Ad-i ur tennum hat-t-it mamẓat-t-it.*

8. *Ad-i ur tennum tubedda n berra.*
9. *A tanagamt-inew a tanaʒdamt-inew.*
10. *Ad ur titkat-t ula tergemt-t-it.*
11. *Nniɣ-ak a bab n cci nniɣ-ak.*
12. *Terwa ur terwi tuɣul-id yelli.*
13. *Warru yeh warru yeh warru warru yeh warru.*
14. *Ddag teɣley tafuyt i ḥedda uḍar.*
15. *Ad-i ur tennum lullu n tedeɣrin.*
16. *Ssiley, afrag-inew a Rebbi.*
17. *Ad yaley am ulgim n waḍil.*
18. *I silewn i wʒrur ar akal.*
19. *Ad-t-ink i ṭelba wenna ɣranin.*
20. *Ad-am isaâd i nem-am waḍu.*
21. *A taɣla i ʒʒuɣruren ilis.*
22. *Amma-nnes ttedâu-yas s-lxir.*
23. *Gimt-as ayenna ur giɣ a lemluk.*
24. *Gimt-as isgar a lemluk.*
25. *Ayaârinew giɣ-as may riɣ.*
26. *A Mulay Buâeʒʒa cerif ɣriɣ-ak.*
27. *Hayy-aɣ g iceḍran-nnek a cerif.*
28. *A tatbirt mi tella taweɣyi g iɣef.*

[1. In the name of God, the merciful, the beneficent.
2. My daughter, God be with you.
3. When I take you, oh brush,
4. To brush Fatima's hair.
5. You help me with everything I do.
6. Oh brusher, please be patient.
7. I don't want her to be in the habit of roaming around.
8. I don't want her to be in the habit of loitering outside.
9. My water fetcher — my wood collector.
10. Don't hit her — don't insult her.
11. I'm telling you, I'm telling you.
12. You get along and she stays or send my daughter back home.
13. [Wordless melody]
14. When the sun sets, the foot must stop.
15. I don't want her to be in the habit of getting money from
   men's leather bags.

16. Oh God, make my destiny climb.
17. Climb like a grapevine.
18. With its bunches hanging to the ground.
19. We offer it to the religious scholars who are educated.
20. God gives you happiness.
21. Oh sheep that drags wool.
22. Oh her mother, wish good things for her.
23. Oh angels, do for her what I could not do.
24. Oh angels, do *isgar* (protection against *imkuraren*) for her.
25. Thanks to God, I did everything I wanted for her.
26. Oh Mulay Buâezza Sherif, I'm calling you.
27. We are under your protection, oh Sherif.
28. Oh bride, you are like a pigeon with yellow coloring on its head.]

Each elder woman in the bride's family is expected to participate in the *iẓlan* performed for the bride as a gesture of respect to the host family. This gathering of the bride's female line lends an intensity to the performance that cannot be conveyed by a description of the text. The slow, steady, drawn-out method of singing gives it an emotional quality that underlies the sincerity of the singers. Midway the text is embellished with a wordless melody that adds emphasis to the singers' emotional involvement with the performance. This song expresses the hopes of the bride's mother and the other women of the family that the bride will be successful in her new home and will be treated fairly by her new husband. Lines 7, 8, and 15 express hopes that the bride will behave herself in her new home and be well taken care of by the groom's family. Most importantly, however, the song is a mother's good-bye to her daughter, making the song even more poignant.

The last line of the song once again uses the metaphor of the pigeon to describe the bride and her hairstyle. The pigeon serves as a symbol of women and the purity of the ritualistic occasion, as discussed earlier;[10] several men and women also told me that the pigeon was used to describe the bride because, like women, pigeons are beautiful. A less obvious metaphorical use of the pigeon appears in line 24, "Oh angels, do *isgar* for her." *Isgar* is a ritualized action for removing any harmful *imkuraren* or sickness from a person that involves a live animal, most typically a bird. The bird is first washed to purify it and then circled over the person's head three times, after which the bird is killed. The bird (or just some of its feathers) is put in a bag with an egg, henna, and some barley and thrown away. Women explained that the feathers symbolized flight and the removal of harm and that the body of the bird is never eaten because it is believed to contain the illness or evil that inhabited the person's body. The description of *isgar* demonstrates that the metaphor of the bird is a powerful one, serving as a metaphor for feminine beauty while protecting the bride from harmful *imkuraren*.[11]

As discussed earlier, I observed that birds are often used metaphorically to reinforce the association of women with fertility, the source of female power in Ait Khabbash society. The dark-colored head covering and white *ahruy* typically worn by married women, for instance, sometimes lead people to compare them to a black and white bird called *um lxir,* translated as "the one of goodness." Women reported to me that if this bird is seen near one's home, it brings fertility, good luck, and blessing. Boddy (1989: 62–65) asserts that in the Sudan there is a strong metaphoric association between the bride and pigeons: both are associated with purity, cleanliness, and beauty. The Ait Khabbash also use the metaphor of the pigeon for the bride, who, it is hoped, will soon bear children. Pigeons and birds in general can further be connected to eggs, a universal symbol of fertility and creation.[12] The egg is often used within the African nomadic tent as a symbol of fertility, and the closed and contained forms of both the egg and the tent echo the aesthetic qualities of fertility and containment found in female-dominated nomadic art in Africa (Prussin 1995: 192).

Some of the silver jewelry worn by the bride also alludes to this connection between women and birds. Married women wear a type of necklace that consists of silver pendants interspersed with colored beads called *tiferfrin* (a term that comes from the Moroccan Arabic word "fly"), whose triangular shape is reminiscent of the tail feathers of a bird (Fig. 1.14). Some other Ait Atta wear silver jewelry that features motifs or figures inspired by birds, such as *isensirn* of the Ait Atta from Tazzarine, which is basically an assemblage of silver money attached to three hooks: a small cast bird is riveted to the central piece of money by a short stem. A similar bird motif is also found on hair pendants worn by Amazigh women in the Dades Valley, an area southwest of the Tafilalet oasis.[13]

Thus the association of the *taqcict* hairstyle with pigeons can also be viewed as a public assertion of the power of women rooted in their ability to give life. The adornment of the bride's head culminates with the performance of a collective dance called *ahidous;* the last line of the song, "Oh bride, you are like a pigeon with yellow coloring on its head," is repeated numerous times. The bride stands in the middle of a line of women facing a line of men that does not include the groom. This dance is thus strictly the domain of the bride and is another example of a wedding activity centered on the bride and her adornment.

Ass Ameggaru: *"The Third Day"*

The last day of the wedding further celebrates the bride's transition from virginal girl to married woman. On this day the bride's face is heavily painted with orange saffron and a black pigment called *ḥargus* and her *aâbroq* is lifted (Fig. 5.10).[14] While the bride's face is painted, she is kept under the confines of a cloth draped over her; women of the bride and groom's family sing for the bride, demonstrating female solidarity across family lines and increasing the crowd's anticipation of finally catching a glimpse of the bride's face. Since this song repeats phrases and themes from several earlier songs, the complete song is included in the appendix. The song ends with the line "Oh my gold, come out," referring to the action of pulling back the bride's *aâbroq* to reveal her saffron-painted face.

Until the 1970s such makeup was worn by all young married Ait Khabbash women on a daily basis, but it has fallen out of fashion and is restricted to use by the bride. Saffron is ground up and mixed with water and painted on the face. A thick line of saffron is drawn around the outside edges of the face and a straight line across the top of the forehead, followed by three horizontal lines extending across the cheeks (Fig. 5.10). Sometimes various geometric motifs are also painted onto the face with thin lines of black *ḥargus*. These motifs are restricted to the central axis of the face and resemble tattoo motifs, such as an *x* on the forehead or between the eyes, four small dots on the top of the nose, and a straight line of small dots on the chin. A small amount of *ḥargus* may also be smeared on the woman's bottom lip. This makeup, once applied, takes almost a week to wear off a woman's face, even after washing. When the bride's face is finally painted, the cloth covering her body is removed. She stands in front of the crowd of women, who push and shove in order to catch their first glimpse of the bride.

UMIDUL: AN EXPRESSION OF COMMUNAL STRENGTH AND COOPERATION

The three-day wedding ceremony concludes with the entire community joining the bride in the performance of *umidul,* a collective dance performed on the last night of the wedding at sunset after the bride's face has been uncov-

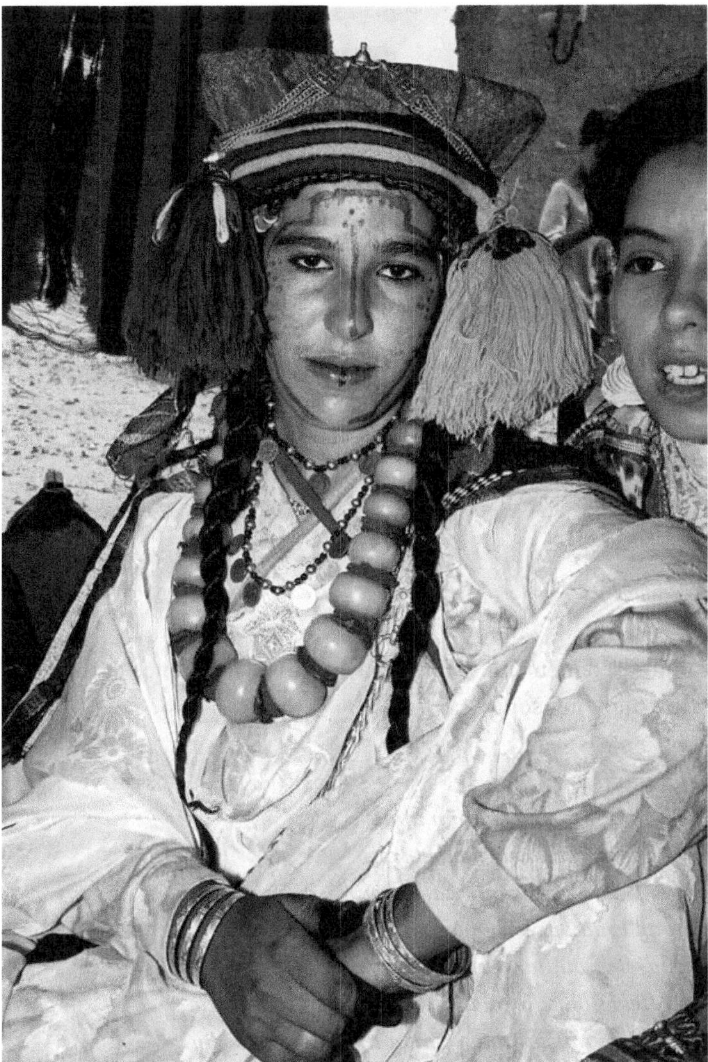

Figure 5.10. An Ait Khabbash bride adorns her face with saffron on the final day of the wedding, 1997.

ered. In some Ait Khabbash areas the bride's face is revealed for both men and women to see; in others, she wears a thin white cloth to cover her face so that unrelated men cannot see her. Almost the entire community participates in *umidul*, a particularly powerful wedding ritual highly charged with expressions of joy and might. The bride, now a symbol of a united community, stands in the middle of the line of women (Fig. 5.11).

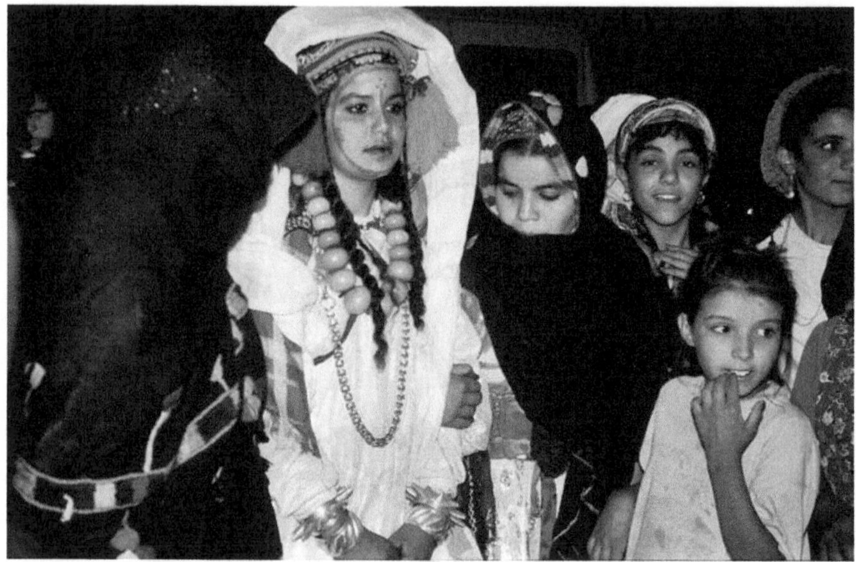

Figure 5.11. A bride's saffron-painted face is revealed on the final day of the wedding, 1996.

More than a hundred men and women may perform this dance at the same time, singing the following song:

Saâdnin a lfal umlil a tiyawsiwin.
Iâdawen-inew ad ur uẓu-n tafaska n imal.
Aâdaw-inew ad ig iẓimer i wucn ad-t-tcin.
Ad-teg m'irban iɣudu uynna-nnes a Rebbi.
Ad-teg m'larbaḥ iɣudu uynna-nnes a Rebbi.
Saâdat-i t saâd-em i bu lfarḥ-inew a Rebbi.
Smunat-ten a Rebbi imkelli tman-emt a tilxudim d'iḍudan.
Smunat-ten a Rebbi imkelli tman-emt a tiyniwin g iâarjan.
Smunat-ten a Rebbi imkelli tman-emt a talwaḥin d-ṭalba.

[Help me, oh white good omen, with everything.
May my enemies not sacrifice their sheep next *âid* (feast).
May my enemy become a sheep for a wolf to eat.
Oh God, may she (the bride) have children and become rich.
Oh God, may she (the bride) have success and wealth.
Oh God, bless me and bless the one who has the party (the groom).
Oh God, unite them as rings are united with fingers.
Oh God, unite them as the dates are united with the bunch.
Oh God, unite them as students are united with their writing boards.]

Umidul is a performative ritual that demonstrates the power and cohesiveness of the community. The words, the rhythms, and the dance steps all play on the emotions of the participants and the audience. The song is a verbal expression of the resistance against domination by outside groups and is rich in visual metaphors of community, such as the reference to a bunch of dates. This performance reflects the values of cooperation and the preservation of group identity, which are key elements in Ait Khabbash weddings.

Umidul uses familiar images (rings on fingers, a bunch of dates, small children with their writing boards in Qur'anic school) to ask God for the successful union of a husband and wife. The silver rings given to women when they marry, for instance, both symbolize their unity with their husbands and suggest a relationship with the past, because they are identical to those given earlier to their mother and grandmothers. Thus the rings given to the brides symbolize a relationship with the past, a unification of families, and their regeneration in the future. All of these images suggest *tamunt* or "unity," a concept that is crucial to the survival of Amazigh communities in North Africa.

This connection of the past, the present, and the future of the Ait Khabbash and reliance upon the fertility of women is further enacted when the *umidul* ends and the bride enters her husband's home for the first time. She breaks an egg, a symbol of fertility and childbirth, on the doorframe or tent pole. She is then literally tied to her mother-in-law with a white turban wrapped around their waists so that the two face each other, representing the cooperative relationship that must exist between the women of the household to ensure a successful marriage. Amid the laughter that accompanies this event, the ritual takes a serious tone when the *isnain* recite the following instructions to the bride:

> *Msisi-mt.*
> *Ad ur tili taẓitt.*
> *Ttcawar tamγart.*
> *Xyar d nâam.*
> *Ad ur tsexsart i tamγart-nnem.*
> *Ad ur tsexsart i wmγar-nnem.*
> *Ad ur tsexsart i γlewsan-nnem.*
> *A xalti.*
> *A âammi.*
> *Nekker ẓik.*
> *Ad ur t-sew-t ard sew-in ilewsan.*
> *Ad ur t-ssu-t ard ssu-n ilewsan.*

[Get along with each other.
Do not fight.
Ask your mother-in-law for her opinion.
Respond with yes.
Do not refuse your mother-in-law's requests.
Do not refuse your father-in-law's requests.
Do not refuse requests from your brothers-in-law
    and sisters-in-law.
Oh, my aunt.
Oh, my uncle.
Get up early.
Do not drink until your brothers-in-law and
    sisters-in-law drink.
Do not lie down until your brothers-in-law and
    sisters-in-law lie down.]

The bride is reminded to obey her mother-in-law and told to call her "my aunt" (*xalti*) and her father-in-law "my uncle" (*âammi*) as terms of respect — good advice since mothers-in-law have the ultimate authority over their son's wives. At this stage of her life, a mother controls the activities of other women in the household, especially those of her daughters-in-law. A new bride's happiness in her new home depends largely on her relationship with her mother-in-law. While the central role that women play in weddings pays tribute to female fertility and procreation, women are also held responsible for controlling the sexuality and fertility of younger women. Young girls are monitored by their mothers, and married women are controlled by their mothers-in-law. Only when their children are grown do women's status and power increase, although their power at this point has less to do with their own fertility than with their ability to control the fertility of others.

The Conclusion of the Wedding

The day after the marriage festivities have ended, young children accompany the bride to a canal, river, lake, or other water source (sometimes a tub of water if there is nothing else). She drinks some of the water and throws some unshelled almonds into it. The small children quickly jump in the water to salvage the almonds, but some almonds are expected to float away to become seeds for future almond trees. The water that the bride drinks represents her sexual encounter with her husband, and the almonds are symbols of the offspring that are expected to result from their relationship. The ultimate purpose of the wedding is procreation, and the visual and performing arts surrounding a wedding emphasize the physical and symbolic continuation of the society through the bodies of women.

As discussed earlier, the public role of women in weddings complicates the public/private dichotomy often used to describe gender roles. Women are not relegated solely to the private/interior/domestic domain but hold important public roles in the society. Yet while the very public association of women with fertility and reproduction during the wedding ceremony gives them considerable power and prestige, it also restricts them to specific roles in the society and limits their life options.

Weddings are central expressions of Ait Khabbash ethnic identity and are used to erect boundaries and maintain distinctions between themselves and others. The clothing worn by the bride and the groom and the songs performed at weddings are oral histories passed on from generation to generation. The Ait Khabbash history was previously nomadic, and references to their nomadic life can be found in many of their wedding songs. In addition, nomadic Ait Khabbash were involved in the trans-Saharan caravan trade, trading salt, dates, henna, and slaves across the Sahara to Timbuktu and other parts of Sudanic Africa (the area of Africa south of the Sahara). The history and legacy of slavery can be found in Ait Khabbash visual and performing arts, especially those of the Ismkhan, who are descendants of the enslaved Sudanic Africans assimilated into the Ait Khabbash and are the topic of Chapter Six.

SIX

Oh, My Sudanese Mother

THE LEGACY OF SLAVERY IN AIT KHABBASH ART

As earlier chapters have shown, Ait Khabbash arts have been shaped by historical changes and contact with other cultures. One such influence not yet discussed has been their participation in the trans-Saharan slave trade. From as early as the ninth century, human beings from Sudanic Africa were forcefully enslaved and brought into North Africa by the trans-Saharan caravan trade. Although slavery was outlawed in southeastern Morocco in the 1930s, the descendants of those enslaved by the Ait Khabbash continued to refer to themselves as Ismkhan, the plural form of the word *ismkh* or "slave" in Tamazight. The Ait Khabbash typically enslaved children, so by the time of manumission the enslaved and their descendants had long since forgotten the name of the ethnic group from which they had come or any of the Sudanic languages that they had originally spoken. They had become assimilated into the Ait Khabbash. Hence the Ismkhan speak the same language as other Ait Khabbash (Tamazight), practice nearly identical marriage ceremonies, and create similar art forms. In fact, an outsider looking at the female-dominated arts of both groups, such as textiles and dress, would not observe any noticeable differences between them. This similarity identifies them as a single people and symbolically reaffirms the crucial role of women's fertility in their cultural identity and survival. Thus Ismkhan women are also artists, creating art that unites these two groups into a single people.

Despite their assimilation, the Ismkhan are dark-complexioned, a constant reminder of the difference in their heritage and bloodline from that of the rest of the Ait Khabbash. As discussed earlier, maintaining the supposed purity of their bloodline is very important to the Ait Khabbash sense of identity; thus the Ismkhan were not allowed to intermarry with other Ait Khabbash, in effect becoming a separate subgroup. As former slaves, the Ismkhan have lower status than other members of the Ait Khabbash. Their position within the Ait Khabbash is elevated by their participation in public healing ceremonies, however, establishing their reputation as gifted healers possessing special *baraka* (divine blessing). In order to elevate their social standing, Ismkhan men and women have come to perform public healing ceremonies, using their ceremonial dress and performances to stress a connection to the Prophet Muhammad and Islam.

As early as the ninth century, the forced migration of enslaved peoples to northern Africa was massive. Based on eyewitness accounts and popular folklore, the Moroccan scholar Mohammed Ennaji (1999) confirms that large numbers of enslaved peoples existed in Morocco throughout history. Many of these slaves entered Morocco through the town of Sijilmasa in the Tafilalet oasis, a stopping point for caravans on the trans-Saharan trade route. In 1353, for example, Ibn Battuta recorded that he traveled across the Sahara from Takadda through Touat on a large caravan carrying six hundred enslaved women that eventually ended at Sijilmasa (Hamdun and King 1994: 73–74).[1] Thereafter, the market of Abou-âam in contemporary Rissani replaced Sijilmasa as the center of commercial life for southeastern Morocco.

In the late nineteenth century maintaining the trans-Saharan slave trade became difficult for people in the Tafilalet oasis due to French occupation of towns on the caravan route, such as Timbuktu, Touat, and Tabalbala. French rule over this desert region was tenuous, however, and their inability to control remote areas of the desert meant that nomadic groups in southeastern Morocco continued to conduct slave raids until the region's colonization in 1934 (Dunn 1977: 112). According to the anthropologist Lloyd Cabot Briggs, long-range raiding (especially of children) was common among powerful nomadic groups. As he noted, raids were commonly

> directed southward into the Sudan, where sedentary negro villagers were seized and carried off as slaves to serve in the camps of their captors. In cases of this kind, however, pursuit was rarely a problem, for the would-be avengers very seldom had the necessary mounts. (Briggs 1960: 121–122)

The people enslaved by nomadic groups such as the Ait Khabbash herded camels, sheep, and goats and performed the difficult domestic chores of fetching water from distant wells and gathering firewood.

The memory of slavery still resonates strongly in and around the Tafilalet oasis of southeastern Morocco, where the Ait Khabbash live. Although most of the people who were actually enslaved and carried across the desert have died, their children and grandchildren know the story of how they arrived in southeastern Morocco even if they no longer recall the names of their ancestors' ethnic groups. The ways in which slavery was practiced in southeastern Morocco also made it difficult for individuals who were enslaved as children to maintain their native language; they often were bought and sold numerous times and very frequently were the only person enslaved by a particular family. Khadija, an elderly Ismkhan woman living in Khamlia, recounted to me the story of her father, who had been enslaved by numerous families before she was born:

> My father was stolen when he was a small boy. He went out with his brother to graze animals and was stolen when he was no more than four or five years old. He was then sold to some Arabs in Tabalbala, where he worked on their farm. He was later sold to a Chleuh [Ait Khabbash] family.[2]
>
> He got his freedom when the French arrived and the man he worked for gave him some land and date palms to farm. Later when the man died, his sons tried to take his land, but, since he had papers giving him ownership of the land, the government said that the man's sons did not have a case.
>
> Later he left the area and worked for some Chleuh nomads near Hafira and married my mother. Only then did he come to Khamlia. I do not have any aunts and uncles from my father's side. If you meet a black person without any cousins, aunts, or uncles, you know that person was stolen. My father was so young when he was stolen that he did not know where he came from or remember his original name.

Despite their diverse origins, the Ismkhan view themselves as an ethnically united community. What binds them to one another is their shared history of enslavement and a common origin myth that connects them not to Dadda Atta, like the rest of the Ait Khabbash, but to Bilal and through him to the Prophet Muhammad himself. Bilal was an Abyssinian slave whose freedom was bought by Muhammad's uncle after Bilal's non-Muslim master mistreated him for becoming Muslim. Despite his status as an ex-slave, Bilal became one of the Prophet Muhammad's first companions and his first *muathin,* the man chosen to perform the Muslim call to prayer five times a day. According to this tradition, Bilal's close relationship with the Prophet gave him and his descendants the gift of *baraka* ("divine blessing"), which transcends their earlier status as slaves.

It is the public invocation of their connection to the Prophet Muhammad and the *baraka* that he has granted them that distinguishes Ismkhan *aḥidous* performances from those of other Ait Khabbash. As noted earlier, each Amazigh group has its own distinct performance style, and the style of the Ismkhan closely resembles that of other Ait Khabbash. This includes men and women standing in parallel lines, with men initiating the performance by singing one line of song that is then repeated by the women, and dancing by stepping from side to side and back and forth in the same parallel lines throughout the performance.

While other Ait Khabbash perform in Tamazight (the language they all share as a people), Ismkhan sing in Moroccan Arabic, linking them instead to Arabs and the Muslim faith. The musical instruments played by the Ismkhan also differ and appear to reflect their larger African roots. These include a large cylinder drum called *ginga* and its smaller counterpart, called *tagingat* (Fig. 6.1). Although the exact origin of these drums is unclear, the word *ginga* probably derives from *ganga* (a term used to refer to any kind of large cylinder drum by the Hausa, who live in the northern part of Nigeria and Benin and the southern part of Niger) (Ames 1965). Ismkhan also play cymbals called *qraqsh* (also called *qraqeb*) made of iron with a straight bar between them, which again suggest a possible Sudanic origin (Fig. 6.2). Akin Euba (1965: 54) has documented a Hausa woman in Nigeria playing a similar instrument called a *sambani,* perhaps related to the term in Hausa, which, as Lois Anderson (1971: 159) notes, also refers to a slave of Arab traders.

The lively dancing, loud drumming, and accompanying rhythms of metal cymbals make *aḥidous* performed by Ismkhan different from that performed by Amazigh groups in Morocco, including other Ait Khabbash. The *aḥidous* begins typically enough with men and women both taking small steps to the side, leading with the right foot and following with the left foot. But as the beat of the drums gradually speeds up, the male performers begin picking up their knees and lifting their *qraqsh* above their heads, making a semicircle around the row of women. A new and even brisker rhythm is the signal for two of the men playing the *qraqsh* to break away from the row and move between the rows of men and women, where they spin counterclockwise then clockwise several times in a squatting position. Gradually the rhythm of the instruments and the dancing increases in speed, ending when the drummer gives the appropriate rhythmic signal. Figure 6.3 illustrates an Ismkhan dance performance photographed sometime between 1930 and 1959. The presence of women, who are not wearing the embroidered head coverings common to both Ismkhan and Ait Khabbash *aḥidous* performances today, further strengthens

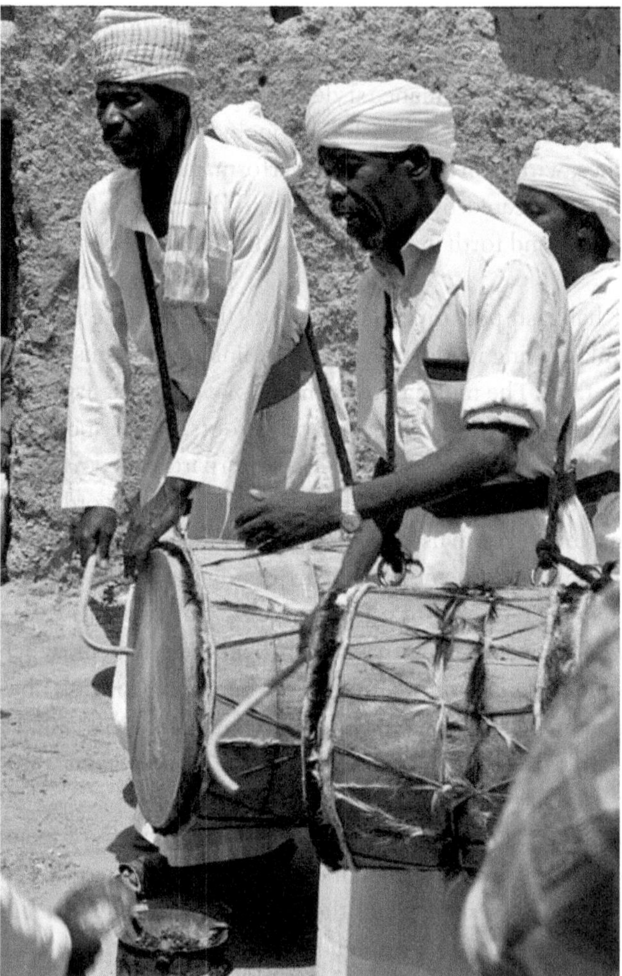

Figure 6.1. Ismkhan men in Khamlia accompany their performances with a large barrel and a small barrel drum called ginga *and* tagingat, *respectively, 2002. These originate from a western African drum called* ganga.

my argument that Amazigh women did not cover while performing *aḥidous* until recent years.

Unlike other Ait Khabbash, Ismkhan repeat one single phrase throughout an entire dance sequence, and these phrases frequently refer to God and the Prophet Muhammad. The Ismkhan view *aḥidous* not just as a form of entertainment but as sacred religious songs, such as the songs below, asking for God's blessing and a release from the suffering that is the legacy of their enslavement:

A Rebi laâfou a bou lalla.
[We ask you, God, for your blessing.]

Ya farraj moula-na.
[Oh our master, release us from suffering.]

Ya Allah, a nabi-na, a Rasul Allah, Allah a nabi-na a Rasul Allah.
[Oh God, our Prophet, messenger of God, Oh deliverer of
God's Message.]

Songs also invoke the name of the Prophet Muhammad's daughter Fatima, whom the Ismkhan claim had a special relationship with Bilal. In a story re-

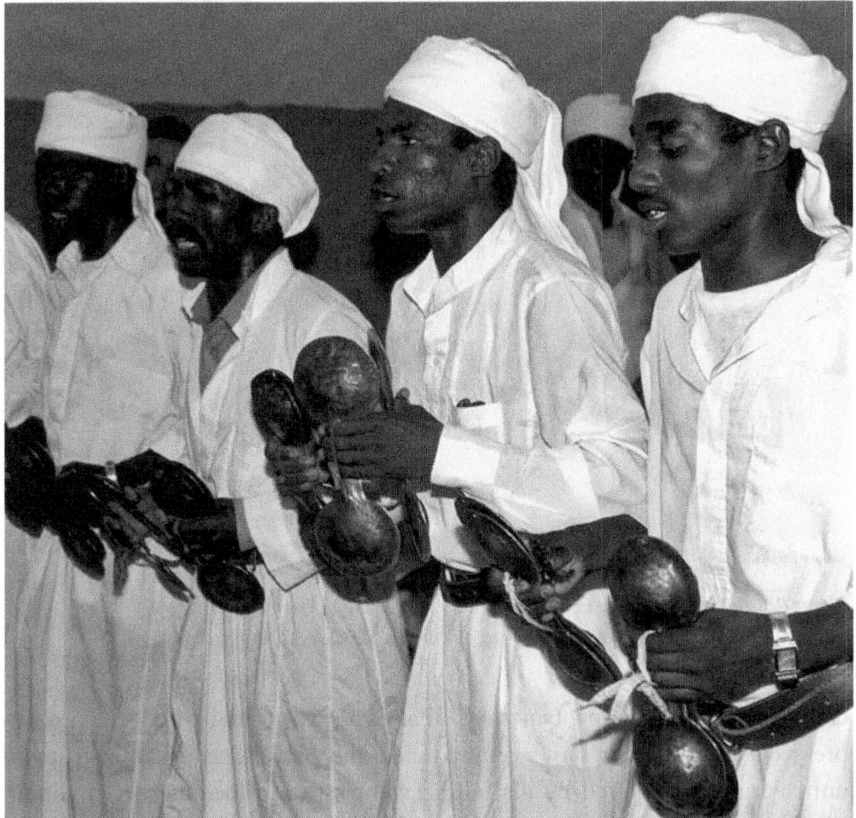

Figure 6.2. Ismkhan men in Khamlia accompany their performances with metal cymbals called qraqsh, *2002.*

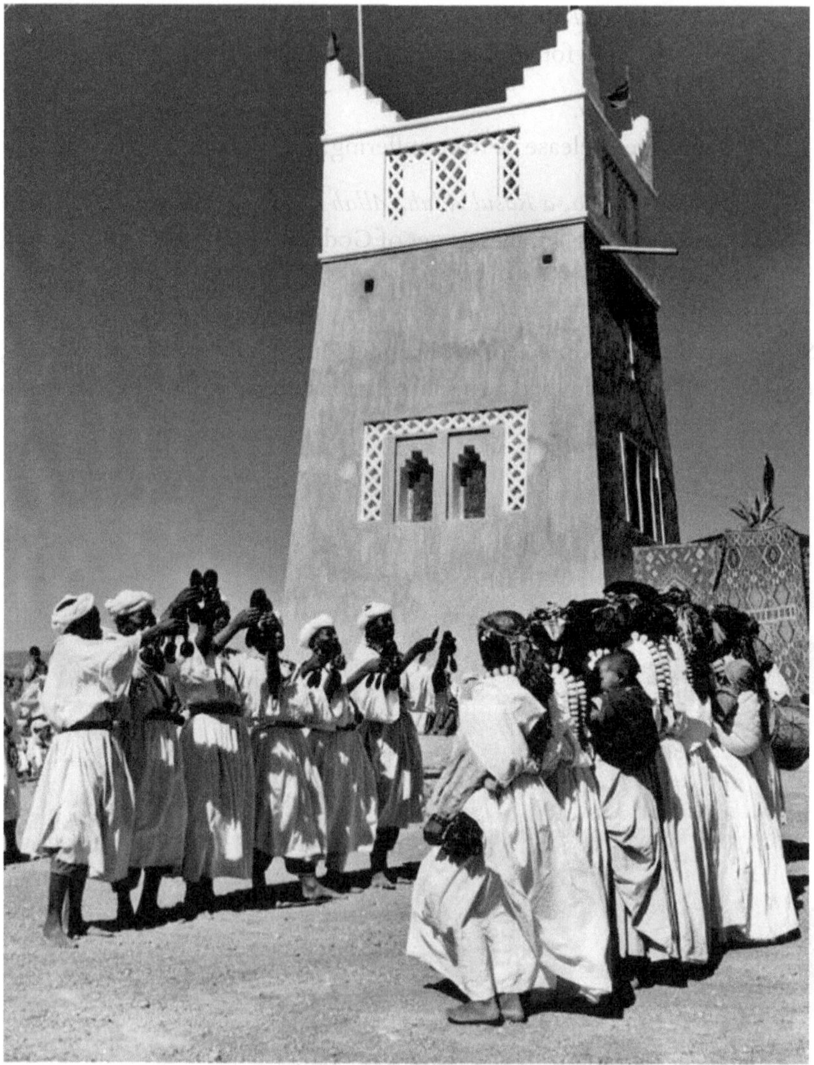

Figure 6.3. An Ismkhan dance in the Draa Valley near Zagora. Photo courtesy of the
National Anthropological Archives, 1930–1959. Smithsonian Institution/04100500.

counted to me by many Ismkhan, Bilal, who was asked to cheer up a depressed Fatima by her father, constructed and played a musical instrument
until Fatima, overjoyed by his music, went into a trance and felt uplifted.
Pleased that his daughter was no longer depressed, the Prophet granted Bilal
and his descendants the gift of *baraka* because of this deed. One Ismkhan song
that recalls this connection to Fatima simply repeats her name:

> *Ah Lalla Fatima ya Fatima ya Lalla Fatima.*
> [Oh Lalla Fatima, oh Fatima, oh Lalla Fatima.]

Much of the distinctive imagery of Ismkhan songs evokes a motherland in the Sudan, as demonstrated by these three songs:

> *Ah Sudanea, Ah ma ya hanna Sudanea.*
> [Oh Sudanese woman, Oh our dear Sudanese mother.]

> *Allah, Allah, Ya Mima, ejeek el khir ya mima.*
> [God, God, oh mother. Blessings to you, oh mother.]

> *Ah ma, ah Bulalla, ah ma dawi-ni.*
> [Oh mother, oh Bilal, oh mother, heal me.]

Such songs are an example of the invented traditions that the Ismkhan have created both to connect them to the Ait Khabbash and to maintain their distinctive heritage. The most significant of these traditions is the annual festival held in Khamlia, a village considered to be the Ait Khabbash homeland of the Ismkhan. Before the 1920s nomadic groups in the region moved across the desert without establishing permanent settlements; but after colonization Ismkhan, employed by the French to work in a nearby lead mine, founded Khamlia. They lived there until the 1960s and 1970s, when the closure of the mine and drought forced them to seek wage-paying employment in the growing cities of Erfoud and Rissani. Although very few Ismkhan live in Khamlia today, it is still considered a special place and serves as home to their annual festival. The festival increases the Ismkhan's special status by providing a service to the larger community. Ismkhan refer to the event as a *sadaka,* which means "gift" or "offering" in Arabic. During the *sadaka* Ismkhan pay tribute to Bilal and their other ancestors and enact their gift of *baraka* by healing the sick and distributing food to the larger community. Many Ismkhan shared with me their belief that drought, famine, or other natural disasters would afflict the region if the *sadaka* was not held each year.

Preparations for the *sadaka* begin after the spring harvest, when Ismkhan men gather for a fifteen-day period of traveling from house to house and village to village playing music and in return collecting food, grain, tea, and sugar. At each house a generous offering is given in exchange for being blessed by the *baraka* of the Ismkhan. One Ait Khabbash man who hosted a dinner for the Ismkhan explained to me that the Ismkhan once healed his sick father, who in gratitude made them dinner each year when they collected for their *sadaka*. Although his father had passed away several years earlier, the man told me that he needed to continue what his father started. Such an attitude toward the Ismkhan is common, and the Ismkhan take care to pass each house in a given village in order to distribute their *baraka* fairly from family to family.

The clothing worn by the men during this fifteen-day collection period is closely regulated. They must wear white turbans, white gowns with a white shirt underneath, brown leather belts, white slip-on shoes, and short, baggy white pants. Anyone who does not dress accordingly must actually pay a monetary fine to the leader or *sheikh* of the Ismkhan. The color white is vital to their association with *baraka* or spiritual blessing, because white is symbolically associated with religious purity in Islam (as discussed earlier). Most men who pray in a mosque wear white clothing, and thus the color associates the Ismkhan men with Islam and the pious behavior connected with prayer. The visual presentation of the body is therefore important to the Ismkhan men because it provides them with a symbol that asserts their Ismkhan identity and their connection with *baraka*. Because ritual purity is considered crucial to participating in the *sadaka,* Ismkhan men purify their bodies by washing as if in preparation for prayer and restrict the participation of women, who might be menstruating and therefore impure.

The healing ceremony of the Ismkhan can be performed upon request, but its most public performance occurs during the three-day *sadaka* itself, which incorporates many elements of the wedding ceremony that the Ismkhan share with other Ait Khabbash. The *sadaka* begins with Ismkhan men, women, and children circling a tent woven from goat hair and set up by men in the same place each year in the middle of Khamlia, in a clearing between houses over a small pile of rocks. The Ismkhan signal the beginning of the *sadaka* in the same way in which the Ait Khabbash signal a wedding: by circling the tent three times clockwise then counterclockwise. There are obvious parallels between Ait Khabbash weddings and the *sadaka* of the Ismkhan, but one major difference is that the procession at Khamlia is led by Ismkhan men rather than by the bride and other women. In both rituals, however, the tent marks the space as liminal. During the *sadaka* Ismkhan are believed to traverse the boundary between humans and spirits to make contact with the spiritual world.

After circling the tent, an Ismkhan man leads the group in prayer, reciting the *fatiḥa* (the opening verse of the Qur'an) and asking for blessings, all in Moroccan Arabic. Although in everyday life the Ismkhan speak the dominant Amazigh language (Tamazight), the recitation of the prayer marks the

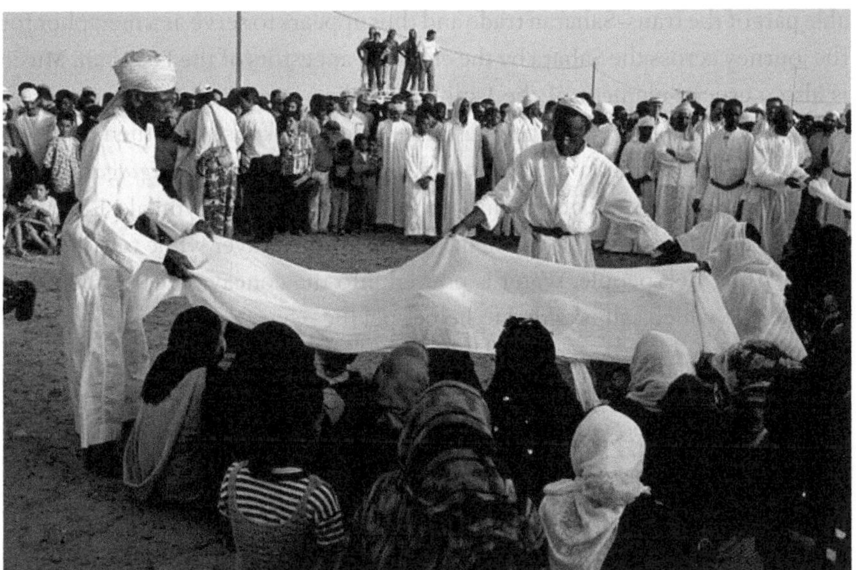

Figure 6.4. An Ismkhan healing ceremony in Khamlia, 2002.

switch from Tamazight to Arabic, from the profane to the sacred. Men next perform an animal sacrifice, which is then followed by a healing ceremony, in which Ismkhan men first ask all sick men, women, and children (both Ismkhan and non-Ismkhan) to come to the area in front of the tent. Ismkhan men are known as particularly adept at healing illnesses caused by the spirits called *jnoun,* which contributes to their relatively high status. Like other Ait Khabbash and Amazigh, the Ismkhan attribute many illnesses to possession by the *jnoun,* and they invoke the *baraka* of their bodies to expel them. The Ismkhan healing ceremony that follows focuses on the heads of the sick, considered the most vulnerable part of the body. The heads of the people who come forth to be healed are covered with white turbans belonging to Ismkhan men (Fig. 6.4). It is believed that this allows the head to absorb *baraka* directly from the Ismkhan. The color white is associated with purity and the turban with honor. As previously mentioned, the Tamazight expression *tbedda tarezziyt-nnek* (which can be translated "your turban is standing up") describes an honorable man.

The healing ceremony itself begins with Ismkhan men eating a morsel of salt to purify their bodies and enhance their ability to expel the *jnoun* from the sick. Not only are white substances such as salt often used as protection against the *jnoun* in southeastern Morocco (as discussed earlier), but salt was a valuable part of the trans-Saharan trade and thus appears to serve as a metaphor for the journey across the Sahara by the enslaved ancestors of the Ismkhan. Music is also a crucial element of the Ismkhan healing ceremony. As the Ismkhan men circle around the sick people three times clockwise and then counter-clockwise, one Ismkhan man beats on *ginga* and another on *tagingat*, which are accompanied by the other Ismkhan men playing metal cymbals. Everyone plays an instrument except one man, who leads the prayer while touching the heads of the sick people. Water is poured into the concave area of the metal cymbals, to which salt is added to help repel the *jnoun*. Each man dips his finger, transferring his *baraka* into the water, which is then consumed by the sick people. The salt in the water and the *baraka* from the bodies of the Ismkhan are believed to be powerful enough to remove the *jnoun* causing the people's illnesses.

Ismkhan are not only skilled at expelling *jnoun;* they also have beneficial relationships with another category of spirits called *mlouk* (singular *malk*). Rather than exorcising the *mlouk*, they are encouraged to enter people's bodies, allowing the possessed person to placate the spirit by performing a dance (called *ḥadra*, meaning "trance") to a particular rhythm, wearing colors that the *malk* prefers, burning certain types of perfumed incense, and consuming particular types of foods. Not every Ismkhan has a relationship with a *malk*, but those who do are required to placate the spirit by occasionally performing the *ḥadra*. If they do not do this, they risk a life filled with misfortune, since a positive relationship with a *malk* guarantees good health and general prosperity. When a person hears a particular rhythm played on the drums and metal cymbals, that individual's *malk* possesses his or her body, causing the person to perform the *ḥadra*. This continues until the *malk* has been satisfied, abruptly leaving the body and causing the person to fall to the ground.

The origin of the *mlouk* and the act of possession-trance is unknown, but, as noted by John Tremearne (1914) when he described the religious beliefs of the descendants of enslaved Africans in Tunisia, it appears to be similar to Hausa *bori* ceremonies. The Hausa believe that spirits enter *bori* participants and control them. Like the *mlouk* of the Ismkhan, each *bori* spirit has its own personality and requires the follower to wear certain clothes and perform particular trance dances that express the disposition of the spirit.[3] Possession by spirits is common among groups in Sudanic Africa, and it is probable that the ancestors of the Ismkhan brought memories of these practices with them across the Sahara. Similar possession occurs during the *holey-hoore* of the Songhai in northeastern Mali (Rouch 1960). In the modern nation of the Sudan, spirit possession and trance are also features of the *tumbura* and the *ʒar* ceremonies (Makris 2000; Boddy 1989).

During the *ḥadra* Ismkhan men who wish to achieve trance stand within a circle of male musicians. Women can also be possessed by the *mlouk*, but social conventions regarding female modesty prevent them from performing the *ḥadra* in public. Women on the verge of going into a trance can sometimes be seen running from the public area so that they can satisfy their *malk* away from the watchful eyes of the crowd.

Although Ismkhan men and women continue to refer to themselves by using the term "slaves," they often told me that they were offended by Ait Khabbash references to their old slaving practices. One event that takes place during the three-day *sadaka* directly reflects the Ismkhan's history as slaves but symbolically turns it on its head. After the *ḥadra* is complete, Ismkhan men act out a slave market and participate in the fictive buying of children. Both Ismkhan and non-Ismkhan parents may request that their children be "bought" by the Ismkhan,[4] which refers to the process of having a child come under the Ismkhan's protection by transferring *baraka* to it. For example, if several of a woman's children have died, she might choose to sell her remaining child to the Ismkhan to protect it. Ismkhan then bid on the child, with the price going higher and higher until the symbolic purchase is made. The Ismkhan present the mother of the child with three small pieces of wood, each representing a different Ismkhan name, and she is told to choose one by which the child must be called for the following three days. Unlike the Ait Khabbash, who often use Amazigh names such as Addi, Moha, and Hugga, the Ismkhan only use particular names that are considered Arab, such as Mbark, Salm, Faraji, Boujamaa, and Bilal for boys and Mbarka, Hajjuba, Oumlkher, and Oumlaid for girls, to align themselves more closely to Islam. These few names are given both to newborn Ismkhan children and to the children fictively sold to the Ismkhan. Although non-Ismkhan children who have been sold may return to their birth name after the three days, many of them choose to use their Ismkhan name throughout their lives. In any case, the children are referred to by the local community as children of the Ismkhan throughout their lives, and each year they are expected to send a small offering to the Ismkhan at the time of the festival. These children are the only non-Ismkhan allowed to participate in Ismkhan activities.

While the art forms practiced by Ismkhan reflect their identity as a distinct group among the Ait Khabbash, the art forms created and used by Ismkhan women are the same as those of other Ait Khabbash women and unite them as

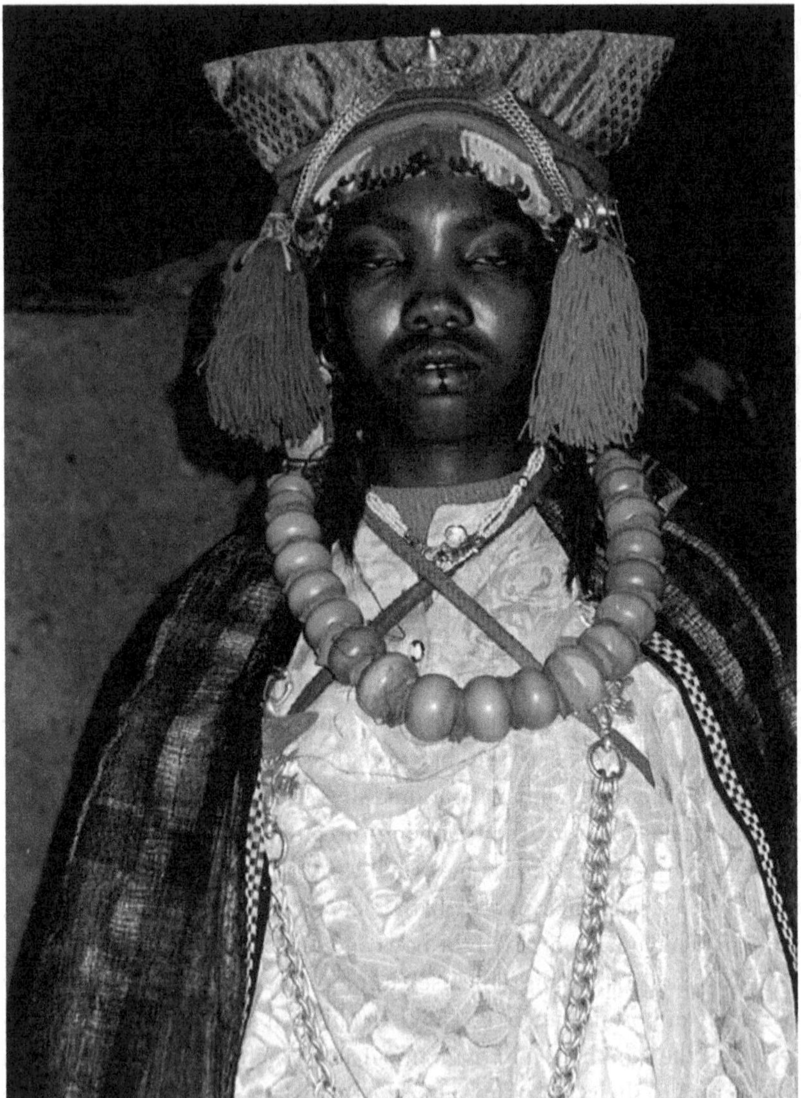

Figure 6.5. An Ismkhan bride in Khamlia, 1997.

a single people. As can be seen in many of the figures used here and in earlier chapters, Ismkhan women weave the same textiles as the Ait Khabbash and wear the same embroidered head coverings. Ismkhan women also take the major role in weddings, which are almost identical to those of other Ait Khabbash, and brides are dressed in similar red silk headdresses and wear silver jewelry and amber necklaces (Fig. 6.5).

While many aspects of Ismkhan *ahidous* performances are similar to those of the Ait Khabbash, a notable exception takes place in the song called *asserked* performed by Ait Khabbash men in honor of the bride and introduced in Chapter Five. During *asserked* men sing for the bride in her tent, expressing their wishes that she be granted a joyous and bountiful married life. The Ait Khabbash lyrics call for the bride to be given numerous gifts that include not only horses and camels but slaves, and Ismkhan refuse to perform this song.

> *Rjiy Rebbi d Nebi ad am kin a tislit,*
> *Meyat naga ayd itggan rhil-nnem.*
> *Meyat bagra ad-t-haleb-t i warraw-nnem.*
> *Meya n tekdift ayd itggan usan-nnem.*
> *A tislit lwajeb ad am ttugin ak-wen sey a krad ismkhan.*
> *Yan ad am ẓẓaden ar am ttagmen ar tsseksa-t sin aliwa.*
>
> [I hope God and the Prophet give you, oh bride, . . .
> 100 camels to move your belongings . . .
> 100 cows to milk for your sons . . .
> 100 carpets to be your spreads . . .
> Oh bride, the essentials will be done for you, we are
>   buying you three slaves.
> One grinds and brings water for you, and you make
>   two your shepherds.]

These lyrics continue to be performed at other Ait Khabbash weddings even though the Ait Khabbash no longer practice slavery. During an Ismkhan wedding that I attended in Khamlia in 1997, Fatima, an Ismkhan woman, explained:

> We don't like *asserked* because it mentions giving the bride slaves. Why are we going to sing that? We do not perform *asserked,* but we sing to the Prophet, which is better.

During Ismkhan weddings, rather than perform *asserked* sitting in front of the bride, one man plays *ginga* and another *tagingat*. The rest play *qraqsh* while performing *ahidous,* repeating a single phrase; they are later joined by women, including the bride (Fig. 6.6):

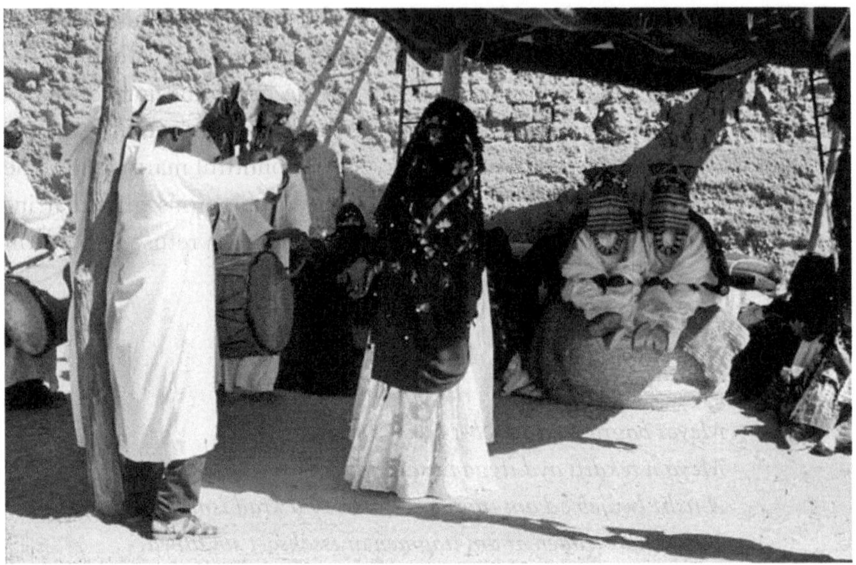

Figure 6.6. Ismkhan in Khamlia perform for the bride, 1997.

Ah ma, ya ma, Allah mṣalli ala Nebi.
[Oh mother, oh mother, God's prayer for the Prophet.]

Rather than recalling their painful history as slaves, this singing of praise to the Prophet reminds the audience of their connection to Islam and the *baraka* of Bilal. In addition, this song performed in honor of the bride uses the word "mother" to refer to their homeland in Sudanic Africa. Although Ismkhan men's dress and healing ceremonies are integral in establishing their connection to the Prophet, women are not absent from identity discourse. Rather, women create the artistic forms that connect them to the Ait Khabbash and at the same time allegorically connect the Ismkhan to their Sudanese motherland. Thus both Ismkhan men and women play a public role in the construction and maintenance of group identity, uniting them with the Ait Khabbash but also expressing their difference.

SEVEN

Contemporary Amazigh Arts

GIVING MATERIAL FORM TO AMAZIGH CONSCIOUSNESS

Amazigh arts in many areas of Morocco have drastically changed since Moroccan independence from French colonization in 1956. As discussed earlier, by the 1960s the majority of Ait Khabbash had abandoned their nomadic lifestyles, settling in towns where Arabic is widely spoken. The result was a dramatic change in Amazigh women's lives and the transformation of Amazigh aesthetic expression. While many forms of Amazigh women's arts, such as tattoos, gradually disappeared, at the same time these arts have been given new life by contemporary Moroccan painters. The painters, both Imazighen and Arab, have turned to the artistic heritage of the Imazighen to create a new painting style that embraces Morocco's cultural and ethnic diversity. These mostly male artists have appropriated indigenous Amazigh art forms and motifs intimately connected to women in their desire to express their postcolonial Moroccan identity, a national identity that is increasingly tolerant of its Amazigh population. These painters pay tribute to the artistic legacy of Amazigh women.

This chapter distinguishes between Amazigh and non-Amazigh contemporary painters because contemporary Amazigh painters remain virtually unknown even within Morocco. Their anonymity is tied to the country's colonial heritage and governmental politics of the Moroccan nation. The French protectorate government, in order to monitor Moroccan economic activity and encourage economic independence from France, restructured Morocco's arts and craft industry (Clancy-Smith 1999; Irbouh 2001). Concerned that artistic production was in decline, they established standards of production to regulate indigenous artistic activity. For example, between 1926 and 1956 Moroccan textile production was reorganized by Prosper Ricard (1923–1927) by region and ethnic group; weavers of a particular group were told to weave carpets and blankets using predetermined colors and motifs that would supposedly represent their group and standardize textile production.[1] Not only did the French thus influence indigenous arts, like textiles, but the French protectorate government also opened art academies, where Moroccans studied European painterly techniques and a European-based history of art. Although painting existed prior to the arrival of Europeans in Morocco, as noted by Toni Maraini (1990: 213), it was primarily restricted to architectural decoration, manuscript illumination, and ceramics.

After Morocco gained its independence from France in 1956, a generation of Moroccan painters who studied European painting abroad grappled with issues of identity, attempting to create a painting style free from European influence. These artists worked according to nationalistic ideas promoted by the Moroccan government and created an artistic style influenced by Morocco's rich artisan industry (Irbouh 1998: 50). They were invited to exhibit in Morocco's museums and galleries and were commonly featured in books about Moroccan contemporary art. By sharp contrast, painters who incorporated Amazigh motifs and designs on their canvases with the intention of consciously promoting their Amazigh heritage were marginalized and rarely invited to exhibit.[2] Their art was considered political and taboo, since any distinction between Imazighen and Arabs was viewed as politically charged and reminiscent of the French colonial attempt to divide Arabs and Imazighen by institutionalizing differences between them. After independence in 1956, the Moroccan government suppressed public expressions of Morocco's Amazigh heritage and instead promoted a homogenous Arab identity for the nation.

Ironically, artists without distinctive Amazigh names or those who did not use their art deliberately to promote their heritage freely incorporated Amazigh motifs into their paintings, achieving considerable fame both within Morocco and beyond. One such painter is Farid Belkahia (b. 1934), one of the most prolific contemporary Moroccan artists, who has been inspired by Amazigh tattoos, jewelry, and textiles. Between 1954 and 1962 Belkahia studied in Europe, returning to Morocco in 1962 and becoming director of the École des Beaux-Arts in Casablanca. Rather than teaching his students European artistic techniques based on three-dimensional representations of the human body and objects from nature, however, he had them study indigenous Moroccan artistic forms such as Amazigh carpets, jewelry, calligraphy, and metalwork techniques. Belkahia himself began to work with indigenous media such as copper leaf, creating dynamic forms that burst out of the conventional four-sided rectangular canvas (Benchemsi 1995: 15). Eventually Belkahia turned to animal skin, stretching the skins over amorphously shaped wooden frames and then painting and dying the skin with natural pigments such as saffron, henna, and sumac to create dynamic compositions as large as six feet tall and five feet wide.[3]

Through his choice of materials, colors, and forms, Belkahia intentionally tried to challenge the dichotomy between artist and artisan. In 1980 he created a series of canvases in the form of a hand decorated with black, deep red, and orange geometric motifs reminiscent of Moroccan women's henna designs. In his *Main (Hand,* featured in Fig. 7.1), Belkahia expressly incorporated the Tifinagh script, using six Tifinagh letters to write a Moroccan Arab woman's name (Saâida) immediately above the centrally placed eye motif.

The Tifinagh script is an Amazigh writing form believed to be related to the ancient Punic script and used primarily by Tuareg women and blacksmiths to write short, intimate messages on household objects and jewelry. The Tuareg are an Amazigh population who live in the Saharan and Sahalean regions of Mali, Algeria, Libya, Burkina Faso, and Niger. It is believed that all Imazighen used Tifinagh in the past; but the Tuareg, the least Arabized of all the Imazighen in Africa, are the only Amazigh group to have retained a written language. Tifinagh letters consist of circles and geometric forms reminiscent of Amazigh women's textile and tattoo motifs (Fig. 7.2 shows the logo of the Royal Institute of Amazigh Culture, using its version of the Tifinagh script). Although the script has not been used for hundreds of years in North Africa, Amazigh activists in Morocco and Algeria adopted Tifinagh to write poetry, songs, and political slogans promoting their Amazigh heritage. Until recently, the public display of Tifinagh was considered to be a politically charged act of aggression against the Moroccan government. In fact, one of the reasons the government gave for arresting members of the group Tilelli in Errachidia in 1994 is that their political banners featured the Tifinagh script.

I would argue that Belkahia certainly realized the political volatility of the Tifinagh script. He confounded this by camouflaging the Tifinagh letters with similar geometric and circular forms, such as repeating triangles, diamond shapes, spirals, arrows, and oval shapes reminiscent of eyes. Hence the Tifinagh letters were reduced to pure decoration, removing the script from its historical and cultural origins and distancing Belkahia from the potential political implications associated with the Tamazight language and Tifinagh. He further did this by spelling out an Arab woman's name rather than an Amazigh one. This is one of the only works where he consciously copied letters from

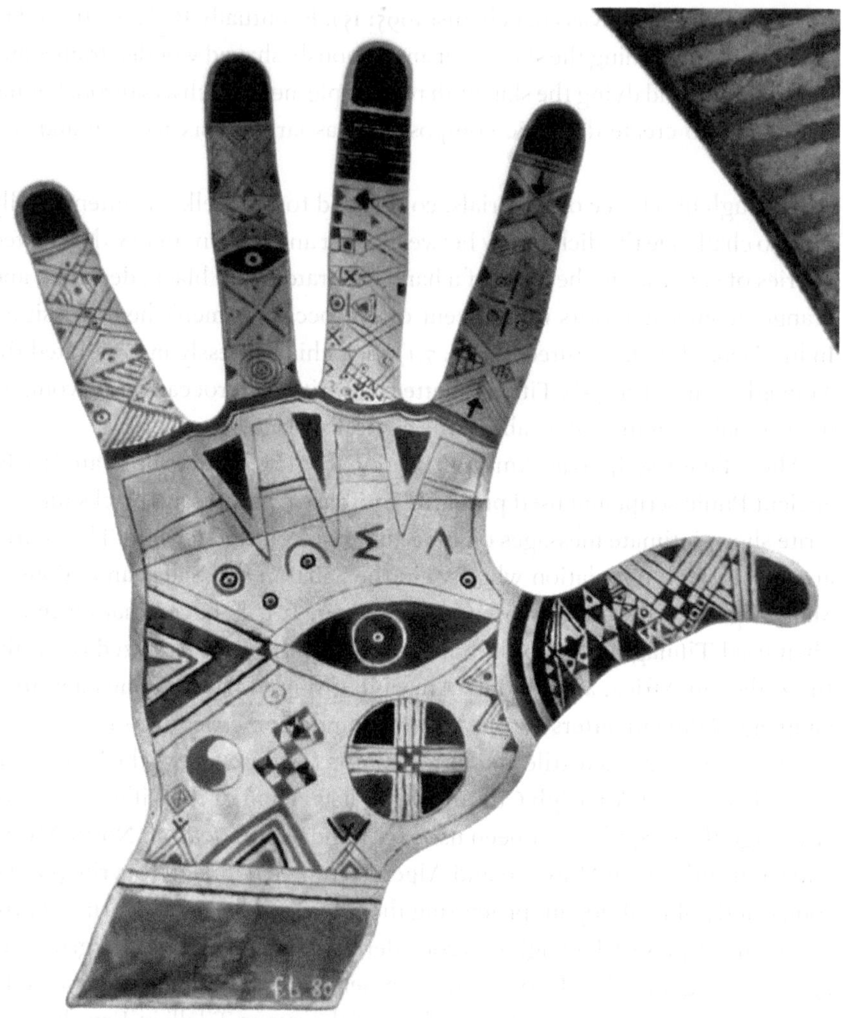

Figure 7.1. Farid Belkahia, Main *(Hand, 1980), henna on skin, 152 cm × 124.5 cm. Collection of the artist. Photo by Abigail Rolland.*

the Tifinagh alphabet onto his skin canvases. Belkahia believes that the geometric symbols and signs that he commonly uses, while similar to those found in Amazigh textiles, ceramics, and tattoos as well as in Tifinagh, are in fact symbols common to many cultures.[4] In other words, Belkahia does not place the motifs that adorn his leather canvas in any particular historical, cultural, or temporal context but uses what he feels are universal artistic symbols that transgress culture and time. As an artist, he sees himself as an intermediary who creates a sense of continuity between the past and the present, bridging and connecting cultures.

Belkahia appropriates an artistic form typically associated with Moroccan women: the henna-decorated hand. He uses henna to adorn his skin canvas, with the goal of using precolonial Moroccan artistic media. These factors coupled with his utilization of leather and Amazigh-inspired motifs represent Belkahia's attempt to create Moroccan art free from colonial influence. His interpretation of Morocco's postcolonial identity as a multicultural pluralistic society does not confront the vision of nationhood created by the Moroccan monarchy, because he reduces Amazigh artistic influence to decorative surface pattern. The Tifinagh script is presented as nonthreatening, apolitical folkloric decoration.

The Moroccan artist Mohamed Nabili (b. 1952) also adorns his canvases with Tifinagh. Nabili, who now lives in Morocco, spent more than twenty years living and working in France. He identifies himself as a "true" Moroccan with a mixed Amazigh and Arab heritage but also considers himself a universalist, who borrows symbols common to many indigenous cultures.

Nabili spent numerous years researching Tuareg art. The rough texture of his sand-covered canvases (such as *Untitled*, 2001) evokes the landscape of the Tuareg's Sahara homeland, and the blue suggests their indigo-dyed clothing (Fig. 7.3).[5] Tuareg men are often referred to as the "blue men" because they cover their faces except for the eyes with a twenty-foot-long indigo-dyed turban (called a *tagelmoust*), which stains their skin blue (Fig. 2.11). Nabili uses

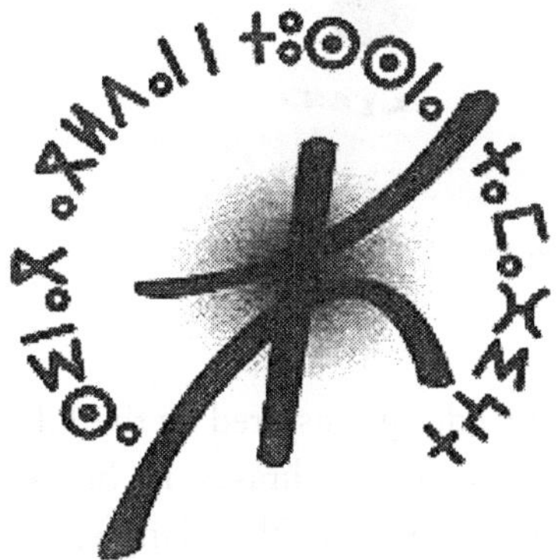

Figure 7.2. The official logo of the Royal Institute of Amazigh Culture (IRCAM). Image courtesy of IRCAM.

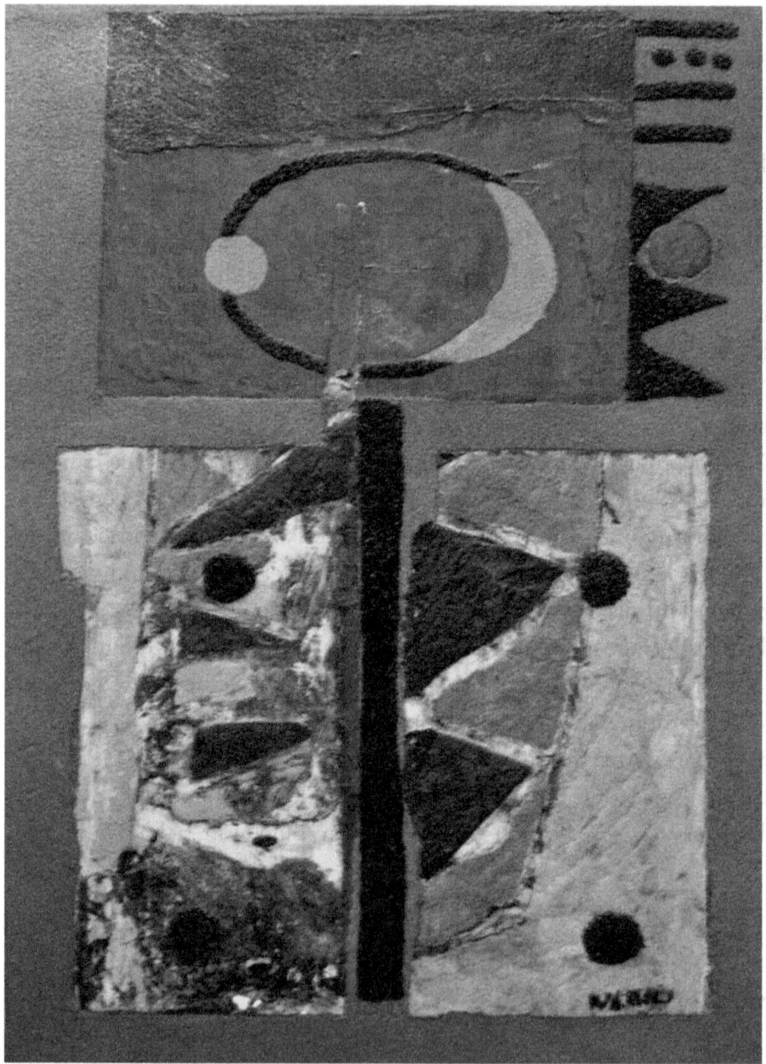

Figure 7.3. Mohamed Nabili, Untitled *(2001), mixed media, 100 cm × 71 cm.*
Photo by Abigail Rolland.

thick lines created from black sand to re-create a design inspired by the Tifi-nagh script. Rather than use Tifinagh to write words or phrases, he breaks the Tifinagh letters down into their basic elements, such as the triangle, the zigzag line, the circle, and the dot. The Tifinagh letters are fused and inter-mingled to create an abstract surface pattern. The circle painted on the top half of the canvas appears to have a full moon on one side and a crescent moon on the other, suggesting the cycle of life. This circular form with its long black stem is at the same time anthropomorphic and is evocative of Tuareg silver jewelry. The long vertical black line has two round dots on either side, however, reminiscent of an Amazigh woman's chin tattoos (Fig. 2.5). Nabili's use of Amazigh motifs formed from sand also implies a metaphoric relationship between women and the earth.

An examination of the art of Belkahia and Nabili reflects the paradoxical situation of Amazigh art in Morocco today. Moroccan artists who freely appropriate Amazigh imagery from its original context and turn it into decorative folkloric surface patterns are invited to exhibit in Morocco's museums and art galleries. Artists who use their paintings to promote their Amazigh heritage, however, remain virtually unknown. This contradiction is slowly changing due to the political actions of Amazigh artists and the creation of the Royal Institute of Amazigh Culture (IRCAM) in 2001 by King Muhammad VI. This royal declaration was the first official recognition of Morocco's Amazigh population and played an important role in enhancing public visibility of Amazigh issues. Amazigh painters have recently discovered new political freedom to express their Amazigh identity in Morocco.

Amazigh painters, writers, and poets are feverishly working, turning to the Amazigh visual and performing art forms once commonly found throughout Morocco for inspiration. By appropriating Amazigh women's visual vocabulary to give material form to their own conceptions of Morocco's Amazigh heritage, contemporary Amazigh painters recognize the association of women, art, and Amazigh identity. This is especially the case for artists in southeastern Morocco, who have been engaged in aggressive political activity to promote their Amazigh heritage. For example, Omar Taws, a male poet and political activist from Goulmima who had both friends and relatives arrested during the now infamous 1994 protest held by the group Tilelli, valorizes women in his poetry. He pays homage to the intimate connection between women and Amazigh identity in his poem entitled "Mma" ("Mother"):

> *Iɣli-nw da t-ttiniɣ s wul*
> *S wul-inw iɣeddigen agensu-nw*
> *Ad iriry ad iniɣ isefra*
> *S wawal netteḍ g uɣu n mma*
> *A mma-nw a tenna yi-yurun*
> *A mma-nw a tenn' aɣ issegman*
> *Tusimt aneɣgum a-nemɣur*

Temḍimt tamara yḥerran
Ussan nnem tarezzift ayd gan
Mar ad di-nxitr mar a-nili
G uyenn'akw iḥlan tgid-aɣ amur
G uyenn'akw illan tgid-aɣ ili
Udem nnem amezduɣ agensu nneɣ
Idammen nnem d wininneɣ yuwen
Tasa t-tayri nnem gant-aɣ afud
Nedda g ubrid tgid-aɣ asidd
Ad iriɣ ad iniɣ isefra
S wawal netteḍ g uɣu n mma
Ussan nnem is nra ad ḥlun
Aɣbalu n tudert ayd aɣ-tgid
Xef wakal g di-temmɣid a yemma
A nezzu digs iledjigen ad jjun
T-tirrugza neddu s afella
Xef tmazirt a-nili tawuri
Afud nneɣ ayd tgid a yemma
Asidd nneɣ ayd tgid a yemma
Awal nneɣ am mma ayd gan
Akal nneɣ am mma ayd gan
Tarwa nnem ayd nga a yemma
Tayri nneɣ ur tedrus, a yemma!

[I sing my songs from my heart.
With my pure heart inside of me.
I sing and recite poems . . .
With words we nursed from our mother's milk.
Oh mother who gave birth to me.
Oh mother who raised me.
You carried the responsibility to help us grow.
You tasted the bitterness of life.
Your days are a gift to us.
So we would grow and exist.
From everything you gave us a portion.
In everything you included us.
Your face lives inside of us.

Your blood and ours are one.
Your liver and your love are our knee (support).[6]
We are on the road, and you are our light.
I sing and recite poems . . .
With words we nursed from our mother's milk.
Your days, we want them to be good.
You are the source of life for us.
Oh mother, on our land . . .
We plant flowers to smell good.
Courageously we advance.
For our Amazigh heritage we work tirelessly.
Mother, you are our knee (support).
Mother, you are our light.
Our word is like our mother.
Our land is like our mother.
Mother, we are your children.
Our love for you is not small!][7]
(Taws 1996: 6)

This poem by Taws appears in his collection of poetry titled *Iledjigen n yigenna,* meaning "Flowers of the Sky." When he wrote this poem in 1992 using the Tamazight language, the social climate in Morocco was such that the poem would have been viewed as politically charged. He raised the funds necessary to self-publish his collection of poems, another political action.

Taws not only valorizes women as the keepers of the Amazigh culture; he also demonstrates the primacy of language in the construction of Amazigh identity, reflecting the goal of preserving and recognizing Amazigh languages. Taws writes that the Imazighen metaphorically receive the Tamazight language while breast-feeding, creating a link between women (specifically mothers), language, and Amazigh identity. He prefers to use poetry rather than prose because poetry is an artistic form historically familiar to the Imazighen. His poem draws from the oral poetry typically performed at Amazigh weddings, circumcisions, and birth ceremonies in order to demonstrate that Amazigh culture is "not only something touristic or something for museums." Amazigh poetry and art, he states, "need to be seen as a living culture and a culture of the future."[8]

Taws, who lives near the rapidly expanding city of Errachidia, is acutely aware of the rapid urbanization influencing the Ait Khabbash and other Amazigh people's lives. Drought and the construction of a dam outside of Errachidia in the 1970s blocked the natural flow of local rivers. The resulting decline in grazing land caused many Ait Khabbash families to sell their livestock and move to Errachidia, the economic capital of the region.[9] Many extended families have been broken up when men moved out of their parents' homes with their wives and children, something that rarely happened in the past. Public education became readily available in the 1970s, resulting in the education of Amazigh children in Arabic. Children speak Arabic on a daily basis at school and to their new neighbors, who are often Arab rather than Imazighen. The result is that many children do not speak Tamazight at all.

As economic subsistence changed, a woman's status became less dependent on her ability to help the family economically through her labor. Women have come to work inside their homes, relying on their male relatives to shop for them in the market, buying vegetables and meat.[10] Women do not fetch water from wells or firewood for cooking; men pay for the running water and bottled gas used in their homes, as Ait Khabbash men find paying jobs in the Moroccan military and elsewhere.[11]

As the Ait Khabbash have become more urbanized, everyday dress has also changed. Men no longer wear handmade wool hooded gowns, instead buying them from the local market. After Moroccan independence from France, Jewish silversmiths moved to urban areas in northern Morocco or to the newly created nation of Israel. In the last decade, most Amazigh women have sold the silver jewelry and the amber necklaces that their mothers and grandmothers wore to European collectors and tourist shops, preferring to wear gold jewelry. Tattoos that were once important symbols of Amazigh identity have disappeared except in the case of the elderly. The Ait Khabbash women who left rural areas to settle in Errachidia or other large towns have assimilated with the Arab population by remaining secluded in their homes; if they do go out, they often wear unembroidered black coverings or the hooded gown (*jellaba*) instead of their embroidered head coverings.

The political activist, artist, and art teacher Muhand Saidi firmly believes that Amazigh women must not forget the traditions of the past; but as a high school teacher in Errachidia he has firsthand knowledge of how rapidly young Amazigh women's lives are changing. He often teaches women in his local Amazigh association how to embroider Tifinagh letters on white cotton cloth. Saidi recognizes that most young Amazigh women today prefer embroidery to carpet weaving, and he hopes to persuade them to embroider Tifinagh letters rather than using the popular Arab styles of embroidery from northern Morocco.[12]

Despite such changes in the arts of everyday life, earlier chapters have shown that arts associated with weddings are slow to change. Weddings are a time when sexuality and reproduction are central concerns, essential to the survival of their ethnic group into the future, since the preservation of one's ethnic group continues to be a concern. An Ait Khabbash bride, even though she may live in a concrete house in the city of Erfoud, still stays in a tent during the three-day wedding ceremony, covering her face with the red headdress for those three days. She also typically wears the amber and silver jewelry (once worn by her mother and grandmother on a daily basis) during the wedding ceremony, although she may remove it on the third day to wear a European-inspired white wedding gown. The comparison of two wedding photos, one from the 1950s (Fig. 3.6) and the other from 1996 (Fig. 5.11), demonstrates how little bridal attire has been modified in more than fifty years, while daily dress (compare the women flanking the brides) has significantly changed. Because women no longer wear silver and amber jewelry after they are married, the groom borrows it from friends and returns it after the wedding is completed. As previously discussed, *ahidous* performances, however, are often sung in Tashelhit, the Amazigh language of southwestern Morocco, rather than in their local language, Tamazight. Ait Khabbash girls often dance to popular music cassettes sung in Tashelhit. The Ait Khabbash still conceptualize their identity on a local scale and desire to maintain their ethnic purity; however, they are at the same time linking themselves to other Imazighen and creating a more global identity.

Mohamed Mallal, a painter, singer, poet, art teacher, and Amazigh activist living in the southern Moroccan city of Ouarzazate, argues that such changes are a necessary part of life. His fear is that Amazigh culture is increasingly viewed as an ancient folkloric culture isolated in remote mountain villages without any usefulness in the contemporary world. He feels that if the Amazigh language and culture can reach a larger population and be commonly featured on the radio and television, for example, then it can become more readily integrated into contemporary life.[13]

Mallal's art reinforces his political views, suggesting that the Amazigh people need to touch a broader audience and recognize their kinship across national boundaries. His paintings promote a transnational Amazigh identity that connects to other Imazighen groups in northern Africa. For example, he often paints images of the Tuareg and refers to them as his brothers in his

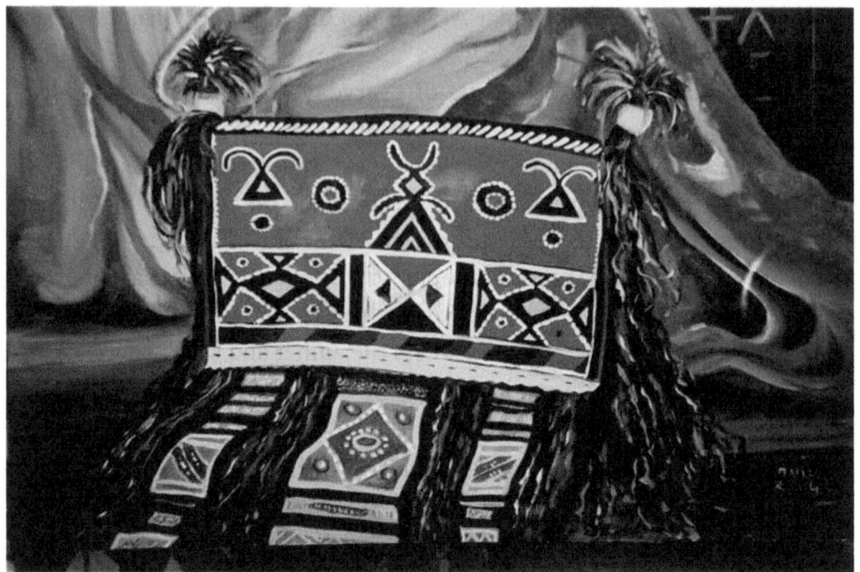

Figure 7.4. Mohamed Mallal, Untitled *(2004), acrylic on canvas, 92 cm × 80 cm. Collection of the artist.*

poetry. In Figure 7.4, he depicts a leather bag immediately recognizable as Tuareg. Mallal perceives himself as part of a large Amazigh community that crosses national borders.[14]

Mallal's painting reinforces the kinship he feels with the Tuareg, who are a minority population within the countries where they live and are struggling for cultural survival.[15] He typically includes the faint letters written in the Tifinagh script on the top right corners of his canvases. Although the Tifinagh letters chosen by Mallal do not spell out particular words, they symbolize his Amazigh identity. The presence of an indigo blue cloth draped behind the leather bag further reinforces his association with the Tuareg. Tuareg leather bags are made by women, and the motifs that he uses to adorn the bag further evoke women's arts, such as the large central triangle common to Amazigh women's arts throughout Africa.

Mallal, like most Amazigh activists, recognizes that Imazighen living in rural areas must be educated in order to increase their political visibility and access to Morocco's economic resources. In the past Amazigh children often began school with no knowledge of Arabic; because classes were taught entirely in this language, students often felt frustrated and abandoned their education. Amazigh activists fought tirelessly for the introduction of Tamazight into Moroccan classrooms, so that their language would be given equal status with Arabic and to help Amazigh children make a smooth transition into school. In September 2004, 317 primary schools began teaching Tamazight to first-year pupils, and the Moroccan government's aim is to teach Tamazight in all schools at all levels within ten years.[16] Amazigh activists feel that the introduction of Tamazight into schools is the first step to ensure the survival of their culture into the future.

Amazigh painters typically incorporate Tifinagh into their canvases, but for them Tifinagh represents more than abstract patterns and folkloric decoration. This is the only form of writing that some Amazigh artists know, and it allows them to express their Amazigh identity. For example, Mohammed Mallal taught his sister, Fatima Mellal (who never attended school and only speaks Tamazight), how to write Tamazight using Tifinagh. Mellal, like most women in her natal village of Tamellalt in southern Morocco, was a carpet weaver. When she initially learned Tifinagh, she began to weave Tifinagh letters into her carpets. In 1998, at the age of thirty, she turned from textile weaving to painting (Fig. 7.5). Mellal turned to painting because she felt that her paintings could touch a broader audience than her woven carpets. This was

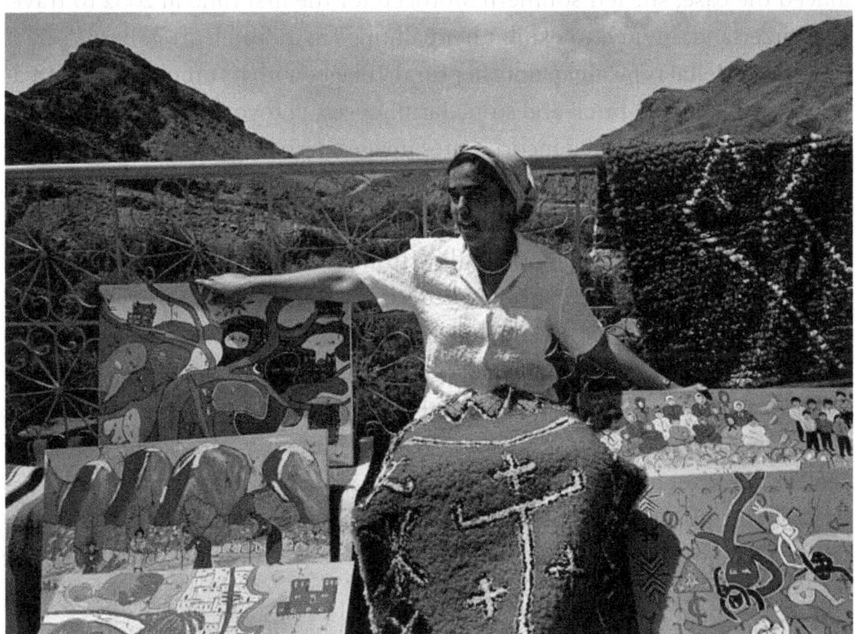

Figure 7.5. Fatima Mellal with her art. Photo courtesy of Fatima Mellal, 2002.

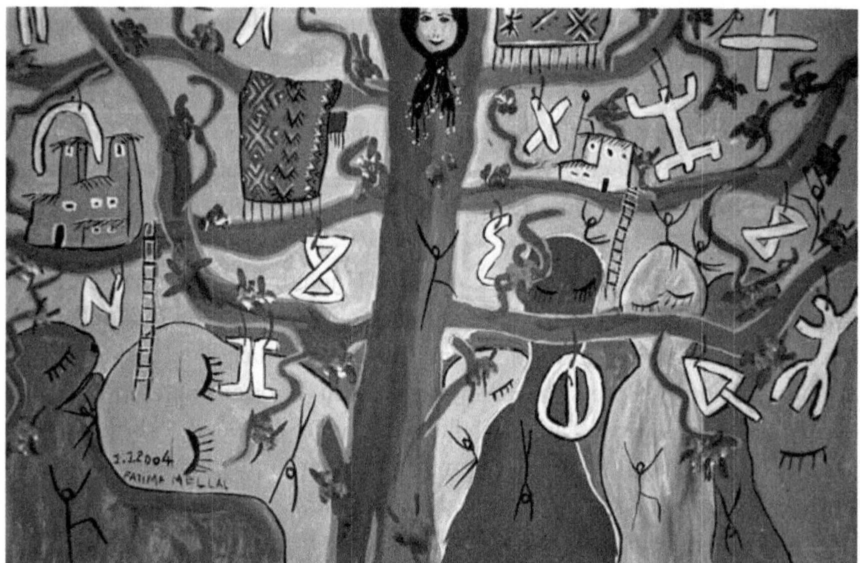

Figure 7.6. Fatima Mellal, Untitled *(2004), acrylic on canvas, 92 cm × 80 cm. Collection of the artist.*

indeed the case; she left southern Morocco for the first time in 2002 to travel to Switzerland, invited to exhibit her paintings in a Zurich art gallery.[17]

Fatima Mellal typically paints her rural village, with its unique rock formations, fortified mud-brick and stone farmhouses, and young children playing in the nearby river. Mellal incorporates images derived from the surrounding landscape as well as colors and motifs from woven textiles (Fig. 7.6). A tree is featured in the center of the composition, topped with a female head wearing a black scarf, with silver sequins dangling from its ends. Bright red carpets with Tifinagh motifs and other geometric designs hang from the tree's branches. She specifically includes the Tifinagh letter *Z*, the central character in the word "Amazigh." This letter has been adopted by the Amazigh movement to symbolize freedom and is also found on the Amazigh flag first presented at the Amazigh World Congress in the Canary Islands in 1997. The same letter is the central character of the IRCAM logo (Fig. 7.2) and one of the thirty-nine letters of the Tifinagh script adopted by IRCAM. Mellal also incorporates a triangular form inspired by a woman's brooch that floats in the bottom right of her mystical landscape.

Mellal's art provides some insight into the future of Amazigh women's arts; however, female painters like Fatima Mellal are rare. Most Amazigh painters are male, but they also pay tribute to Amazigh women on their canvases. Mellal paints a tree with large overhanging branches in the middle of her canvas and transforms it into a woman to express the central role that women play in giving birth to and maintaining Amazigh culture.

Mohamed Ziyani, a self-taught male artist living in Tinghir, also pays tribute to Amazigh women in his canvases. In his acrylic canvas from 2004 entitled *Tudert* (meaning "Life" in Tamazight), Ziyani divides the face of his anthropomorphic triangular figure into two halves: male and female (Fig. 7.7). He paints the female side with a brooch or fibula on her shoulder and rain falling behind her, making a connection between women and fertility. Additionally, the female half is accompanied by women's tattoo designs floating above blue waves of water at the bottom of the canvas. On the male side, Ziyani draws inspiration from the motifs that adorn the region's mud-brick architecture, which he paints on the bottom left of his canvas.[18]

This discussion of Amazigh painters in Morocco illustrates how artists look across national borders yet remain regionalized at the same time, drawing inspiration from the ancient and the contemporary as well as the local and the global. Hamid Kachmar, an Amazigh artist transplanted from Goulmina to the United States, demonstrates the multifarious nature of contemporary Amazigh identity. Kachmar, who has been studying art at Howard University since 2003, expresses his heritage through his paintings. He incorporates motifs and symbols reminiscent of his deceased mother to represent the collective Amazigh visual memory. Kachmar dutifully promotes the Amazigh culture in the United States, explaining that he paradoxically "had to travel to the occident in order to come back" and return to his Amazigh origins.[19]

In his 2005 painting *Imi n war imi* (Mouth of the Mouthless), Kachmar covered the canvas with pieces of African barkcloth that he sewed together with exaggeratedly large stitches to create the sense of an aged and restituted surface, suggesting the antiquity of the Amazigh culture and its struggle to survive (Fig. 7.8). He dyed the barkcloth with natural pigments made from henna, madder, and ground walnut root to create warm red and ochre hues reminiscent of the earth tones found in southeastern Morocco. Kachmar transformed the canvas into the door of a *qsar* (mud-brick village typical of southeastern Morocco, called *ighrem* in Tamazight) and added a metal panel at the bottom left with the words *tagurt n tilelli* (door of freedom) engraved in Tifinagh.

The center of the painting features a large oval face. The face, which has one large elliptical eye and one small circular eye, pays tribute to his much-

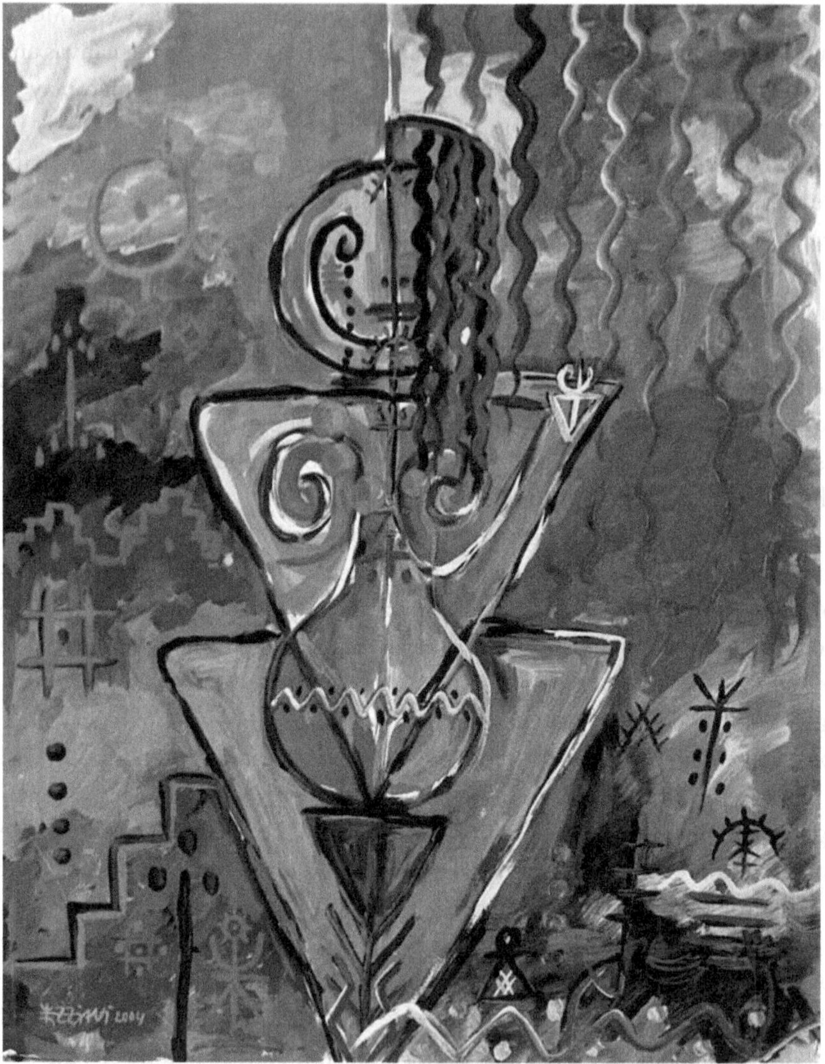

Figure 7.7. Mohamed Ziyani, Tudert *(2004), acrylic on canvas, 65 cm × 50 cm.
Collection of the artist.*

loved mother, who was blind in one eye. The two sets of three parallel dots
running vertically at the bottom of the face (where her chin would be) further
indicate that this figure represents a tattooed Amazigh woman. Her face is
covered with various Amazigh symbols inspired by both Tifinagh and the textiles that Kachmar watched his mother weave when, as a small boy, he rested
his head on her lap. His use of balance and symmetry in the visual composi-

tion suggests the anthropometry of the human body. The surface texture of the canvas also creates the impression that his mother's face was marked by a life of hard work and exposure to the harsh climate of southeastern Morocco. His mother's difficult life is a metaphor for the situation of the Amazigh people, who are struggling to preserve their heritage and identity. He visually creates a correlation between women's bodies and the Amazigh culture, reinforcing the idea that women shape Amazigh identity.

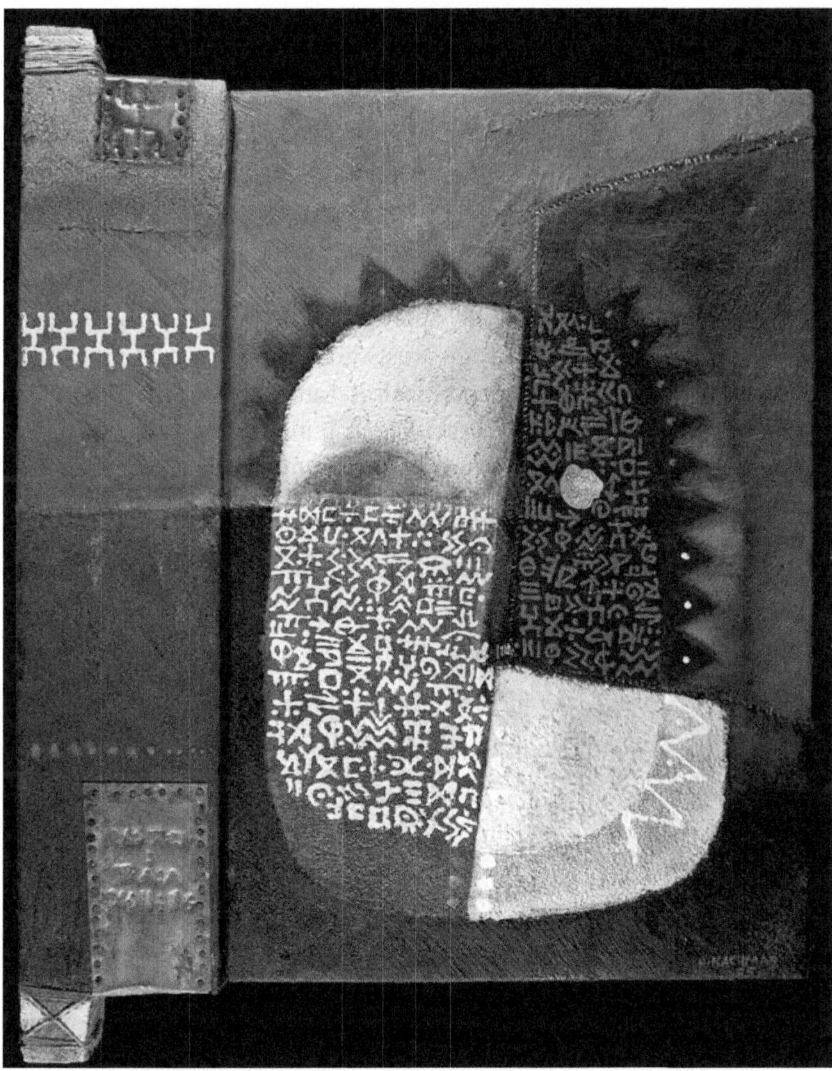

Figure 7.8. Hamid Kachmar, Imi n war imi *(2005), mixed media on canvas, 58 cm × 45 cm.*

According to Kachmar, the image of the door itself has multiple meanings. The door can represent a literal passage or opening and suggests the important role that mothers play in guiding their children into the future. A door is often referred to metaphorically as the opening or "mouth" of a house. The image of a door, the mouthless face of the female figure, and the title, *Mouth of the Mouthless,* suggest that the painting's subject refers to the current situation of the Amazigh people.[20] Kachmar feels that the Amazigh people have been rendered voiceless by political and social discrimination but are on the threshold of a cultural renaissance.

Kachmar and the other artists discussed here honor the creative power of women and their role in shaping Amazigh identity, but they also reflect the paradoxical situation of Amazigh arts in Morocco today. Amazigh women's arts are rapidly changing, due to economic, social, and political factors. This often results in their transformation and disappearance, even as an active political movement in Morocco calls for the recognition of the Amazigh language and heritage and the official acknowledgment of the Imazighen's contribution to Morocco's history and culture. By appropriating Amazigh women's visual vocabulary, both Arab and Amazigh artists give material form to their own conceptions of Morocco's distinct multicultural and pluralistic heritage. Contemporary painters recognize the crucial contribution of the artistic legacy of Amazigh women to Morocco's history and contemporary identity.

Selected Songs from Ait Khabbash Weddings

Asserkeḍ: *Men Honor the Bride*

1. *Iffu lḥal ur iffu manẓa-kmin a tislit?*
2. *Iffu lḥal ur iffu manẓ-iken a yigerramen g ikḍif?*
3. *Iffu lḥal ur iffu manẓa-kmin am wulli?*
4. *Iffu lḥal ur iffu manẓa-kmin am tleymin?*
5. *Iffu lḥal ur iffu manẓa-kmin am iysan?*
6. *Iffu lḥal ur iffu manẓa-kmin am truka?*
7. *Rjiɣ Rebbi d Nebi ad am kin a tislit,*
8. *Kin-aɣ kin i mayd ibeddan tama n ikḍif.*
9. *Rjiɣ Rebbi d Nebi ad am kin a tislit,*
10. *Sebâa n warraw Ait iwedjan tifaliwin.*
11. *Rjiɣ Rebbi d Nebi ad am kin a tislit,*
12. *Sebâa n warraw imnayn gin kullu laciax.*
13. *Rjiɣ Rebbi d Nebi ad am kin a tislit,*
14. *Meyat beyla ad-t-kerreẓt i warraw-nnem.*
15. *Rjiɣ Rebbi d Nebi ad am kin a tislit,*
16. *Meyat âawda ad-t-serrejt i warraw-nnem.*
17. *Rjiɣ Rebbi d Nebi ad am kin a tislit,*
18. *Meyat naga ayd itggan rḥil-nnem.*
19. *Rjiɣ Rebbi d Nebi ad am kin a tislit,*
20. *Meyat bagra ad-t-ḥaleb-t i warraw-nnem.*
21. *Rjiɣ Rebbi d Nebi ad am kin a tislit,*
22. *Meya n tekḍift ayd itggan usan-nnem.*
23. *Rjiɣ Rebbi d Nebi ad am kin a tislit,*
24. *Meyat âawda ayd itggan tiruka-nnem.*

25. *Rjiɣ Rebbi d Nebi ad am kin a tislit,*

26. *Meya n teɣrart ayd itggan leâwil-nnem.*

27. *Rjiɣ Rebbi d Nebi ad am kin a tislit,*

28. *Meyat melyun ayd itggan lusul-nnem.*

29. *Rjiɣ lfal-nnem ad ig imkilli tggen iârrimen ig ufan tagerẓa s-waman n unẓar.*

30. *Rjiɣ lfal-nnem ad ig imkilli teggen ilâiqen ig ufan tiferdi s-waman n unẓar.*

31. *A tislit lwajeb ad am ttugin ak-wen seɣ a krad ismkhan.*

32. *Yan ad am ẓẓaḍen ar am ttagmen ar tsseksa-t sin aliwa.*

33. *Nuẓen akabar ad-dik lhidj ariaɣten i lxuf a Rebbi.*

34. *Riɣ ad-d nẓur mas-kwen ujiɣ a yisemḍel n Mulay Âli.*

35. *Igan tifeẓâin ig imnayn tbubbat awa tedda tka iɣf i lexla.*

36. *Ayayd iwiɣ iḍan awiɣ aẓal ad-d nawey tiyni n-usekriɣ.*

37. *Ayayd usiɣ ikḍif asiɣ adar ilin icirran afella.*

38. *Ayayd-ten ssegm-iɣ tawit-ten s agari a yaḥenḥan.*

39. *Yilwa ẓẓin n yan isertinni yiweḍ waẓẓar ar attay n ikâa.*

40. *Yilwa ẓẓin n tafuyt yaɣenn iɣir n tuga ar tikki s-lanwar.*

41. *Tabuqest n leḥrir dda s-tt-ageln imnayen tifra.*

42. *A tattast g isrus ugellid i warraw-nnes arrial aliwa.*

43. *Âniɣ tirwed imnayn annayɣ ageḍrur tamẓem rrma a yistran.*

44. *Mek ɣurneɣ iney bu lman qqa-dd nawey sin imurn neɣ nemmut.*

45. *Is iney bu tẓibba qqa-dd uɣulɣ iqqen tama n uxam.*

46. *Numeẓ aseggawer ur nggid i waskarn mek llan.*

47. *I silew i yfrawn a tamedda han amnay kiɣt-in i luḍa.*

48. *Manẓimt tiɣrarin nyigr mid is ur llint a tiwetmin.*

49. *Illa kan lfal ɣur ait daddeɣ macan ur iḥli iwaḍu.*

50. *Lawla xes id msew aḥrir i tggudimt ils n teɣratin ur illi.*

51. *Âtti aḥ n bab-nnem arim-d lluẓ.*

52. *Âtti ayiɣf n-ẓerri it-t-inign tadwunt saɣ-d ibawn mek-am laḥ lluẓ.*

53. *Âtti isuggurn s-taẓẓirt a taqmut n-mush.*

54. *Âtti amr a Rebbi tegnugit seg-bougafer irreẓ uɣanbub-nnem ad ig idammen.*

55. *Âtti n-ssudda Laâyoub-nnem samḥ-i âadri.*

Asserkeḍ: *Men Honor the Bride*

[1. Has the morning come yet or not? Where are you, bride?

 2. Has the morning come yet or not? Where are you, blood on the carpet?

 3. Has the morning come yet or not? Where are you, owner of sheep?

 4. Has the morning come yet or not? Where are you, owner of camels?

5. Has the morning come yet or not? Where are you, owner of horses?

6. Has the morning come yet or not? Where are you, you with many cooking pots?

7. I hope God and the Prophet give you, oh bride,

8. They give us and give to all those standing around the carpet.

9. I hope God and the Prophet give you, oh bride,

10. Seven sons with horses and swords.

11. I hope God and the Prophet give you, oh bride,

12. Seven sons who are cavaliers and who are leaders.

13. I hope God and the Prophet give you, oh bride,

14. 100 mules for your sons to farm with.

15. I hope God and the Prophet give you, oh bride,

16. 100 horses to saddle for your sons.

17. I hope God and the Prophet give you, oh bride,

18. 100 camels to move your belongings.

19. I hope God and the Prophet give you, oh bride,

20. 100 cows to milk for your sons.

21. I hope God and the Prophet give you, oh bride,

22. 100 carpets to be your spreads.

23. I hope God and the Prophet give you, oh bride,

24. 100 horses to be your saddles.

25. I hope God and the Prophet give you, oh bride,

26. 100 bags to be your supplies.

27. I hope God and the Prophet give you, oh bride,

28. 100 million to be your wealth.

29. We hope what you want will be plentiful as when young men cultivate from rain.

30. We hope what you want will be as successful as lambs are when they find pasture that grows with water from rain.

31. Oh bride, the essentials will be done for you, we are buying you three slaves.

32. One grinds and brings water for you, and you make two your shepherds.

33. We sent a caravan to Mecca; God protect them from fear.

34. I want to visit the tomb of Mulay Ali.

35. Horses in groups, what a large number of cavaliers on their backs facing the vast desert.

36. How many nights and days I traveled to bring the *askriy* dates (highly valued and a metaphor for the bride).

37. How many times I loaded the carpets (on a camel) and the palanquin with the children inside.
38. How I raised my sons and you, leader, send them to the bullets.
39. The beauty of one horse's tail: its hair reaches down to its ankles.
40. The beauty of the sun when it shines on a mountain full of colorful flowers.
41. Cords of silk the cavaliers use to hang their *koummiyat* (daggers with curved blades).
42. Oh bowl, where the king puts money for his children.
43. Maybe the cavaliers are coming. I saw the dust. Get your arrows ready for battle.
44. If God helps us and grants us luck, we will come back with two shares or die.
45. If weak people go with us, I will come back and tie my horse next to the tent.
46. We have cover. We are not afraid of the horses' hooves if they come.
47. Oh hawk, spread your wings and land. I'm knocking down the cavaliers for you.
48. Women, where are the sacks from the farm (for almonds) or aren't there any?
49. There are few (almonds) offered by these people, but it's not enough.
50. There are only soup eaters, tongues of *tyratin* (ululation) do not exist.
51. Oh aunt, we are warning you, give us the almonds.
52. Oh aunt, with a head resembling the head of a cockroach, searching for fat, go and buy fava beans if you can't afford almonds.
53. Oh aunt, who is looking into a jar with a face like a cat's.
54. Oh aunt, we wish that you may fall down Bougafer Mountain, break your face, and become covered in blood.
55. Oh aunt, your weaknesses are clear to us, we forgive you.]

Taqcict: *Dressing the Bride as a Pigeon*

1. *Bismi Allah rraḥman rraḥim.*
2. *Yelli ẓẓur-ɣ ẓar-em Rebbi.*
3. *Asra g da-yemma-ɣ i tislit.*
4. *Asra g kem-id usiɣ a tiseksit,*
5. *An-kerḍ adlal-nnes i Fatima.*
6. *Ayenna-d usiɣ tâawenem-it.*
7. *A tamaccaṭ-inew lḥarma-nnem harru.*

8. *Ad-dinawiy yelli ar didda ge-d ulin.*

9. *Yelli-new yelli dag-d ulin.*

10. *Ad iwert-nnum hat-it manẓat-it.*

11. *Ad iwert-nnum tubedda n berra.*

12. *Ayaârⁱ-new giɣ-as may riɣ.*

13. *Ggeẓ-imed a lmalayka ar ɣur yelli.*

14. *Ait igenna d ait wakal.*

15. *Hayaɣ g iceḍran-nnek a ccix.*

16. *Tisent am iẓyan a yelli.*

17. *Tisent am ibrurin wala.*

18. *Gimt-as isgar a lemluk.*

19. *Gimt-as ayenna ur giɣ a lemluk.*

20. *Ayaârⁱ-new giɣ-as may riɣ.*

21. *Feɣ-d a yureɣ-inew.*

Taqcict: *Dressing the Bride as a Pigeon*

[1. In the name of God, the merciful, the beneficent.

2. My daughter, God be with you.

3. When I put henna on the bride.

4. When I take you, brush,

5. To brush the hair of Fatima.

6. What I do, help me with it.

7. My brusher, please be courageous.

8. We bring my daughter to her new home.

9. My daughter, my daughter, when they (the husband and his male relatives) come home.

10. I don't want her to get into the habit of roaming around.

11. I don't want her loitering outside.

12. What happiness! I did what I wanted for her.

13. Oh angels, come down near my daughter.

14. Those angels of the sky and those of the earth.

15. We are by your side, oh Sheikh.

16. Salt stays on you, oh my daughter.

17. The salt that is on you makes you look beautiful.

18. Do *isgar* (protection against *imkuraren*) for her, oh angels.

19. Do what I haven't done for her, oh angels.

20. What happiness! I did what I wanted for her.

21. Oh my gold, come out.]

Notes

Introduction

1. In contrast, David Crawford (2002) argues that rural Berbers living in monocultural rural areas of Morocco are unconcerned with asserting their Berber identity since they do not define their identity in opposition to other groups.

2. Until the last forty years, the living situations of the majority of Berbers were rural; and rural themes persist in Berber literature, which is primarily oral. Berbers do have a writing system called Tifinagh that was preserved by the Berbers (Tuareg) living in the Saharan regions of Africa. Although it appears that the Tifinagh script greatly influenced Berber art, especially textiles and ceramics, it was never used to write history and literature (Ennaji 1997: 25).

3. Regardless of the existence of three distinct languages, the term "Tamazight" is used here as an overarching term to describe all three languages.

4. Gabriel Camps (1995: 66–67) writes that the word "Imazighen" probably derives from the words "Mazic" and "Mazica," commonly found on ancient funerary inscriptions in northern Africa referring to the indigenous population.

5. Dadda Atta is a genuine sixteenth-century historic figure whose tomb is located in the Upper Draa Valley 25 km north of a town called Tagunit. Not much is known about the early history of the Ait Atta, but scholars trace their history to the sixteenth century, when a number of nomadic Amazigh groups from the Sahara banded together to eject Arabs from the region of the Saghro Mountains. Ross Dunn (1977) and David Hart (1981) have written extensively on the early history of the Ait Atta. Hart (1981: 62) estimates that in 1960 the Ait Atta population was approximately 135,000.

6. Rebecca Popenoe's *Feeding Desire* (2004: 92–93) discusses the role that Azawagh Arab women in Niger play in preserving group identity.

7. The Ait Khabbash, one of the subgroups within the Ait Atta, recognize that they are part of the Ait Atta but also have their own origin story that exposes how the desire to maintain ethnic purity organizes their society. Khabbash, one of Atta's descendants, had four sons who founded four subgroups within the Ait Khabbash. In the nineteenth century, three other non–Ait Khabbash Amazigh groups were eventually adopted into the group. While these seven groups are all

united today, the four original groups consider themselves to be purer than the others. According to Marie-Luce Gélard's study of Ait Khabbash kinship, intermarriage between the three "adopted" groups is prohibited in order to keep the nonpure population within the Ait Khabbash from growing too large. There are no social restrictions prohibiting marriage between members of the four original groups, however, who also intermarry with the three adopted groups (Gélard 2003: 173). While Ait Khabbash identity is flexible enough to allow non–Ait Khabbash to become integrated into their group, revealing the process of identity construction, their marriage patterns are colored by the desire to preserve the integrity and purity of their bloodline.

8. For example, in the late nineteenth century the Ait Khabbash entered into a business relationship with the Bani Mhammed, a group of Arab caravan merchants, and agreed to guard their caravans for a protection fee. They solidified this agreement through the exchange of breast milk of nursing women from both groups.

9. For a further discussion of the importance of women's breast milk in the creation of kinship bonds, see Altorki (1980), Boddy (1989), and Popenoe (2004: 95).

10. For more information about the connection between women and identity, see Moghadam's book *Identity Politics and Women* (1994).

11. This book argues that such a search for the remnants of a pre-Islamic "pure" Amazigh art is not possible, as historical interactions between the Imazighen and other peoples make it impossible and largely irrelevant to identify "authentic" Amazigh art and culture.

12. King Hassan II, confronted with social unrest in the 1960s and 1970s, integrated Arab-speaking officials from the Arab-dominated Istiqlal political party that con-

trolled Moroccan politics after independence into positions of power in the nation's rural Amazigh areas. This policy of undermining Amazigh political influence, in addition to others that attempted to restrict Amazigh control over land tenure, angered many Imazighen and led to their political mobilization (Venema and Mguild 2003: 42–43).

13. Amazigh activists also called for the teaching of Amazigh languages in schools, which would increase the potential participation of the Imazighen in Moroccan political and economic life. Many Amazigh children drop out of school because they are taught in a language foreign to them, Arabic; the language barrier eventually limits their involvement in governmental dealings, which are conducted in Arabic or French.

14. For more information about the Amazigh language in Morocco, see Ennaji (1997). See Crawford (2002) for a survey of the academic literature on Imazighen in Morocco and Maddy-Weitzman (2002) for a history of the Berber movement in North Africa.

15. These demands were made in a letter to the prime minister of the Rabat Council by the Amazigh group of Rabat (the capital city of Morocco) on May 1, 2002. The demands were published on the Internet at the website of the World Amazigh Action Coalition (http://www.waac.info).

16. Errachidia is the province capital of southeastern Morocco, the focus of this book.

17. While Hassan II began to tolerate the idea of cultural pluralism within Morocco, at the same time he carefully controlled the political activities of the Imazighen and frequently asserted the monarch's supremacy and his role as ultimate decision maker (Denoeux and Maghraoui 1998: 124). The teaching of Tamazight in schools never did materialize during Hassan II's reign. In fact, despite Hassan II's promises, many Imazighen felt

that he was also intensifying his Arabization campaign. For example, the state-controlled television news, previously broadcast in Classical Arabic, began to summarize the news for the nation's Amazigh population; but it broadcast summaries of the news for only five minutes in each of Morocco's three Amazigh languages. While more newspapers and books began to be published in Tamazight, official registrars were instructed by the government not to register children who were given Amazigh names. Parents were told to choose names from a list of primarily Arab names. In other words, the government allowed the Imazighen certain concessions but tried to prohibit them from developing into a unified political movement.

18. Some Amazigh activists are not happy with IRCAM because they feel it is an organization controlled by the monarchy to neutralize the Amazigh Cultural Movement.

19. See Fatima Sadiqi's book *Women, Gender and Language in Morocco* (2003) for more information about women and their association with the Amazigh language.

20. See Julia Clancy-Smith (1999) for a discussion of the impact of colonialism on women's artistic production in North Africa.

Chapter One

1. For more information concerning the horizontal loom and tent construction, see Laoust (1920), Reswick (1981), and Sorber (2002).

2. French colonial records, travel accounts, and my personal interviews clarify that in the late nineteenth century nomads in southeastern Morocco purchased indigo-dyed cotton cloth to make clothing (Gaulis 1928: 182; Harris 1895: 289). Prior to this point, Ait Khabbash wore hand-woven wool clothing.

3. Jim Miller's *Imlil: A Moroccan Mountain Community in Change* found a similar arrangement of cooperation, which is referred to as *touiza* in the area of southwestern Morocco where Imlil is located (Miller 1984: 70).

4. Forelli and Harries (1977) provide a more detailed description of loom manufacture.

5. See Bynon (1966) for more information about Amazigh riddle telling.

6. For a further discussion of this, see Messick (1987: 213).

7. For similar beliefs, see the discussion of weaving in Tunisia in Reswick (1981: 60).

8. This English translation of *sura* 15, verses 26–27, comes from Muhammad Ali's English translation of the Qur'an (1991: 511).

9. For a thorough discussion of Moroccan beliefs concerning the *jnoun,* see Westermarck ([1926] 1968, 2: 262–301).

10. In "The Rugs of Settled and Nomadic Peoples: A Contrast in Expression," Flint argues that the patterns, colors, and forms of the textiles of nomads and settled peoples reflect the differing ways of organizing time and space. He claims that nomadic textiles, unlike those of settled people, do not have a precise center and are not framed by borders. Instead they demonstrate a repeating succession of horizontal patterns that reflect "an evenly sustained succession of equal parts. This can perhaps be related to a non-hierarchic society and a nomad life style" (Flint 1980: 58).

11. See the book *The Fabric of Moroccan Life* for more examples of Moroccan textiles from different regions and times (Paydar and Grammet 2002).

12. Abu-Lughod (1986: 131).

13. See Antoun (1968), Bourdieu (1977), Combs-Schilling (1989), Davis (1983), Dwyer (1978), and Joseph (1980).

14. This practice is found throughout North Africa and has been noted by numer-

ous authors, such as Doutté (1909), Messick (1987), Reswick (1981), and Westermarck ([1926] 1968).

Chapter Two

1. My definition of dress follows the designations established by Joanne Eicher and other scholars (Barnes and Eicher 1992; Eicher 1995).

2. According to the *Encyclopaedia of Islam* (Gibb 2003) the *ihram* consists of two pieces of white seamless cloth that also symbolize a man's unity with other members of the Muslim community and the equality of its members.

3. Harmel, *Peganum harmala*, is a common Moroccan plant that is ground and mixed with salt to protect against the *jnoun*.

4. Westermarck ([1926] 1968, 1: 441–478) includes a thorough description of the evil eye.

5. Belief in the evil eye is common around the Middle East. Its existence is even mentioned in the Hadith, the words and deeds of the Prophet Muhammad. Many Hadith have been compiled and interpreted. Some are more reliable than others. One of the most reliable is *Sahih al-Bukhari*, which is the Hadith referred to in this study, from a readily available English/Arabic translation entitled *The Translation of the Meanings of Sahih al-Bukhari: Arabic-English*, edited by Muhammad Muhsin Khan. The parenthetical numbers indicate the volume and page of Khan's translation. For example, (5: 87) indicates volume 5, page 87. The citation for the evil eye is (7: 426–427).

6. This sentiment, recited by both Arabs and Imazighen in southeastern Morocco, is primarily Moroccan Arabic, with the addition of the Tamazight word *ʒarri,* which means dung beetle.

7. The word *sbuâ* has the same root as the number seven, which is *sbaâ.* The ceremony

is named *sbuâ* because it is performed seven days after a child's birth.

8. Doutté (1909: 348), Laoust (1920: 143), and Westermarck ([1926] 1968, 2: 408) also noted similar practices, claiming that shaving the child's head purified the child.

9. See Champault (1953, 1956, 1969) for information about similar necklaces in southern Algeria.

10. The back of the necklace consists of a piece of thick plastic, because a thin string may cut into the boy's shoulders and back.

11. Westermarck ([1926] 1968, 2: 380) describes similar practices elsewhere in Morocco.

12. People throughout Morocco and the Middle East use the hand motif, which can realistically resemble a hand or can be represented abstractly by five lines or dots. The crucial thing is that five repeating motifs be included for an object to be considered a *khamsa* or *afous.*

13. For an overview of hairstyles in different regions of Morocco, see Jarrot (1935: 267), Langel and Marcais (1954: 8), Laoust (1920: 142–145), and Westermarck ([1926] 1968, 2: 409).

14. See Westermarck ([1926] 1968, 2: 416–433) for a detailed discussion of circumcision practices in Morocco.

15. In *Sahih al-Bukhari,* circumcision is described as *fitra* (7: 777, 7: 779). The word *fitra* means "to create" and "to bring into being," suggesting being born into a state to accept Islam.

16. In some areas of Morocco, elderly women may serve as tattoo specialists; they consecrate their status by performing a pilgrimage to a local shrine (Herber 1948).

17. The following passages from *Sahih al-Bukhari* condemn tattooing: (3: 242, 7: 533, 7: 535, 7: 536).

18. Herber (1921) provides a thorough review of tattoos and their prohibition in Islam.

19. Basset (1963), Herber (1948), Laoust

(1920: 138–142), and Searight (1984) also discuss the tattooing process in Morocco.

20. Searight (1984: 219) writes that "this absence of blue in the colour scheme of some informants is a personal idiosyncrasy, physiological, educational or psychological."

21. See Kapchan (1993) and Vonderheyden (1934) for more information on the use of henna in Morocco.

22. Janice Boddy (1989) describes the value placed on the desire to close and contain the human body among Sudanese Arabs as the quality of "interiority"; and Rebecca Popenoe (2004), in her discussion of Azawagh Arabs, describes this value as "closedness."

23. The Hadith *Sahih al-Bukhari* instructs menstruating women to limit their daily participation in religious activities. For instance, menstruating women cannot perform the *hajj*, "pilgrimage to Mecca" (1: 178), perform their daily prayers (1: 146, 1: 181), or engage in sexual intercourse with their husbands (1: 177). Women are directed to wash themselves after their menstrual cycle is complete to resume their daily prayers (1: 186).

24. Marcus (1992: 74) and Kapchan (1996: 160) also note that items with *baraka* purify the inner, spiritual body.

25. According to Coon (1931), Doutté (1909), and Searight (1984: 252), a woman's origin could be determined by the style of her tattoo. While Bons (1936: 177) and Searight (1984: 226) recognize the problem of assigning a specific meaning to tattoo motifs, Westermarck ([1926] 1968, 1: 466) interprets them as representations of either the eye or the hand motif that protected women against the misfortune of the evil eye. Cola Alberich (1949) claims that tattoos represented the ancient Amazigh sun cult forgotten by the current Muslim population; and Marcy (1931: 52) holds that some tattoos were based on the Phoenician symbol for the goddess Tanit.

26. Because of the controversy and mis-appropriation of the term "veil," I choose not to use it in this study to refer to Ait Khabbash head and body coverings. Instead, I use the phrase "head covering." For more information concerning the subject of the "veil," see Ahmed (1992), El Guindi (1999), Hale (1989), and Mernissi (1987).

27. For a listing of groups who use indigo, see Besancenot (1990).

28. Boddy's *Wombs and Alien Spirits* (1989: 62–64) similarly argues that there is a strong metaphorical association between unmarried women and pigeons in the Sudan, where both are associated with purity, cleanliness, and beauty.

29. Moroccan women living in urban areas first wore the *jellaba*, a garment seen as liberating for women, in the 1940s. Its form was based on men's hooded gowns.

30. The term "girl" is appropriate, because in southeastern Morocco the word "woman" is used strictly for married women.

Chapter Three

1. For more information about *ahidous* in Morocco, see Harries and Raamouch (1971), Hart (1981, 1984), and Lortat-Jacob (1981).

2. Bernard Lortat-Jacob (1981: 88), who writes about Amazigh music in the High Atlas Mountains, also notes that music fosters positive intra- and intergroup relations by belonging to everyone in the community.

3. See Kapchan (1996), Lortat-Jacob (1980b), and Schuyler (1984, 1985) for a discussion of professional musicians in Morocco.

4. Hoffman (2002) and Schuyler (1984, 1985) both write about how Amazigh music in Morocco reinforces collective moral and social norms.

5. The methodology used to compare and contrast male and female dress is adopted from Michelman and Erekosima's (1992) analysis of the Kalabari dress in Nigeria.

6. For a detailed description of the *allun* and playing techniques, see Lortat-Jacob (1980b), Thornton (1936), and Woodson (1974).

7. See Lortat-Jacob (1980a, 1980b, 1981) and Harries and Raamouch (1971) for examples of men's oral poetry performed elsewhere in Morocco.

8. See Hoffman (2002) for a similar discussion of generational change in Berber women's songs in southwestern Morocco.

Chapter Four

A version of this chapter was previously published in an edited volume entitled *Wedding Dress across Cultures* (Foster and Johnson 2003).

1. See Combs-Schilling (1989: 212) for a further discussion of the Moroccan bride and her alleged passivity.

2. Many Ait Khabbash women explained that in the past marriages would be arranged. Until the last decade, the bride could be as young as sixteen and the groom eighteen. Today young men and women often see each other briefly before consenting to marry. A young man typically visits the house of his potential bride with his mother, having the opportunity to see and possibly talk with the potential bride. Once he expresses interest in marrying the girl, his mother proposes the idea to her family, who may or may not accept the offer.

3. See Prussin (1995) for a discussion of nomadic arts in Africa and the central role that women play in these female-dominated arts.

4. It is not socially acceptable for women to look for husbands for their daughters.

5. Rasmussen (1995) writes that Tuareg rites of passage, such as birth and marriage, are also staged around the nomadic tent, paralleling the Ait Khabbash wedding.

6. As discussed in the previous chapter, Ait Khabbash women are less likely to receive formal education in Arabic. Since women were responsible for most of the childcare, women teach the Tamazight language to their children. The link between women and the Tamazight language is especially obvious during the wedding ceremony.

7. The word *tirggiyin* refers to people with west African origins living in the region of Alnif, Morocco, who are descended from enslaved peoples. Prior to colonization of the area in the 1930s, the Ait Khabbash were actively involved in the trans-Saharan slave trade.

8. The central Moroccan city of Fez has provided southeastern Morocco with textiles, jewelry, and other items for centuries. Often caravans left Fez, passed through southeastern Morocco, and headed across the Sahara.

9. In the past these belts were woven from silk, but today synthetic silk is common.

10. I am using the term "girl" here to refer to an unmarried woman, since in Morocco the word "woman" is equated with a female who is either married or divorced.

11. Current laws in Morocco require that a woman have permission from her husband to receive free birth control pills from her local clinic. Many women, uncertain about the future of their marriages, wish to postpone childbirth until their marriages are more secure. If a woman is unable to secure her husband's permission to buy birth control pills, she often tries to hide the pills from him. Women may wish to purchase birth control pills secretly in the local pharmacy but struggle to find the money to buy them.

12. Ait Khabbash women also explained to me that smells can directly influence a person's physical well-being. A person who smells something bad can become physically sick. Small children are believed to be especially sensitive to smells, and women often

place strings of cloves around their children's necks to prevent them from falling ill due to bad odors.

13. While this cloth is an important symbol of Ait Khabbash group identity, Ait Khabbash women do not weave it. Rather, the *tasebniyt n uâbroq* is made in the northern city of Fez, shipped into the area, and purchased in the market of Rissani.

14. As previously discussed, green is associated with fertility because it is the color of vegetation.

15. Prussin (1995: 194) also notes that red is used throughout the African nomadic world and may have its origin in the red dyes from tannins used to make leather pliable.

16. See Dubin (1987: 291–296) for a more thorough discussion of amber.

17. See Bynon (1984) for a further discussion of fibulae and their supposedly prophylactic abilities.

18. See Bynon (1984) and Westermarck ([1926] 1968) for a discussion of the significance of the triangle in Amazigh art.

19. See Abu-Lughod (1986: 136) and Michelman and Erekosima (1992: 175) for further discussion of women's belts and their relationship to female sexuality.

20. Kapchan (1993: 10) and Combs-Schilling (1989: 212) both describe the henna ceremony in Morocco as a painfully long process for the bride.

21. See Abu-Lughod (1986: 165). Kapchan (1996: 192) notes that in Morocco emotions are not publicly revealed except during celebrations, such as weddings.

22. In her book *Beyond the Veil,* Fatima Mernissi (1987: 121–122) further describes how Moroccan women typically try to control their sons' wives.

23. The Tamazight word *imkuraren* is the equivalent of the Arabic word *shur,* often translated as "conjuring" (Kapchan 1996: 239). Wehr (1980: 465), in *A Dictionary of*

Modern Written Arabic, translates *shur* as "sorcery" and "magic." See Kapchan (1996: 241) for a detailed discussion of *shur* in Morocco. Because of the negative connotations associated with the words "sorcery" and "magic," I prefer to use the indigenous terminology.

24. Men believe that women practice *imkuraren* to control them, and a groom is vulnerable for reasons of revenge or jealousy (Kapchan 1996: 236).

25. Davis (1983: 114–117), in her book *Patience and Power: Women's Lives in a Moroccan Village,* writes that (although men and women can practice *shur*) the practice of *shur* by women is one of their main sources of power and allows them to control the behavior of their husbands through fear of reprisal.

26. See Combs-Schilling (1989: 190) and Westermarck ([1914] 1972: 97) for a more thorough discussion of the groom in Moroccan weddings.

27. Westermarck ([1926] 1968, 1: 572) writes in great detail about the types of *thiqaf* that can cause the groom's impotency.

28. It may be tempting to analyze the seclusion of the groom and the public role of the bride as a reversal of gender norms, but Ait Khabbash women, like most Amazigh women in Morocco, have never been confined to their homes or tents. Amazigh women perform much of the heavy labor typical of women living in rural settings, requiring them to traverse the open landscape unrestrictedly.

29. Scholars such as Antoun (1968), Bourdieu (1966, 1977), Dwyer (1978), and Joseph (1980) use the public/private dichotomy to describe gender roles in North Africa.

Chapter Five

1. See also Westermarck ([1914] 1972: 188) for a discussion of how the bride's female relatives protect her from harm.

2. In his early twentieth century descrip-

tion of Ait Atta weddings, Laoust (1993: 102) also notes that the men of the groom's village playfully refuse to allow the bride to enter the village (*qsar*) until the *isnain* agree to give them a portion of meat.

3. In her discussion of Tuareg weddings, Rasmussen (1995) notes that many rites of passage are accompanied by the counter-clockwise movement of women around the nomadic tent, which she believes is a pre-Islamic practice. Before the Tuareg bride and groom enter the nuptial tent, they circle it three times, suggesting a parallel with the Ait Khabbash practice of circling the bridal tent before entering.

4. The discussion of the physical aesthetic of fattening among Arabs in Niger by Pope-noe (2004: 50) and the examination of spirit possession among Sudanese Arabs by Boddy (1989) both emphasize the positive value placed on female bodies that are closed and contained.

5. This contrasts with Arabs, who consummate weddings at sunrise.

6. Gélard (2003: 97) writes that among the Ait Khabbash in Merzouga before intercourse the groom must find a needle hidden in the bride's clothing.

7. Abu-Lughod (1986: 41) demonstrates in her study of Bedouin culture that blood relationships based on descent from a common ancestor are a concept that binds nomadic groups, because "blood both links people to the past and binds them in the present."

8. Combs-Schilling (1989: 11) argues that the ritual deflowering of a virginal bride during a wedding ceremony mimics the Moroccan monarch's annual sacrifice of a sheep for the good of the nation on the day of the Great Sacrifice; thus, she contends, deflowering of a bride in a Moroccan wedding ritually reinforces the strength of the Moroccan kingship.

9. Abdellah Hammoudi (1993: 121–122), in his book *The Victim and Its Masks: An Essay on Sacrifice and Masquerade in the Maghreb,* also recognizes that the bride's blood defloration is necessary to create a marital union, just as an animal sacrifice is necessary.

10. As noted earlier, the metaphor of the pigeon is also used to refer to the groom when he is dressed in white clothing on the day before the wedding.

11. Seeing a connection between birds and the supernatural is common in Morocco. According to Westermarck ([1926] 1968, 2: 337), some Amazigh groups in Morocco do not eat either tame or wild birds, because a pigeon may be the earthly form of a *jinn* or a dead person. Anyone responsible for its death risks considerable danger. My mother-in-law, whose house happened to be located near the village cemetery, explained that birds seen at the cemetery house the souls of dead people, coming to console their family members who are mourning at their graves.

12. Boddy (1989: 62–63) and Prussin (1995: 192) also associate women, birds, and fertility.

13. Jacques Rabaté and Marie-Rose Rabaté (1996: 149–150) interpret the bird motif on the jewelry from Dades as the representation of a pigeon or dove.

14. See Joseph Herber (1929) for more information about *ḥargus.*

Chapter Six

Another version of this chapter was previously published in the *Journal of North African Studies* (Becker 2002).

1. Sijilmasa thrived due to the caravan trade but began to decline with the demise of the Songhai empire in the sixteenth century. Its final abandonment is believed to have taken place in 1818, after warring groups in the area destroyed it. Walter Harris (1895: 265), an English journalist and traveler to the Tafilalet oasis, reported that the acres of shapeless

ruins that dotted the landscape were the only reminder of the once-great Sijilmasa.

2. "Chleuh" is a term commonly used by Arabs to refer to the Imazighen. Some Imazighen feel that the term is derogatory.

3. See Fremont E. Besmer (1983) and John Tremearne (1914) for more information about the *bori*.

4. See Amélie Marie Goichon (1927: 46–47) for information concerning a similar event performed in the Mzab in southern Algeria.

Chapter Seven

1. Prosper Ricard during the colonial period based much of his reorganization on discussions with merchants and onsite visits to areas of textile production. Not every region participated in the market economy. Many areas were not fully safe for French travel (for example, the High Atlas and southeastern Morocco), leaving large regions such as the Tafilalet oasis uninfluenced by French efforts at classification.

2. An exception to this is the Amazigh artist Mahjoubi Aherdan, the leader of the National Popular Movement (MNP), a political party that represents rural Moroccans, including many Imazighen. For more information on other Moroccan artists who used Amazigh motifs to form abstract patterns in their paintings, see Irbouh (1998).

3. See Irbouh (1998) for more information about Belkahia's artistic process.

4. Farid Belkahia, interview by author, Marrakech, June 6, 2004.

5. Mohamed Nabili, telephone interview, January 25, 2005.

6. The liver is believed to be the place where people's sentiments are located.

7. Translation by Addi Ouadderrou.

8. Omar Taws, interview by author, Goulmima, June 24, 2004.

9. See Miller (1996) for information about

the drought and how this has changed life in southeastern Morocco.

10. Unlike the situation in other areas of Morocco, Ait Khabbash men have not left the region to work in northern Morocco or even Europe. Female-run households are not common.

11. See Nashat and Tucker (1999: 102–104) for more information about the evolution of pastoral nomadic women's lives in North Africa and the Middle East.

12. Muhand Saidi, interview by author, Errachidia, June 25, 2004.

13. Mohamed Mallal, interview by author, June 10, 2004.

14. This idea of a transnational Amazigh identity is relatively new among Imazighen in Morocco and is largely due to the Internet. In 1992 the electronic mailing list Amazigh-Net was established, allowing Imazighen from Algeria, Morocco, France, and other African countries to communicate, share information, and establish a sense of community across national borders. In addition, several dozen websites have recently emerged that are concerned with the question of Amazigh identity and strategies to incorporate Tamazight into each nation's educational curriculum and mass media.

15. French colonization, the creation of national borders, and successive droughts resulted in the gradual disintegration of many fundamental characteristics of Tuareg society, including nomadism. Tuareg armed rebellions in Mali and Niger in the 1990s led to the exile of many Tuareg to refugee camps. Today most Tuareg refugees have returned to their prospective countries, and peace reigns. Several contemporary Tuareg musical groups, including Tartit and Tinariwen from Mali, sing not only traditional Tuareg songs but also songs about the aspirations of young Tuareg and the struggle for survival.

16. Tamazight is taught in Moroccan

schools using the Tifinagh script. Many Amazigh activists criticize IRCAM's decision to use Tifinagh rather than the Latin alphabet, which is the convention in France. Critics feel that the use of Tifinagh is a ploy by the Moroccan government with the goal of further marginalizing the Imazighen and the Tamazight language.

17. Fatima Mellal, interview by author, Ouarzazate, June 10, 2004.

18. Mohamed Ziyani, interview by author, Tinghir, July 4, 2004.

19. Hamid Kachmar, interview by author, Portland, Oregon, May 14, 2005.

20. Ibid.

Abu-Lughod, Lila. 1986. *Veiled Sentiments*. Berkeley: University of California Press.

Ahmed, Leila. 1992. *Women and Gender in Islam*. New Haven: Yale University Press.

Ali, Maulana Muhammad. 1991. *The Holy Qur'an*. Columbus, Ohio: Lahore, Inc.

Allen, Sheila. 1998. "Identity: Feminist Perspectives on 'Race,' Ethnicity and Nationality." In *Gender, Ethnicity and Political Ideologies*, ed. N. Charles and H. Hintjens, pp. 46–64. New York: Routledge.

Almasude, Amar. 1999. "The New Mass Media and the Shaping of Amazigh Identity." In *Revitalizing Indigenous Languages*, ed. J. Reyhner, G. Cantoni, R. St. Clair, and E. Yazzie, pp. 117–128. Flagstaff: Northern Arizona University.

Altorki, Soraya. 1980. "Milk-Kinship in Arab Society: An Unexplored Problem in the Ethnography of Marriage." *Ethnology* 19 (2): 233–234.

Ames, D. W. 1965. "Hausa Drums of Zaria." *Ibadan* 21: 62–80.

Anderson, Benedict. 1991. *Imagined Communities: Reflections on the Origin and Spread of Nationalism*. London: Verso.

Anderson, Lois Ann. 1971. "The Interrelation of African and Arab Musics: Some Preliminary Considerations." In *Essays on Music and History in Africa*, ed. Klaus P. Wachsmann, pp. 143–169. Evanston: Northwestern University Press.

Antoun, Richard. 1968. "On the Modesty of Women in Arab Muslim Villages: A Study in the Accommodation of Traditions." *American Anthropologist* 70 (4): 671–697.

Arnoldi, Mary Jo. 1995. "Introduction." In *Crowning Achievements*, ed. Mary Jo Arnoldi and Christine Mullen Kreamer, pp. 9–25. Los Angeles: Fowler Museum of Cultural History, University of California, Los Angeles.

Balfour-Paul, Jenny. 1997. *Indigo in the Arab World*. Richmond, Surrey: Curzon.

Barnes, Ruth, and Joanne B. Eicher, eds. 1992. *Dress and Gender: Making and Meaning in Cultural Contexts*. New York: Berg.

Basset, André. 1963. *Textes berbères du Maroc*. Paris: Geuthner.

Becker, Cynthia. 2002. " 'We Are Real Slaves, Real Ismkhan': Memories of the Trans-Saharan Slave Trade in the Tafilalet of South-Eastern Morocco." *Journal of North African Studies* 7 (4): 97–121.

———. 2003. "Gender, Identity, and Moroccan Weddings: The Adornment of the Ait Khabbash Berber Bride and Groom." In *Wedding Dress across Cultures,* ed. H. Foster and D. Johnson, pp. 105–122. Oxford: Berg Press.

Benchemsi, Rajae. 1995. "Farid Belkahia: Tradition Is the Future of Mankind." In *Vital: Three Contemporary African Artists,* ed. J. Nesbitt, pp. 13–45. Liverpool: Tate Gallery.

Besancenot, Jean. 1990. *Costumes et types du Maroc.* Aix-en-Provence: Édisud.

Besmer, Fremont E. 1983. *Horses, Musicians & Gods: The Hausa Cult of Possession-Trance.* South Hadley, Mass.: Bergin & Garvey Publishers.

Boddy, Janice. 1989. *Wombs and Alien Spirits: Women, Men, and the Zar Cult in Northern Sudan.* Madison: University of Wisconsin Press.

Bons, Gilbert F. 1936. "Tatouages berbères." *Réalisations* 2 (6): 176–178.

Bourdieu, Pierre. 1966. "The Sentiment of Honour in Kabyle Society." In *Honour and Shame: The Values of Mediterranean Society,* ed. J. G. Péristiany, pp. 191–241. Chicago: University of Chicago Press.

———. 1977. *Outline of a Theory of Practice.* Translated by Richard Nice. Cambridge: Cambridge University Press.

Brett, Michael, and Elizabeth Fentress. 1996. *The Berbers.* Cambridge, Mass.: Blackwell Publishers.

Briggs, Lloyd Cabot. 1960. *Tribes of the Sahara.* Cambridge, Mass.: Harvard University Press.

Bynon, James. 1966. "Riddle Telling among the Berbers of Central Morocco." *African Language Studies* 7 (1): 80–104.

———. 1984. "Berber Women's Pottery: Is the Decoration Motivated?" In *Colloquies on Art & Archaeology in Asia No. 12,* ed. J. Picton, pp. 136–161. London: University of London.

Camps, Gabriel. 1995. *Les Berbères: Mémoire et identité.* Paris: Éditions Errance.

Chaker, Salem. 1984. *Textes en linguistique berbère: Introduction au domaine berbère.* Paris: Centre National de la Recherche Scientifique.

———. 1998. *Berbères aujourd'hui.* Paris: Éditions L'Harmattan.

Champault, Francine Dominique. 1953. "La naissance à Tabelbala." *Journal de la Société des Africanistes* 23: 87–101.

———. 1956. "Un collier d'enfant du Sahara algéro-marocain." *Journal de la Société des Africanistes* 26 (fasc. 1 & 2): 197–209.

———. 1969. *Une oasis du sahara nord-occidental, Tabelbala.* Paris: Éditions du Centre National de la Recherche Scientifique.

Charles, Nickie, and Helen M. Hintjens, eds. 1998. *Gender, Ethnicity and Political Ideologies.* London: Routledge.

Clancy-Smith, Julia. 1999. "A Woman without Her Distaff: Gender, Work, and Handicraft Production in Colonial North Africa." In *A Social History of Women and Gender in the Modern Middle East,* ed. M. Meriwether and J. Tucker, pp. 25–62. Boulder, Colo.: Westview Press.

Cola Alberich, Julio. 1949. *Amuletos y tatuajes marroquíes.* Madrid: Instituto de Estudios Africanos.

Combs-Schilling, M. Elaine. 1989. *Sacred Performances: Islam, Sexuality and Sacrifice.* New York: Columbia University Press.

Coon, Carleton. 1931. *Tribes of the Rif.* New Haven, Conn.: Human Relations Files.

Courtney-Clarke, Margaret, and Geraldine Brooks. 1996. *Imaⁿighen: The Vanishing Traditions of Berber Women.* New York: Clarkson Potter.

Crawford, David. 2002. "Morocco's Invisible Imazighen." *Journal of North African Studies* 7 (1): 53–70.

Crawford, David, and Katherine Hoffman. 2000. "Essentially Amazigh: Urban Berbers and the Global Village." In *The Arab-African and Islamic Worlds: Interdisciplinary Studies,* ed. K. Lacey and R. Coury, pp. 117–134. New York: Peter Lang.

Davis, Susan Schaefer. 1983. *Patience and Power: Women's Lives in a Moroccan Village.* Cambridge, Mass.: Schenkman Publishing Company, Inc.

Davis, Susan Schaefer, and Douglas A. Davis. 1985. *Adolescence in a Moroccan Town.* London: New Brunswick.

Denoeux, Guilain, and Abdeslam Maghraoui. 1998. "King Hassan's Strategy of Political Dualism." *Middle East Policy* 5 (4): 104–130.

Doutté, Edmond. 1909. *Magie et religion dans l'Afrique du Nord.* Algiers: A. Jourdan.

Dubin, Lois Sherr. 1987. *The History of Beads: From 30,000 B.C. to the Present.* New York: Abrams.

d'Ucel, Jeanne. 1932. *Berber Art: an Introduction.* Norman: University of Oklahoma Press.

Dunn, Ross. 1972. "Berber Imperialism: The Ait Atta Expansion in Southeast Morocco." In *Arabs and Berbers: From Tribe to Nation in North Africa,* ed. E. Gellner and C. Micaud, pp. 85–108. London: Duckworth and Co., Ltd.

———. 1977. *Resistance in the Desert: Moroccan Response to French Imperialism, 1881–1912.* Madison: University of Wisconsin Press.

Du Puigaudeau, Odette. 1967, 1968, 1970, 1972, 1980–1981. "Art et coutumes des Maures." *Hespéris-Tamuda* 8: 111–196; 9: 329–427; 11: 5–82; 13: 183–224; 16: 185–211; 19: 169–220.

Dwyer, Daisy. 1978. *Images and Self-Images: Male and Female in Morocco.* New York: Columbia University Press.

Eicher, Joanne, ed. 1995. *Dress and Ethnicity: Change across Space and Time.* Oxford: Berg Press.

El Guindi, Fadwa. 1999. *Veil: Modesty, Privacy, and Resistance.* Oxford: Berg Press.

Ennaji, Moha. 1997. "The Sociology of Berber: Change and Continuity." *International Journal of the Sociology of Language* 123: 23–40.

Ennaji, Mohammed. 1999. *Serving the Master: Slavery and Society in Nineteenth-Century Morocco.* Translated by Seth Graebner. New York: St. Martin's Press.

Euba, Akin. 1965. "Preface to a Study of Nigerian Music." *Ibadan* 21: 53–62.

Fernea, Elizabeth. 1998. *In Search of Islamic Feminism: One Woman's Global Journey.* New York: Doubleday.

Fisher, Angela. 1984. *Africa Adorned.* New York: Harry Abrams.

Flint, Bert. 1980. "The Rugs of Settled and Nomadic Peoples: A Contrast Expression." In *From the Far West: Carpets and Textiles of Morocco,* ed. Patricia L. Fiske, W. Russell Pickering, and Ralph S. Yohe, pp. 57–64. Washington, D.C.: Textile Museum.

Forelli, Sally, and Jeanette Harries. 1977. "Traditional Berber Weaving in Central Morocco." *Textile Museum Journal* 4 (4): 41–60.

Foster, Helen Bradley, and Donald Clay Johnson, eds. 2003. *Wedding Dress across Cultures.* Oxford: Berg Press.

Gaulis, Lieutenant. 1928. "Le Tafilalet." *Renseignements Coloniaux (Bulletin du Comité de l'Afrique Français)* 3: 180–189.

Gélard, Marie-Luce. 2003. *Le pilier de le tente: Rituels et représentations de l'honneur chez les Ait Khebbach (Tafilalt)*. Paris: Maisons des Sciences de l'Homme.

Gellner, Ernest, and Charles Micaud. 1972. *Arabs and Berbers: From Tribe to Nation in North Africa*. London: Duckworth and Co.

Gibb, H. A. R., ed. 2003. *The Encyclopaedia of Islam*. Leiden: Brill.

Goichon, Amélie Marie 1927. *La vie féminine au Mzab: Étude de sociologie musulmane*. Paris: Geuthner.

Hale, Sondra. 1989. "The Politics of Gender in the Middle East." In *Gender and Anthropology*, ed. Sandra Morgen, pp. 246–267. Washington, D.C.: American Anthropological Association.

Hamdun, Said, and Noel King. 1994. *Ibn Battuta in Black Africa*. Princeton: Markus Wiener Publisher.

Hammoudi, Abdellah. 1993. *The Victim and Its Masks: An Essay on Sacrifice and Masquerade in the Maghreb*. Translated by Paula Wissing. Chicago: University of Chicago Press.

Harries, Jeanette, and Mohamed Raamouch. 1971. "Berber Popular Songs of the Middle Atlas." *African Language Studies* 12: 52–70.

Harris, Walter. 1895. *The Tafilet: The Narrative of a Journey of Exploration in the Atlas Mountains and the Oases of the North-West Sahara*. London: Blackwood and Sons.

Hart, David. 1981. *Dadda 'Atta and His Forty Grandsons: The Socio-political Organization of the Ait Atta of Southern Morocco*. Cambridge: Middle East and North African Studies Press.

———. 1984. *The Ait 'Atta of Southern Morocco*. Cambridge: Middle East and North African Studies Press, Ltd.

Herber, Joseph. 1921. "Tatouages marocains — Tatouage et religion." *Revue de l'Histoire des Religions* 83: 69–83.

———. 1929. "Les peintures au Harqus." *Hespéris* 3–4: 323–351.

———. 1948. "Onomastique des tatouages marocains." *Hespéris* 1: 31–56.

Hoffman, Katherine. 2002. "Moving and Dwelling: Building the Moroccan Ashelhi Homeland." *American Ethnologist* 29 (4): 928–962.

Irbouh, Hamid. 1998. "Farid Belkahia: A Moroccan Artist's Search for Authenticity." In *Issues in Contemporary African Art*, ed. Nkiru Nzegwu, pp. 46–68. Binghamton, N.Y.: International Society for the Study of Africa (ISSA) at Binghamton University.

———. 2001. "French Colonial Art Education in Morocco." *Ijele: Art eJournal of the African World* 2:1.

Jarrot, Jean. 1935. "Coiffures d'enfants." *Réalisations* 1 (10): 265–268.

Jereb, James F. 1995. *The Arts and Crafts of Morocco*. London: Thames & Hudson.

Joly, F. 1951. "Les Ait Khebbache de Taouz." *Travaux de l'Institut de Recherches Sahariennes* 7: 129–159.

Joseph, Terri. 1980. "Poetry as a Strategy of Power: The Case of Riffian Berber Women." *Signs: Journal of Women in Culture and Society* 5: 418–434.

Kapchan, Deborah. 1993. "Moroccan Women's Body Signs." In *Bodylore,* ed. Katharine Young, pp. 3–34. Knoxville: University of Tennessee.

———. 1996. *Gender on the Market: Moroccan Women and the Revoicing of Tradition.* Philadelphia: University of Pennsylvania Press.

Khan, Muhammad Muhsin. 1983. *The Translation of the Meanings of Sahih al-Bukhari: Arabic-English.* 9 vols. Lahore, Pakistan: Kazi.

Kratochwil, Gabi. 1999. "Some Observations on the First Amazigh World Congress (August 27–30, 1997, Tafira, Canary Islands)." *Die Welt des Islams* 39: 149–159.

Langel, A. M. M., and Ph. Marcais. 1954. "Les coiffures à Tindouf (Sahara occidental)." *Travaux de l'Institut de Recherches Sahariennes* 12 (2): 113–121.

Laoust, Ernest. 1920. *Mots et choses berbères: Notes de linguistique et d'ethnographie—dialectes du Maroc.* Paris: A. Challamel.

———. 1993. *Noces berbères: Les cérémonies du mariage du Maroc.* Aix-en-Provence: Édisud.

Lightfoot, Dale, and James Miller. 1996. "Sijilmasa: The Rise and Fall of a Walled Oasis in Medieval Morocco." *Annals of the Association of American Geographers* 86 (1): 78–101.

Lortat-Jacob, Bernard. 1980a. "Music as a Collective Enterprise: The Case of Berber Music of the High Atlas." *World of Music* 21 (3): 62–67.

———. 1980b. *Musique et fêtes au Haut-Atlas.* Paris: Centre Nationale de la Recherche Scientifique et du Musée de l'Homme.

———. 1981. "Community Music as an Obstacle to Professionalism: A Berber Example." *Ethnomusicology* 25 (1): 87–98.

Maddy-Weitzman, Bruce. 2002. "Contested Identities: Berbers, 'Berberism,' and the State in North Africa." In *Middle Eastern Minorities and Diasporas,* ed. M. Ma'oz and Gabriel Sheffer, pp. 153–178. Portland, Ore.: Sussex Academic Press.

Makris, G. P. 2000. *Changing Masters: Spirit Possession and Identity Construction among Slave Descendants and Other Subordinates in the Sudan.* Evanston: Northwestern University Press.

Maraini, Toni. 1990. "Morocco." In *Contemporary Art from the Islamic World,* ed. W. Ali, pp. 211–218. Northampton, Mass.: Interlink Publishing Group, Inc.

Marcus, Julie. 1992. *A World of Difference: Islam and Gender Hierarchy in Turkey.* London: Zed.

Marcy, Georges. 1931. "Origine et signification des tatouages des tribus berbères." *Revue de l'Histoire des Religions* 102: 13–66.

Mernissi, Fatima. 1987. *Beyond the Veil: Male-Female Dynamics in a Modern Muslim Society.* Bloomington: Indiana University Press.

———. 1989. *Doing Daily Battle: Interviews with Moroccan Women.* Translated by Mary Jo Lakeland. New Brunswick, N.J.: Rutgers University Press.

———. 2004. *Les Sindbads marocains: Voyage dans le Maroc civique.* Rabat: Éditions Marsam.

Messick, Brinkley. 1987. "Subordinate Discourse: Women, Weaving, and Gender Relations in North Africa." *American Ethnologist* 14: 210–225.

Michelman, Susan O., and Tonye V. Erekosima. 1992. "Kalabari Dress in Nigeria: Visual Analysis and Gender Implications." In *Dress and Gender: Making and Meaning in Cultural Contexts,* ed. R. Barnes and J. Eicher, pp. 164–182. New York: Berg.

Miller, James. 1984. *Imlil: A Moroccan Mountain Community in Change.* Boulder: Westview Press.

———. 1996. "Sustained Past and Risky Present: The Tafilalt Oasis of Southeastern Morocco." In *The North African Environment at Risk,* ed. Will D. Swearingen and Abdellatif Bencherifa, pp. 55–69. Boulder: Westview Press.

———. 2001. "Trading through Islam: The Interactions of Sijilmasa, Ghana and the Almoravid Movement." *Journal of North African Studies* 6 (1): 29–58.

Moghadam, Valentine, ed. 1994. *Identity Politics and Women.* Boulder: Westview Press.

Moore, Henrietta. 1990. *Feminism and Anthropology.* Minneapolis: University of Minnesota Press.

———. 1993. "The Differences Within and the Differences Between." In *Gendered Anthropology,* ed. Teresa del Valle, pp. 193–204. London: Routledge.

Morin-Barde, Mireille. 1990. *Coiffures féminines du Maroc: Au sud du Haut Atlas.* Aix-en-Provence: Édisud.

Munson, Henry, Jr. 1993. *Religion and Power in Morocco.* New Haven: Yale University Press.

Murphy, R. F. 1964. "Social Distance and the Veil." *American Anthropologist* 66: 1257–1274.

Nashat, Guity, and Judith Tucker. 1999. *Women in the Middle East and North Africa: Restoring Women to History.* Bloomington: Indiana University Press.

Paydar, Niloo Imami, and Ivo Grammet, eds. 2002. *The Fabric of Moroccan Life.* Indianapolis: Indianapolis Museum of Art.

Péristiany, John G., ed. 1966. *Honour and Shame: The Values of Mediterranean Society.* Chicago: University of Chicago Press.

Popenoe, Rebecca. 2004. *Feeding Desire: Fatness, Beauty, and Sexuality among a Saharan People.* London: Routledge.

Prussin, Labelle. 1986. *Hatumere: Islamic Design in West Africa.* Berkeley: University of California Press.

———. 1995. *African Nomadic Architecture: Space, Place, and Gender.* Washington, D.C.: Smithsonian Institution Press.

Rabaté, Jacques, and Marie-Rose Rabaté. 1996. *Bijoux du Maroc: Du Haut Atlas à la vallée du Draa.* Aix-en-Provence: Édisud.

Rasmussen, Susan. 1995. *Spirit Possession and Personhood among the Kel Ewey Tuareg.* Cambridge: Cambridge University Press.

Reinisch, Helmut, and Wilfried Stanzer. 1991. *Berber: Tribal Carpets and Weavings from Morocco.* Hauptplatz: Helmut Reinisch.

Reswick, Irmtraud. 1981. "Traditional Textiles of Tunisia." *African Arts* 14 (3): 56–65.

———. 1985. *Traditional Textiles of Tunisia.* Los Angeles: Craft and Folk Art Museum.

Ricard, Prosper. 1923–1927. *Corpus des tapis marocains.* 4 vols. Paris: P. Geuthner.

Rohlfs, Gerhard. 1874. *Adventures through Morocco and Journeys through the Oases of Draa and Tafilet.* London: S. Low, Marton, Low, and Searle.

Rouach, David. 1989. *Bijoux berbères au Maroc.* Paris: ACR Édition.

Rouch, Jean. 1960. *La religion et la magie Songhay.* Paris: Presses Universitaires de France.

Rovsing Olsen, Miriam. 1989. "Symbolique d'un rituel de mariage berbère: Une approche ethnomusicologique." *Annuario Musical* 44: 259–291.

Sabatier, Camille. 1891. *Touat, Sahara et Soudan: Étude géographique, politique, économique et militaire.* Paris: Société d'Éditions Scientifiques.

Sadiqi, Fatima. 1997. "The Place of Berber in Morocco." *International Journal of the Sociology of Language* 123: 7–21.

———. 2003. *Women, Gender and Language in Morocco.* Leiden: Brill.

Schuyler, Phillip. 1984. "Berber Professional Musicians in Performance." In *Performance Practice: Ethnomusicological Perspectives,* ed. G. Behague, pp. 91–148. Westport, Conn.: Greenwood Press.

———. 1985. "The Rwais and the Zawia: Professional Musicians and the Rural Religious Elite in Southwestern Morocco." *Asian Music* 17: 14–31.

Searight, Susan. 1984. *The Use and Function of Tattooing on Moroccan Women.* New Haven: Human Relations Area Files.

Sijelmassi, M., A. Khatibi, and A. Brahim. 1989. *L'art contemporain du Maroc.* Courbevoie: ACR.

Simon, H. 1934. "La pacification du Maroc." *Journal of the Royal African Society* 33 (133): 329–337.

Sorber, Frieda. 2002. "Weavings for Rural Life." In *The Fabric of Moroccan Life,* ed. N. Paydar and I. Grammet, pp. 129–132. Indianapolis: Indianapolis Museum of Art.

Spillman, Capitaine Georges. 1936. *Les Ait Atta du Sahara et la pacification du Haut Dra.* Rabat: Éditions Félix Moncho.

Taws, Omar. 1996. *Iledjigen n yigenna (Flowers of the Sky).* Rabat: Isefra.

Thornton, Philip. 1936. *Voice of the Atlas: In Search of Music in Morocco.* London: A. Maclehose & Co.

Tremearne, John. 1914. *The Ban of the Bori: Demons and Demon-Dancing in West and North Africa.* London: Heath, Cranton, and Ouseley, Ltd.

Trout, Frank E. 1969. *Morocco's Saharan Frontiers.* Geneva: Droz Publishers.

Venema, Bernhard, and Jogien Bakker. 2004. "A Permissive Zone for Prostitution in the Middle Atlas of Morocco." *Ethnology* 43 (1): 51–62.

Venema, Bernhard, and Ali Mguild. 2003. "Access to Land and Berber Ethnicity in the Middle Atlas, Morocco." *Middle Eastern Studies* 39 (4): 35–54.

Vonderheyden, M. 1934. "Le Henné chez les Musulmans de l'Afrique au Nord." *Journal de la Société des Africanistes* 4: 179–202.

Wehr, Hans. 1980. *A Dictionary of Modern Written Arabic.* London: MacDonald and Evans.

Westermarck, Edward. [1926] 1968. *Ritual and Belief in Morocco.* 2 vols. New York: University Books.

———. [1914] 1972. *Marriage Ceremonies in Morocco.* London: Macmillan and Co.

Woodson, Craig. 1974. "The Effect of a Snare on the Tone of a Single-Headed Frame Drum, the Moroccan Bendir." *Selected Reports in Ethnomusicology* 2: 103–117.

Yuval-Davis, Nira. 1998. "Beyond Differences: Women, Empowerment and Coalition Politics." In *Gender, Ethnicity and Political Ideologies,* ed. N. Charles and H. Hintjens, pp. 168–189. New York: Routledge.

Index

Page numbers in italics indicate illustrations.

Printed and bound by CPI Group (UK) Ltd, Croydon, CR0 4YY

31/05/2026

14889700-0003